HIKE366

A Woman's Tales of Hiking
Adventures All Year Round

JESS BEAUCHEMIN

Hike366
Copyright © Jess Beauchemin 2021

First Edition

Paperback ISBN: 978-1-945587-71-9
Library of Congress Control Number: 2021917464

1. Hiking; 2. Outdoors; 3. Pacific Northwest; 4. Oregon; 5. Maine.

Book design & production: Dancing Moon Press
Cover design & production: Dancing Moon Press
Photos: Jess Beauchemin
Illustrations: Jess Beauchemin

Manufactured in the United States of America

Dancing Moon Press
dancingmoonpress.com

Bend, Oregon
Lincoln City, Oregon

DANCING
MOON
PRESS

Contents

Acknowledgements

My husband, Aaron, whose endless support and encouragement throughout this project, as well as his companionship on many of my hiking adventures, has made this book possible.

My Dad for inspiring me to get outside and explore, and for helping me complete the final hike on this journey.

My climbing mentors and friends, including Rick Craycraft, Lee Davis, John Godino, Brad Farra, Tom Kline, Leora Gregory and Monty Smith.

All the people who accompanied me on my hikes: Jamie Anderson, Sarah Allen, John Bannon, Lindsay Bean, Darlene Beauchemin, Jake Beauchemin, Frank Bock, Russ Born, Tracy Byers, Amy Card, Theresa Conley, Preston Corless, Sarah Gribionkin, Nadine Grzeskowiak, Scott Hinderman, Ryan Jayne, Karen Lashenske, Mary Ellen Lessard, Eugene Lewins, Josh Liberles, Woody Keen, Amanda Long, Matt Mioduszewski, Linda Musil, Don Nelsen, Luke Newby, Jill Perry, Sue Peters, Karl Peterson, Lauretta Prince, Tommy Rawlins, Amber Reese, Vanessa Robinson, Kevin Rooney, Mike Saporito, Marc Sanchez, Kelcie Sirois, Karen Swanger, Sandra Thompson, Anthony Veltri, Steve Vigne, Lisa Marie Warren, Julie Weiss, Guy Wheaton and countless more.

My friends who spent many hours providing feedback on this book.

Mariah Wilson, who patiently, methodically and professionally edited my first book.

The Balch Hotel in Dufur, Oregon, for providing a quiet retreat where I could sit and start telling my story.

Introduction

Summers are for hiking. At least, that's what I thought all through childhood and into early adulthood. As a novice hiker, I met people who shared stories about hiking in the winter, and I became curious. I asked people for advice about how to prepare for hiking in the winter. One hiker said, "Just keep hiking through the fall and notice how things change." That sounded so simple and reasonable. Seasons blend into each other, so by hiking every weekend I learned from experience how my gear, skills and planning strategies needed to adapt to seasonal changes. I did hike that fall, and the following winter and spring. I began to appreciate the variety of conditions that come with year-round hiking, writing down my observations in a journal.

Throughout this book, I share excerpts from these handwritten pages. It is important to me to share not only current memories, naturally distorted by time and distance, but also the feelings of being in the moment that only a journal entry can convey. In addition, I recorded some basic information about each hike in a spreadsheet. I enjoyed tracking the data from my outings well before GPS watches and social media sharing became so popular. I also started a blog and took photos on my hikes, which provided me with a rich primary source of visual hiking history dating back to 2005.

While browsing the posts on an internet hiking website one day, I came across the idea of experiencing a hike every day of the calendar year. I was intrigued; most hiking lists are place-based, not time-based. Going through my spreadsheet, I realized that my random hikes over the years had gotten me pretty close to completing this unusual list. I made a goal to fill in the "missing calendar dates," and on that day Hike366 was born. Finishing the list was an intriguing and accessible challenge that would motivate me to get out on days I wouldn't normally hit the trails.

Given how much I love hiking, I was confident I would finish the project in the following year. Little did I know the challenges I'd face and the many things I'd learn while working on this project. Over the next few years, I dedicated myself to filling in the gaps and finding new hikes to add to my growing list. If I missed a day due to illness or scheduling conflicts or anything else, it set my project back a full year. This, unfortunately, happened several times.

As *Hike366* was nearing completion in May 2018, I reflected upon my experiences with hiking. I noticed a few themes, and I realized that over the years my motivations and interests changed. What started as a cheap and easy hobby morphed into an identity and a way of life. My time on the trails, on the beaches, in the woods and in the mountains has made me who I am today. Hiking has shaped my values and provided a lens through which I see the world. In writing this book, I hope to use my experiences to share with you some insights and skills that I learned along the way.

How to Read This Book

As you make your way through this book, you will see an evolution of skills, experiences, philosophies and ideas. Meaningful moments from my three hundred and sixty-six individual hikes come together to tell one story. In an effort to dive more deeply into specific hikes, I have not included each separate hike in the book. (If you're curious, a complete list of all the hikes in the project can be found in the appendix.)

Chapter One begins with recollections from my formative years. In these early stages, I attempted to define hiking for myself. I learned how I could shape my own body and sense of self by pushing my limits in the outdoors.

In Chapter Two, I explore the theme of hiking with other people, from going with friends to joining groups to leading groups. And in Chapter Three, I take a sharp turn, sharing my experiences hiking solo. Take time absorbing these particular stories and evaluate your thoughts on concepts such as risk, danger and personal choice. I have had some transformative experiences while solo hiking. And while most land managers and hiking organizations do not advocate hiking alone, I heartily believe that everyone should at least give it a try.

In Chapter Four, I examine what makes a hike a "hike." I present stories of hikes on the long and short end of the mileage spectrum and reflect on how being injured can change one's perspective of what defines a hike.

In Chapter Five, I begin to explore what it takes to cross technical terrain and develop climbing skills within a team. Included are tales of mountaineering and rock-climbing adventures. I continue to question definitions, such as what distinguishes a "climb" from a "hike" or a "scramble."

In Chapter Six, I share stories of managing joy, risk and comfort in adverse conditions. Neither snow nor rain nor sleet nor hail has kept me from hiking. You'll also find many tips to help you stay happy and safe on the trail, no matter the weather conditions.

Precipitation and clouds can play a role in the ease of

navigating trails, which leads right into Chapter Seven. Here I explore a range of topics and scenarios related to route finding and navigation. These stories are coupled with useful advice and suggestions for learning how to stay found while hiking, on or off the trail. This is one skill that can benefit both novice and experienced hikers, and is something that many of us, myself included, should practice more often.

In Chapter Eight, I share some of the most unique outdoor experiences that I've had over the years. They have one thing in common: The time or place is particularly special. Urban hikes, full-moon ambles, sunrise walks, cave explorations and sand dune traverses all showcase the diversity of hiking opportunities on this planet.

And finally, Chapter Nine ties it all together with stories that highlight the Seven Principles™ outlined by the Leave No Trace Center for Outdoor Ethics (LNT). The LNT principles provide a guiding ethic for interacting with our world's wild spaces. In more than a decade of hiking, I have seen over and over again the negative impact that people can have on the environment. Through this book, I hope to spread the word about LNT and inspire you to look to these principles each time you hike, camp, backpack or otherwise explore our remaining wild public lands.

Throughout the book you will find several call-outs and sidebars that provide more information on a variety of topics. Some sidebars define words and ideas that only experienced hikers and climbers may know. Others provide tips on navigation, packing, Leave No Trace and other hiking-related skills. And some are just for fun. If you're as obsessed with hiking as I am, you may not find these sidebars useful, so feel free to skip them. It is my intention that *Hike366* be readable by anyone—regardless of prior knowledge and experience—so that my stories may resonate with a larger audience.

While you're reading this book, check out the companion photos and stories on the Hike366.com website and on Instagram @hike366. There you'll see this project come to life, with images from each hike posted to Instagram on the date they were taken. Plus, I continue to share hiking tips, inspiration, lessons and thoughts.

During the course of this project I experienced several setbacks. Despite illness, scheduling conflicts, feelings of apathy and self-doubt, I persisted in reaching my goal. On May 10, 2018, I completed the list. This is my story.

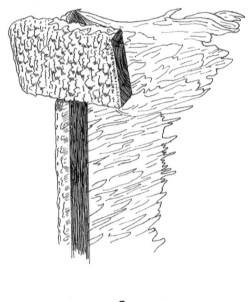

1

Getting Started

I was alone, soaking wet from the moisture-laden vegetation. The familiar songs of white-throated sparrows, hermit thrushes and chickadees pierced the silence. Each slippery step took me through a magical fairyland brought to life. Here in Maine, in a quiet forest, I got bitten really hard—by the hiking bug.

I remember that day very clearly: July 1, 2005. I'd just finished teaching summer school, and it was my first free weekend in a very long time. I had driven to Maine the previous afternoon to go on a camping trip. I tossed the idea out to several friends, but no one was interested in coming with me. With my mind set on this adventure, I borrowed some camping gear from my dad and headed out on my own.

When I arrived at the campground, I realized I was going to have to set up camp, my first time as an adult. I wrestled with the tent poles, figured out how to make a fire and scribbled quietly in my journal:

The sun is setting on my fire. The breeze is cool. I think I'll sleep well tonight. My eyelids and my brain are battling it out. The people in the cabin next door are just getting wound up, but I am ready for bed. Daylight still clings to the gray sky so it must be early. I didn't bring a watch, and my cell phone is useless out here. Time has become irrelevant. I'll wake with the robins tomorrow. Adventures await; this is only a beginning...

Writing gave me something to do while I was alone and it was a way to help keep me grounded. A classic introvert, I have always struggled to communicate with the spoken word. Instead, I buried my thoughts between the bindings of a blank book. Sometimes my words were brief, listing only the birds I'd seen on a hike or describing the trail conditions. Other times I wrote furiously, capturing the mood and lessons learned as well as detailed observations of the landscape, weather and wildlife.

I had no idea I was about to embark on a long and personal journey, one that was rooted in childhood memories but also had branches reaching far into the future. I awoke to a damp forest and hiked, alone, on empty trails. Stomping through mud and walking across granite bedrock all day long, I filled my brain with the scenery, smells and sounds of the mountain forest. On the drive back to camp I screeched to a halt to stare at a moose poised on the side of the road. She stared back at me for a few moments before disappearing into the woods. How could something that big vanish without a trace? Back at camp, I devoured my dinner while poring over a map to plan my next hike. My legs were tired after six hours of walking on rugged New England trails, but I was determined to get back out there again.

The next day, I took off on yet another solo hike just over the border in New Hampshire. Although I was pretty new to hiking, I was not afraid to get out there by myself. I'd hiked and explored as a kid with my family and on scout trips, but not much on my own. I was comfortable enough, and risk-averse enough, to feel confident that I could take care of myself in the woods, but I had no idea how many lessons I had yet to learn.

After barely making it to the top of South Baldface in New Hampshire's White Mountains, I decided to take a little detour on my way down to find a waterfall I'd noticed on my map the night before. But I took a wrong turn and walked about a mile and a half out of the way before running into a man who was working on the trail. He kindly pointed out my mistake, and I grumpily headed back the way I came. As I slowly retraced my steps, I stopped to check out a snake I saw on the trail. It was unlike any garter snake I'd seen before; it had caught a frog! It was a big frog, all puffed up in self-defense. I was so excited to have stumbled across this sight that I soon forgot to continue berating myself for taking the wrong trail. Had I not made that "mistake," I would not have had this opportunity. My weekend trip tapped into something I needed so deeply, and set off a chain of events that would make hiking a central part of my life from then on.

Long before this project began, I hiked without collecting much data. This was well before smartphones, the ubiquity of social media and other technological innovations that have developed in the years since. I hiked for fun. I hiked to spend time with friends. I hiked to be outside. I loved all of that. On May 28, 2005, I unknowingly went on what would come to be the first trip in my hiking log. I took only six photos. I wrote down where I went and the name of the person I went with and that was it! From those scant pieces of information I tried to piece together the experience years later. I remembered that we only carried one backpack between the two of us. My friend would hike up ahead of me on the bouldery sections and then reach down his hand to help me up. I felt so offended by this innocuous gesture. The gall of a man to assume that I couldn't do what he could, ha! While I still have that spicy attitude, I have since developed the habit of carrying my own backpack, no matter what.

In the beginning, I longed for hiking partners. I would see groups of people hiking together, laughing and talking, and wanted to be a part of that too. I took my search for adventure buddies to the Internet and found several people through a local hiking message board. Somehow, I often ended up hiking with people who really liked to push themselves physically: mountaineers, ultramarathon runners and otherwise very fit and motivated individuals. This shaped the type of hiker I would become.

Just a few months after my "shared backpack" hike with a friend, I ended up hiking a whopping twenty miles in a day with a new hiking buddy, Frank. He planned a version of the Franconia Ridge Traverse that crossed six White Mountain summits and descended the ridge by means of an old, unmaintained trail. Much of the hike was quite enjoyable. We hiked well together. At times, we stayed close and conversed. At other times, we gave each other some space and walked in quiet solitude. I liked having this mix of both. We hiked at a similar pace and enjoyed each other's company.

On the way back down, we struggled to find the old trail. Once we did, we quickly discovered it was overgrown with vegetation and difficult to follow. One particularly large downed tree sent us way off course, leaving us lost in the woods.

Lost. Isn't that everyone's greatest fear? Getting lost in the woods? I followed my partner's seemingly aimless wandering for the next hour as we tried to regain the route. It was exhausting work. We climbed over tree branches, pushed through thick brush and slogged through muddy soil. I focused on keeping within eyesight of my hiking partner. Somewhere along the way, as the branches and brush scraped against my body, they dislodged the fleece top I'd shoved into the outside pocket of my pack. I was left without a jacket as well as the gloves and map that were stored in its pockets. The day was going from bad to worse.

Frustrated by our lack of progress, we ultimately backtracked to our last known location and followed the maintained trail back out, ending up in an unfamiliar parking area. However, our car sat three miles up the road in another lot. Due to sheer luck, we ran into another group of hikers who were finishing up their walk and were willing to drive us to our car. Despite it being a long and exhausting day, my memories are more positive than negative.

Instead of letting these early experiences deter me from going hiking, I treated each hardship as a challenge, and I relished the adventure. As a not-naturally-athletic person, hiking was the only activity I enjoyed that made my body feel good and capable. Even if my knees hurt and my lungs burned, I knew I could take one more step. I understood that the physical pain in the moment would go away in the future. Each misadventure left me craving the next outing.

Taking stock after the White Mountain trip, I learned the value of knowing when to turn back as well as the value of packing the ten essentials; we needed our headlamps to get out of the woods.

TEN ESSENTIAL SYSTEMS

The list of the ten essentials was first published in *Mountaineering: The Freedom of the Hills* in 1974. In 2017, the list was revised to contain ten systems instead of ten items, allowing hikers to plan more specifically for their trips. The ten essentials for a short day hike look pretty different than the ten essentials for an overnight snow-camping trip. Some examples of must-have items are included next to the categories below. How many of the essentials do you usually carry?

Navigation: map, compass, GPS, altimeter

Headlamp: or flashlight, spare batteries

Sun protection: sunscreen, hat, clothing, lip balm with SPF

First aid: gauze, bandages, medications, blister pads, insect repellant

Knife: tape, cord and other repair supplies

Fire: matches, lighter, tinder, stove and fuel

Shelter: tarp, rain shell, emergency blanket

Nutrition: food for the trip plus emergency food

Hydration: water for the trip, water filter, electrolytes

Extra clothes: jacket, hat, gloves, plus a way to keep spare clothes dry

---

The day after my epic hike on Franconia Ridge, I woke up to a dark camp and drove to another trailhead, where I met my next hiking partner. With wobbly legs, I struggled to keep up with Jamie's long stride as he bounded up the steep trail. On that day, we intended on hiking to one particular highpoint, but we were so inspired by being in the mountains that we kept going, all along the ridge, reaching one peak after another. I was amazed that although I'd hiked twenty miles the day before, I just wanted to keep walking. In the words of John Muir, "The mountains are calling and I must go."

※

In the beginning, mistakes came easily; my ambition far surpassed my skill. But I was dogged and determined, ready to tackle whatever obstacles came my way.

Navigation was not my strong suit. Surprisingly, this didn't slow me down very much. I anticipated that I would make mistakes, having to course correct along the way. My errors were due to poor planning, novice map-reading skills and tricky trail conditions. It was the latter that left me scratching my head in September 2005. Recent rain had flooded the trail, leaving what looked like paths in every direction. I was hiking with a new partner I'd met online. Between the two of us, we eventually got our bearings and hiked to a prized off-trail destination: the Arrow Slide.

Our unofficial hiking route led us to the summit of North Hancock, one of forty-eight 4,000-foot peaks in the White Mountains. This list of peaks guided my hiking choices while I lived on the East Coast. We chose the Arrow Slide route over the standard trail for the increased challenge. I was actually scared on this hike as I scrambled up steep, wet rock. Despite the fear, I discovered early on that I prefer off-trail scrambles to manicured routes for two reasons. First, they are more interesting and demand more thought than simply walking up a trail. I have to use my hands and feet along with my brain. Second, they are way less popular than the main trails. And, as crowd-averse as I am, this is a huge advantage. I have greater adventures and have a better chance of being in the woods on my own.

But I needed people. Winter scared me. Before meeting people in the hiking community, winter hiking was completely off my radar. Once I had a set of friends who had the equipment and experience to help me get out safely in the winter, I set a goal to keep hiking through the fall and winter of 2005.

One of the highlights that season was a hike up Mt. Carrigain, another 4,000-foot peak on my list. I went with a familiar hiking buddy in order to glean as much trail wisdom as I could. The trails were wet and sometimes hard to follow; we got off-track a few times. I was enamored by the colors of the foliage and the crisp air—it was stunning. Above the tree line, with a panoramic view of the surrounding mountain range, we stopped to look at the peaks. My partner pointed to several little bumps and ridges in view, rattling off their names from memory. I tried to remember a few of those names, but it was overwhelming. I felt very new there, and I realized I had much to learn. On the return hike, I appreciated the signs of the season: golden leaves, swollen streams and chilly air. Yes, fall hiking is worthwhile too!

A few weeks later, I met up with a hiking group for a grueling hike up to the North and South Twin Mountains. I was put face to face with one of my biggest nemeses: a stream crossing. The creek was running high and fast. I was incredibly nervous. There is something terrifying about moving water. There I was, among a large group of experienced hikers, near the start of the trail, apprehensive about what came next. I felt like the newbie, like I didn't belong with these people. No one else was deterred by the stream, but I stared at it, fear in my eyes, wondering how I was going to rally the courage to hop across the rocks and continue hiking.

I couldn't do it myself. My teammates stepped in to coach me across. Someone handed me a hiking pole, since I did not carry poles at that time. Using the pole and every ounce of gusto I had, I strode across the stepping stones that poked out of the water's surface. On the other side of the stream, I felt a wave of relief as well as a small boost in confidence. This was a skill I'd need to practice many more times before I'd be confident doing it on my own. However, the experience taught me that I didn't have to do everything completely on my own. That's what partners and teammates are for.

Many times I'd hike with a person or a group once and then never again. In July 2005, when I was really itching to find partners, I joined up with a group hiking the Mt. Tripyramid Loop. The hike was challenging, especially the North Slide. These slides were created by a large force—such as an avalanche or mudslide—ripping a tear into the side of the mountain. The end result is a steep jumble of boulders that basically stripped free any large vegetation from the slope, creating a straight path from bottom to top. Nature, not humans, engineered these passageways, so there are no waterbars, switchbacks or other features to make the trail easily passable for humans. To me, this was part of the charm.

All of my senses were engaged while climbing these slides. I used my hands and feet to scramble up the rock, craning my neck up to see what was ahead. I anticipated the joy of coming out on top and searching for the peak's summit. Mostly though, I enjoyed turning around to see the unobstructed view of the surrounding mountains. On this trip, the company wasn't memorable, but the landscape was. In the distance, I saw endless tree-covered peaks and wide blue skies. I knew I had to keep doing whatever it took to get myself out there.

꙰

My first taste of winter hiking came in late October 2005 with a hike on the Davis Path in the White Mountains. I once again joined my hiking partner Frank and loaded up my backpack with borrowed gear. We intended on summiting several mountains that day. I had hiking poles, snowshoes, traction devices for my boots and (in hindsight) too many extra layers of clothing. I was dressed for the cold, wearing long underwear beneath ski pants and several upper-body layers. I quickly heated up and had to strip off clothing during several rest stops.

I wore a new pair of boots, and I carried a much larger pack than usual to accommodate all my gear. This winter hiking stuff was a lot of work! The entire experience was a comedy of errors. My partner's clothing got soaking wet from the snow. We struggled to push through the snow and ice on the ground in an efficient way. And at least one of us was grumpy at any given time. After reaching just two highpoints, we decided we'd been whooped and retreated back down the trail.

This was the first time I realized that being over-prepared could be harmful. All that extra weight slowed us down and heated us up. Before that day, it didn't occur to me that I could be too hot while hiking in the snow. All of my previous experience with winter activities involved being too cold. In over-preparing to fend off the cold, I created a new problem. In the future, I'd need to learn how to find balance: bringing the right amount of gear, wearing the right amount of clothing for the conditions and having the right mindset.

I took these lessons and applied them to my next big challenge: a winter-like ascent of the notorious Mt. Washington.

Mt. Washington is the tallest peak in New Hampshire. At only 6,288 feet tall, its height pales in comparison to the high mountains in Colorado, Washington and California, but this highpoint is well known for its bad weather. Winter conditions on Mt. Washington challenge even the seasoned mountaineer. With temperatures that drop well below freezing and wind speeds far higher than most places on earth, the summit of this mountain can be just as inhospitable as a peak twice its size.

With that in mind, it was with some trepidation that I decided to join a team of five others on a climb up Mt. Washington. On November 12, 2005, I did my first real hike in winter conditions on a difficult mountain.

Again, I needed to borrow gear. One of my companions loaned me an old ice ax and crampons. I learned about crampons from conversations with other year-round hikers. They are spiked, metal devices that strap onto the bottom of your boots, providing traction on hard-packed snow and ice. I'd never used them before, but I trusted my hiking partners to teach me how they work on the trail.

We started in the dark, trudging up the trail by headlamp. I had overdressed and started sweating during the first mile. Despite my internal heat, it was cold outside. My water-bladder hose froze solid. Once we broke out of the forest and into the alpine zone, the wind became very apparent. I had to put my layers back on, including a balaclava to shield my face. My mind was on high alert—things felt serious. I'd been on these mountains before, but only in the summer. This was a whole new world, like nothing I'd ever seen before. The meadows and boulders were covered in snow and wind-sculpted ice. I could see no obvious trail and nothing looked familiar.

I watched the other hikers in front of me and tried to mimic their behavior. I put on crampons when they did; I stepped where they stepped; I watched how they used their ice axes to brace themselves against the wind. This was alpine school, and I was learning how to climb in the mountains.

Our route to Mt. Washington took us up and over Mt. Monroe

first. From this summit, we could see the ocean. The sky was so clear and blue!

My heart raced in excitement. I continued up the mountain, following my companions. At this point, there were only three of us. Two members of the group turned back while we were still in the forest, unable to keep pace, and one turned around after summiting Monroe, uncomfortable with the steepness of the snowfields beyond. Would I bail too?

The leader of the trip decided to take a path up a slope that got steeper and steeper. This felt like the most dangerous part of the day. I watched carefully as my partners made their way up the snow slope in a switchback-type pattern. The man in front would walk at a slight uphill angle to the right for several feet, then turn and walk uphill to the left. We zig-zagged in that fashion up the steepest section of the mountain.

They seemed to take a lot of care in choosing their steps wisely and taking their time. I remembered a story I'd read in *Deep Survival* about how an injured ice climber traversed difficult sections of a hike by "sticking to the pattern." That's exactly what I did. I made sure I had good contact with two points before moving to a third: plant ice axe, step left foot, step right foot, plant ice axe . . .

Any time I veered from the pattern, I got freaked out. I couldn't look down below me, only up towards our destination. Step, step, axe. Step, step, axe.

BOOK RECOMMENDATION

Deep Survival: Who Lives, Who Dies, and Why by Laurence Gonzales, 2004.

Read fascinating stories about real-life survival scenarios and how the choices people make impact the outcome.

When I stood next to the iconic sign at Mt. Washington's summit, I felt a sense of triumph. I made it! The sign was covered in a thick layer of rime ice, something I'd never seen before. Rime ice forms when the moisture in the air freezes onto a surface. The result is a beautiful sculpture of frozen crystals covering trees, boulders and any other objects outside. The wind blew steadily, fingers of rime pointing into the wind. Small chunks of ice whizzed by my face. We didn't stay there long. The descent was hard but unremarkable. I returned to survival mode: make no mistakes, rest when needed, follow the leader. I just wanted to get off of the mountain safely. When I got back home, I checked the day's statistics from the Mt. Washington Observatory. The weather instruments recorded sustained winds at 40 mph, with 99 mph gusts at the summit. Now I could say I knew what 40 mph winds felt like.

I was incredibly grateful for the kindness and patience my partners showed me on this trip. I may not have had the skills and experience necessary to be a good trip leader, but I could follow directions and keep up with the team. I trusted my leaders to let me know if I needed to turn back or if I could continue with them. Their safety was intricately entwined with my own; it was in their best interest to make sure I would not bring them harm. That sense of solidarity inspired me to keep seeking out hiking experiences with other people.

I continued to be a good follower for many years in order to develop the skills I needed to get out in extreme conditions. But I was terrified about the increased risks of hiking in the snow and ice, so I reached out to anyone who would take an eager beginner out in the winter.

My January trip up Mt. Moosilauke was one of these small-group adventures. This ten-mile hike begins in the forest, tops out above the tree line on a wind-swept summit and dashes back down along an old road, which was slick with ice that day. My partners helped me maintain a comfortable hiking pace that was neither too fast nor too slow. They stopped to put on layers before we entered the wind-whipped summit area. They ate and drank regularly to maintain their hydration and body temperature. I soaked all these strategies in like a sponge. I began to see that finding a comfortable middle ground between being under- and over-prepared and too hot or too cold depended on preparation. Knowing the route ahead of time and being able to anticipate changes in weather conditions proved to be key factors in how we experienced a hike.

Although it was exciting to me to seek out new places and explore unfamiliar territory, I began to see the value in studying the route in detail before beginning a hike, an insight that took me some time to develop. But back then, I trusted my partners to fill in the gaps so that I could continue hiking year-round.

In August 2006, I packed up my car and drove across the country in search of a different lifestyle. I had met so many great people in the White Mountains who shared my passion for spending time outdoors. During the previous year, I felt most like myself when I was walking in the woods. But I became tired of the long commute out of the city and into the wilderness. After meeting several hikers who were visiting from the West Coast, I started thinking about making the move.

I'd always lived in the East; growing up in Rhode Island, mountains were not in my blood. I went to college in New Jersey, lived for a short while in Pennsylvania and North Carolina, took a few short vacations to Virginia and Florida. My only experience in the country was along its eastern shores. Living in the Boston Metro area, I grew weary of sitting in traffic and spending most of my time on pavement. I counted down the hours and minutes until I could leave school and head for the hills. The high cost of living, population density and focus on material things above experiences didn't suit me. I found myself restless and discontent in both my job and my living situation. After connecting with people who exuded a passion and love for life I hadn't seen in others before, I thought that maybe I could build a life that was more than just showing up to work and getting a paycheck.

For months, I schemed an escape plan; I'd move to the west coast. But, where? I eliminated Seattle (too much rain) and the entire state of California (mostly based on what little I knew of the immensely diverse state), settling on Portland, Oregon. I had a college friend who was living there and who also had an empty room in her apartment for me when I arrived.

Once the school year was over, I seized my opportunity: I quit my teaching job, loaded up a trailer and drove to Oregon in search of a new life and a new community.

Moving to the Pacific Northwest was a huge change. I quickly discovered that hiking there was physically easier because of thoughtful trail design and well-placed signs. I found myself disappointed in the classic "difficult" hikes in the area since they just didn't compare to the rugged and demanding trails back east. If I wanted to be challenged, I needed to learn new skills to get off the pedestrian trails and into the big mountains.

In December 2006, a friend invited me to go play in the snow on Mt. St. Helens. We got a late start, so we were not attempting to reach the summit. As I strolled around in my snowshoes, gazing upwards towards the shoulder of the volcano, I longed to climb higher. The sun shone brightly through the cold winter air, making the snow crystals sparkle like a disco ball. Simultaneously intimidated and inspired by the sheer size of Mt. St. Helens, I knew I needed to find my way to the top soon. That hike was a tease; walking on those broad, sweeping snowfields was enough to stoke a fire in me. I was determined, not only to get to the summit of that mountain, but to climb all the mountains I could see on the horizon. I knew in that moment that I'd made the right move in coming to Oregon.

Since that first hike in the White Mountains I had grown so much. I found my edges, learning just how far my legs and lungs could carry me. I discovered the limitations of my knowledge and experience. On each outing, I took time to reflect on what went well and what did not. Eager to learn more about my craft, I sought out mentors and people who were willing to answer my questions and push me further. Those early hiking partners were fit, hard-charging athletes who taught me that hiking is mostly about ticking off the miles. In my first year, I defined hiking by how far and how fast I walked through the mountains. But, as I would come to learn, hiking is about much more than covering distance in the woods.

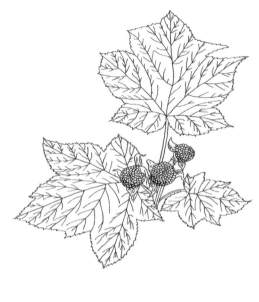

2

Hiking With Others

The flower show began as we approached the first rocky outcrop in the woods. Pink buckwheat, purple larkspur, yellow stonecrop and red paintbrush delighted our eyes. The droplets of dew clinging to each leaf and flower brought a depth of color that you just can't get on a hot, dry day. The sky was dark and gloomy and thick clouds filled the air overhead, obscuring the nearby peaks and ridges. The moist air felt sticky on my skin and brought a chill to my body. As it turned out, this was the perfect kind of weather to explore this wild garden.

I hiked with my friend Lauretta across sprawling alpine meadows on our way to the rocky pinnacle of Iron Mountain in the Oregon Cascades. We were in no rush. Sometimes it takes a friend to help me slow down and notice all of the beauty around me instead of focusing on pounding away the miles. I was very grateful to have her with me. Little patches of flowers sprung up everywhere. We stopped at each one to identify any flowers we hadn't seen yet. Neither of us were flower experts, so sometimes the ID was simply "big yellow flower" or "little yellow flower."

At the summit the clouds began to disperse, creating ephemeral pockets of blue sky. We savored some solitude there, enjoying each other's company as much as the scenery we overlooked from our perch. Together it felt like we were on top of the world.

Hiking is often a social activity. I hike with friends, family and strangers from the Internet. I go on group hikes; I lead group hikes; I meet up with climbing groups. All of these experiences contribute to a richness and diversity in my time outdoors. There's one person in particular who first got me on the trails and whom I cherish any opportunity to hike with—my dad.

When my brother and I were young, our parents took us camping during the summer. We'd head out for a weekend or longer to a campground not far from our home in Rhode Island. This was far from any mountain wilderness, but to a six-year-old, it felt like being transported to another world. We'd play catch, jump rope, catch frogs, go swimming, grill hot dogs and take nature walks. I never carried a backpack or learned how to navigate the forest. I simply learned to enjoy being outdoors.

My favorite childhood hike was to the Wolf Den in Connecticut's Mashamoquet Brook State Park. All along the way I recall stopping to investigate curious plants and fungi, look under rocks for bugs and scramble over boulders near the trail. When we arrived at the "wolf den," my dad would tell us the story of how a pioneer killed Connecticut's last wolf right there. Although wolves hadn't been in the cave for 200 years, I still remember feeling chills running down my spine when I stood in that spot.

As I grew older I lost this visceral connection with the outdoors. My high school and college friends were never interested in exploring the woods, and I was much too timid to go out on my own. But I'm grateful that my dad planted the seed. While it lay dormant for many years, it took only a little water to sprout. With steady nurturing its roots have come to intertwine, strengthen and guide many aspects of my life.

Since we now live on opposite sides of the country,

opportunities to hike with my father are limited. Every time I venture back to the East Coast, I make time to go hiking. In 2009, I hiked up the uber-popular Mt. Monadnock with my dad. On another trip, in 2014, I took him on a 15-mile hike in Connecticut. The hike was flat, with only 800 feet of elevation gain. I had a delightful time, ambling through the forest at a quick yet comfortable pace. The best part of the experience was the amount of quality time I got to spend with my dad. To be back in Connecticut walking with him was something special. On the trail, we talked. We shared moments of joy, laughter and challenge. Being in nature with another person helps deepen connections in some mysterious way. It's not like going to the movies or grabbing a meal at the corner restaurant. The act of hiking creates an opportunity to share a meaningful experience with someone. I'm not sure whether it's being outdoors, being physically active, seeing beautiful places, having extended conversations or a combination of all of the above that makes hiking such a valuable relationship tool.

Although my brother, Jake, also lives on the East Coast, we have gotten to hike together quite frequently since those childhood camping trips. Since I moved to Oregon, he's come to visit me for one weekend almost every single year. When he is in town, I happily plan hiking adventures for the two of us. On our first foray in the west, we went to Mt. St. Helens in Southern Washington. We began our hike on the north side of the mountain, where we could see the blast zone from the 1980 volcanic eruption right in front of us. We hiked through wildflower meadows and across ridgelines. We gazed down on a huge herd of elk, looked away, and in an instant they were gone. It was a surreal landscape. I hoped I hadn't set the bar too high for future visits!

A few years later we headed toward the Oregon Coast. The weather was perfect, but the trail was very muddy. I found it entertaining watching my brother try to keep his shiny white sneakers from getting dirty along our walk to Cape Lookout. This beautiful spit of sand overlooks the Pacific Ocean, providing a clear view of the water and rugged coastline. Spending these short but intense times with my brother, just one weekend a year, has been a great way to stay connected and talk more deeply than we ever could on a quick phone conversation.

In 2014, Jake brought his partner, Vanessa, along on his annual Oregon trip. This time I decided to show off Central

Oregon. We drove through lava fields, frozen in time, to tackle a route described in one of my favorite hiking books. I thought it would provide a nice sampler of Central Oregon's notable terrain features. We walked past shimmering lakes, wildflower meadows, summit viewpoints, rocky lava fields and burnt forest. We walked all day through this beautiful and diverse scenery, appreciating the bright, warm summer sun. I'm grateful to have family members who are interested in sharing the things I love. They trust me to find a good route, make a plan and ensure the group stays on track.

⁂

I appreciate friends who share my interest in hiking. I can classify my friends into two distinct groups: hikers and non-hikers. The distinction isn't always crystal clear, but I can get a good sense of where people fit based on what I know about them.

> PRO TIP
>
> If you're looking for somewhere to take a hike, start with a hiking book. Written hiking guides are excellent resources, with maps, regulations and suggested routes. Check your local library or gear shop for books about your area.

After moving to Oregon, I noticed something interesting; everyone here says they like hiking. I have come to understand that this is a meaningless statement, since hiking is an ill-defined activity (How many miles? How many hours? What kind of terrain? In what kinds of weather?). So when I call a friend a "hiker," it usually means they have enough experience on a good variety of trails that I don't need to tell them what to pack or how to prepare for an outing. It also usually means that they have the stamina to get out and walk all day without complaining, getting hurt or feeling exhausted. My "non-hiker" friends may have gone hiking previously, but I know that they do not have the same level of skill, endurance or foresight as my "hiker" friends.

They don't salivate over maps and hiking books like I do. They probably don't pack the ten essentials or hike in the rain or snow. That doesn't mean that they're bad people or that I don't like hiking with them; it's quite the opposite. I love going hiking with less experienced people when they're excited to get outside, and it's especially fun when they're open to learning new things.

In January 2017, my friend Amanda wanted to check it out Steelhead Falls in the snow. She falls into my "non-hiker" category, partly because she's not as obsessed with hiking as I am. She'd gone on many hikes in the past but still had a lot to learn. I took this as an opportunity to build on the skills we practiced on a previous snowy hike earlier that month.

The trail was absolutely treacherous, as old footprints turned the fluffy snow into sloping death ice. We were grateful for our Yaktrax but wished for better traction. Amanda asked, "What would you do if I slid into the river?" That led to an interesting conversation about decision making, the ten essentials and when/how to call for help. I think she was only partly joking when she asked, but that is what makes a good hiking buddy: someone who wants to have the conversation about problem solving and emergency scenarios before they happen. We had a great hike—no one slid into the river, we discovered a bloody deer carcass and we chattered the whole time about all sorts of stuff. Every hike presents new opportunities, and you never know exactly what you're going to get into.

WINTER TRACTION

Yaktrax®: tire chains for your boots

MICROspikes®: (more aggressive than Yaktrax®), made with chains and small metal spikes that dig into the ice

Snowshoes: provide both traction and flotation for walking on deep snow

Crampons: provide the best traction on ice but are heavier, more expensive and more technical than the first two options

---

I frequently hear people say, "Oh, I'd love to go hiking with you!" But only a small percentage of them ever follow through. In June 2014, one of my non-hiking pals actually did follow through, and we met up for a short walk at Bald Hill in Corvallis, Oregon. It was a hot day in July, and I was grateful to find some tree-shaded trails. We hiked quickly up to the summit viewpoint and then meandered down on an erratic network of trails, some user-generated and some not. With no real time crunch, we simply enjoyed each other's company and the opportunity to have a mini-adventure close to home.

Partway down the hill I stopped in my tracks. All around me were thimbleberry bushes thick with bright red berries. I introduced my friend to this local berry, and we started gorging ourselves on the sweet, seedy fruit. Finding wild foods is just one of many reasons to get out hiking in your own backyard!

And here's a word of advice: If you're one of those people who won't go out with your experienced hiker friends out of fear that you aren't knowledgeable or fit enough, just go. If they invited you to go hiking, then they're prepared to walk at your pace, hook you up with the gear you forgot at home, teach you how to stay on track and share what they're passionate about.

I made an unexpected hiking friend in late 2015. After I'd given up my career teaching high school science, I longed to find a way to stay connected to youths in some capacity. I interviewed at the local youth shelter in Corvallis to learn more about their mentoring program. When I told them I was interested in working with teenage kids, they said they really didn't have a good match for me because most of their kids were elementary-aged. Much later, I got a phone call from them about a 14-year-old girl who might be a good fit. They warned me that she was on the autism spectrum and was a difficult child to work with. They did not seem confident that it would work out. I told them I'd give it a try.

Let's call her Anna. When I first met Anna, she hardly said a word. She wouldn't admit to liking anything, wanting anything or knowing anything about herself. But it appeared that she and her dad wanted to be matched with a mentor, so we started meeting a couple of times each month.

I tried everything I could think of, but I struggled to connect with Anna. One day, as I was out of any better ideas, I asked if her dad would drop her off at a park so we could take a walk. Anna hated it at first, but very soon we were able to establish a rapport on these walks. She'd start out talking about this or that drama occurring between her favorite anime characters, but it didn't take much effort to redirect her attention to the scenic drama we were walking through.

In January 2016, we took a walk at Fitton Green, a local natural area. On the trail, Anna looked for birds and squirrels. We picked up unusual rocks and admired the trees. She was curious about all the things she found on our walk, and she wove creative stories about them. It was beautiful to see how Anna engaged with the natural world—I admired her for it.

As we strolled up the hill to the bench in the meadow, I had to stop several times to let Anna catch her breath. She was young and thin and weak. She feared exertion, thinking she was going to overdo it and get hurt. It was strange to see. A girl of her age should be running circles around me, but she wasn't an athlete and was probably never pushed to do many physical things. I felt like these walks were good for her on so many levels.

Once we reached the bench, we took off our backpacks and dug around for snacks. I had taught her how to pack for a hike: food, water, jacket. Anna had a nice sandwich that she had made earlier that day but she really wanted what I had: a bag of mixed nuts. I was happy to share. She ate ravenously, as if we'd just run a marathon. The breeze blew; the crows soared overhead; the tall grass undulated. We sat in silence—neither of us needing to talk. It was close to a perfect moment.

As we turned back, Anna immediately resumed telling stories. I listened intently as she blurred reality with fantasy, incorporating the objects in front of us with the dreams in her head. Anna, who could not connect with people in the real world, had this incredible ability to see beyond what I saw. I struggled to understand how she would make a life in this society, a society that operates differently than she does. I hoped that in some small way, I had played a positive role in Anna's journey, allowing her to express herself in nature without judgment.

I have always enjoyed taking young people out hiking. In December 2012, I met up with one of my former high school students to hike in the Columbia River Gorge. Despite living in Portland, she had never been there before. I took her to the Cape

Horn Loop and Wahclella Falls, two of my favorite hiking spots. Both hikes travel through iconic scenery, with steep cliffs, river views, thick trees and dramatic waterfalls. While I'd hiked these trails many times before, walking with her was like unwrapping a Christmas present. She was pleasantly surprised and curious about everything we saw on the trail. As we passed by a large root mass of a tipped-over tree, she stopped in her tracks. "I've never seen anything like it," she said. On my own, I would have strolled right by it without a second glance. I paused to appreciate its shape, its size and its unique beauty. I thought about how much I missed when I was solely focusing on moving quickly along the trail to get a "fast time" for my spreadsheet.

While these occasional experiences are very meaningful, I mostly plan hikes with a regular group of friends. When I moved to Portland, Oregon, in 2006, I established some steady hiking partners from within my friend group. I had known Sue since college, and somehow we'd both ended up living in Portland. Shortly after my relocation, we hiked up Devil's Peak in the Mt. Hood National Forest. After that, we met up for regular weekend hikes all over Northwest Oregon and Southern Washington.

Through Sue, I met other people who became friends and hiking partners. In March 2007, I hiked with Sue and a couple of other friends on a loop trail in the Columbia River Gorge. All of us shared a real love of the outdoors. Since we had different academic backgrounds and life experiences, we were able to learn from each other as we hiked. One pointed out interesting geological features, another taught us how to find edible plants, and another listened for bird songs to identify. While our pace was comfortably fast, we did take time to stop and snap photos and investigate interesting things we found along the way. I was happy that I'd found such a fun, silly and adventurous group of people so soon after moving west. I would hike many, many more times with this group over the following years.

Occasionally, I convinced a friend or two to take off on a hiking road trip with me. While I was a high school teacher, it was easy to find stretches of time during the summer to go further into the backcountry. In August 2012, I drove across Oregon with Sue and Karen, another friend living in Portland, to check out some unfamiliar places. We hiked up Four-in-One Cone and Belknap Crater, located in the sun-baked lava flows of Central Oregon. I particularly enjoyed our adventures on Belknap and Little Belknap Craters because we wandered around off-trail, exploring the landscape. It's important for me to have friends who are up for some exploration. I'm much too curious to be confined to a trail.

After moving away from Portland, hiking served as a convenient way to stay connected with the friends I'd left behind. Sue and I took a trip to the Oregon Dunes National Recreation Area in 2013, hiking across endless sand dunes, through coastal forests and out to the Umpqua Lighthouse. Part of the dunes is off-limits to vehicle traffic, making it a perfect place to hike. Amidst rolling hills of sand and the distant sound of crashing waves, we wandered slowly, stopping to investigate interesting sand shapes and sculptures.

In July 2015, we spent a few days in the Willamette National Forest. Stretching across densely wooded areas in the central portion of the Cascade Range; this area has many trailheads and campgrounds to choose from. I chose a few mountains to hike with trails leading up to their summits, and Sue gladly accompanied me. Between peaks, we enjoyed quiet time at our camp and explored short trails nearby. Highlights of this trip and others like it include beautiful hikes, warm fires, good food and great conversation. As life takes us in geographically different directions, I think it's important to make time to stay connected.

One of my longest-running hiking relationships is with Rick. I met Rick on one of the first winter hikes I did with the Mazamas in 2006. The Mazamas is a nonprofit mountaineering club that formed on the summit of Mt. Hood over a hundred years ago. Based in Portland, Oregon, the club now provides classes, workshops, events, climbs and social events for climbers and hikers across the Pacific Northwest. I came to the Mazamas as a curious young hiker eager to broaden her skills, and I was very lucky to connect with Rick so early in my climbing career.

Over the years, Rick and I have completed a number of hikes and climbs together. And now that we live hours apart, we try really hard to meet up for one good adventure each summer. In 2015, our destination was a highpoint on the flanks of Mt. Rainier in Washington. It was going to be a long and grueling outing, but we were confident that we could make the best of it. The mountain weather did not cooperate, so we trudged through a thick fog all day. With little to no visibility in the wet, heavy air, we decided that attempting a loose scramble with route-finding challenges would not be a good idea. We did, however, hike all the way out to a great viewpoint near Panhandle Gap that was shrouded in clouds. From there, we turned around and headed back since the conditions were not right for our original plan. When things don't go as expected, it's nice to have a trusted friend along for the journey.

Not every trip is my idea of a good time. In 2012, I reluctantly decided to join Sue and her husband, Scott, on a two-day backpacking trip around Mt. St. Helens. I have never enjoyed backpacking—my body hates carrying heavy loads. I always prefer traveling light and fast on long day hikes rather than slogging along with an overnight pack. However, my interest in spending time with my friends outweighed the pounds on my back, so I decided to go.

NASCAR backpacking, I call it, where you just go around in a pointless circle. I wanted to reach the tops of mountains, not walk around them. So my head was in the wrong place right from the outset of our trip. We marched eighteen miles on that first day. The sun beat down hard as we walked through the barren, treeless blast zone. Between the heat, the mileage and the slippery gravel, I was delirious by the time we reached camp. The only thing on my mind the next day was getting out. It took forever to walk that final ten miles. I was toast!

Two years later, I decided to turn the tables and invite my dear friends on an adventure of my design. We booked a stay at a fire lookout in Central Oregon that required a bit of snowshoeing to get to. The pace on this trip was much more relaxed. After a few hours of hard work getting there, we were able to spread out and relax, playing games, drinking wine and stoking the campfire. That was my idea of a good time.

My husband, Aaron, is always a willing adventure partner. He is a quick study in learning new skills and he is naturally curious about his environment. We take road trips together at any opportunity. Whether it's a weekend getaway or an epic vacation, we always find ways to have a good time outdoors. In spring 2015, our annual vacation took us to Southern Utah, where we visited several national parks. Since national parks are typically crawling with mobs of tourists, we had to plan creatively to find some semblance of solitude. The Fairyland Loop in Bryce Canyon was a good place to start. To me, Bryce came across as a "drive-through park." Most people simply stepped out of their vehicle at each viewpoint, took a photo and then drove on to the next one. I was surprised by how few people were actually out hiking. We even did the Figure 8 Loop at Bryce Canyon, which is one of the more popular hikes in the park. There were some people out hiking but it never felt too crowded. Then again, the scenery may have been so spectacular that we hardly noticed the people. We enjoyed the cool weather and light dusting of late-April snow at this incredibly beautiful national treasure. Plus, we were on the lookout for benchmarks park rangers placed throughout the park like a scavenger hunt. It was clearly an activity designed for kids, but we had fun searching for those hidden treasures. After finding a certain amount, we were eligible for a special prize at the visitor center. (It ended up being a little disappointing: a pin). I can always count on Aaron to participate in these sorts of silly activities!

As the years roll by, we continue to accumulate more days spent on the trails together. I especially enjoy taking Aaron to places in his home state of Oregon that he has never seen before. Together, we have traveled to coastal forests, volcanic highpoints, alpine lakes and remote deserts. We have camped in the snow, rain, wind and sun. We'll drive for miles to reach quiet hot springs in the middle of winter. No matter what crazy plan I come up with, Aaron is up for just about anything. We've even gone on frigid hiking adventures—the winter season has never shut him down. Early in our relationship, we hiked up Marys Peak in the snow. That was just one step towards bigger and bolder mountains that we'd face together in the coming years.

Upon moving to Oregon, I learned that one simple way to find new partners and facilitate getting out more often is to join organized hiking groups. Through these groups I was able to learn new skills, explore unfamiliar places and meet like-minded individuals. I participated in many Mazamas hiking trips while living in Portland, including an outing to Larch Mountain in March 2009.

PRO TIP

Hiking and climbing organizations offer group outings, hiking education and trail-work opportunities to help you connect with your hiking community.

In Oregon, the Mazamas have led the charge, exploring the mountains in the Pacific Northwest and across the globe since 1894. Do an Internet search to find more information about local clubs in your area.

I had hiked up Larch Mountain before, so I knew the route, but I thought the excursion might be a nice way to connect with other people who enjoy challenging snowshoeing. The team was strong and up to the task. I was surprised at how efficiently our group was able to complete fourteen snowy miles in a reasonable amount of time. I enjoyed being out with my own people, reveling in our shared passion.

I always keep my eyes open for similar types of trips. In December 2010, I joined a group hike of the Elk Mountain-Kings Mountain Traverse in the Oregon Coast Range. This hike is difficult enough when the trail is bare, so I was excited to see just how treacherous it would be covered in snow. For this trip, a very eclectic and under-prepared group showed up. They did not understand how much harder they'd have to work to move along a trail that was covered with wet, heavy snow. Our experienced leader, Rick, did his best to keep the party moving. It was an interesting contrast from my experience on Larch Mountain the previous year.

Several years later, I participated in a yoga retreat led by one of my favorite Mazamas leaders, Eugene. After the yoga sessions were over, Eugene offered to lead a hike through the forest near the lodge. Another eclectic group gathered, taking him up on his offer. But unlike the difficult conditions we encountered on the Elk-Kings trip, the trail was snow-free and clear of obstacles. The sun was shining; the sky was cloudless. We had no lengthy agenda or serious time constraints. We walked casually among the trees and streams, simply enjoying our time in nature. The people I met through organized hikes and classes with the Mazamas turned out to be good adventure partners outside the club as well. In 2007 I climbed Mt. Shasta with a couple I had met through the Mazamas. The climb was beautiful. All went according to plan. My fondest memory from this trip was my experience at Shasta's summit. Atop this 14,000-foot peak, I found myself encapsulated in a swirling mass of butterflies. As I lay back on the rock and let my gaze shift upwards, I watched a flurry of little orange wings fill the sky. Bright beams of sunlight danced between the flying insects, coaxing me into a quiet, blissful state of relaxation. I took a brief summit nap in the warm sun. All that remained was the long walk back in the blistering July heat.

These experiences highlight various circumstances that can arise when hiking in organized groups. At that point, I didn't know how much I still had to learn about the differences between attending a hike versus leading a hike.

Throughout my life, I never saw myself as a leader. But something grabbed a hold of me early in my hiking days, when I signed up to take charge of a group participating in the Flags on the 48 memorial hike. On September 11, 2005, forty-eight teams planned to hike up each of the 4,000-foot summits in New Hampshire to fly the American flag. The event was organized to honor those lost on 9/11, just a few years prior. I decided it was a good opportunity to try on a leadership role, and to coax my dad out on a hike with me.

I tasked him with designing a contraption that would hold the flag once we got to the summit. He dreamed up a telescoping device that could be collapsed for the hike and expanded when needed to serve as our mountain-top flagpole. A motley crew of hikers joined us for the event. I chose North Kinsman for our hike, which we accessed from the popular Lafayette Place Campground. As we trekked up the steep and rocky trail, I tried to pay attention to how everyone was doing. Some people walked faster than others. Some had to take many rest breaks to catch their breath. Some needed reminding to drink water. I learned that being a leader means minding the needs of other people in addition to taking care of myself. Fortunately for me, this was a relatively easy group that did not need much from me. Once our flag was situated on the summit, a few of us walked over to the South Kinsman summit, chatting with the group gathered on top.

This was the first of many group hikes that I would end up leading over the years. I would need to learn much more in order to be an effective leader, able to deal with the different personalities that would end up on my teams in the future.

Many years later, while working as a high school teacher, I connected with a small group of women working at the school who wanted to organize a women's weekend retreat. We decided to drive from Portland to Bend to explore the Central Oregon mountains and other sights while we were there. I became the de facto hike leader for this small group of people with whom I'd never hiked before.

Knowing full well that there'd be various degrees of fitness and hike preparedness among the group members, I tried to lead a hike at Smith Rock State Park that is a bit more challenging than the usual pedestrian loop. I'd hiked it previously with a group of friends who knew the way. There is one steep hill and some brief off-trail scrambling, but I thought it would be within reach of the women on the retreat.

One person called it quits on the very first hill climb. Called Misery Ridge, this steep section of switchbacks can take anyone's breath away. But walking at the right pace, most people are able to make it up just fine. However, she had planned on a much easier day and decided to stay behind, strolling around the park taking photos while the rest of us finished the hike. Oops, lesson number one for me: talk to group members ahead of time to learn more about the type of experience they want and are able to do.

The rest of the day went off without a hitch, as the other hikers enjoyed the scenery, the terrain and the challenges of the route. I felt successful leading most of the team on the intended hike, but I also felt a little twinge of failure for not being able to accommodate everyone. I knew I had to be more thoughtful about my hike choice for the next day so that everyone could complete the planned trip and feel successful.

That next day led us to Scout Camp. At only 2.5 miles and 700 feet of elevation gain, I thought it would be a great hike for all to enjoy. While the elevation change was a little challenging for some, the hike was so short that we could really take our time and soak in the scenery. For a January day, it felt really hot in the canyon and everyone ended up stripping off layers of clothing to stay comfortable. But we all survived, got great pictures, made interesting observations and spent some quality time together in the great outdoors.

Knowing the abilities of a group beforehand is a luxury not always afforded in group hiking. In 2013, I tagged along with some people I'd never met before. One of the group's members advertised an extra permit for Mt. St. Helens on a hiking website. I had climbed this mountain a few times before and felt comfortable enough with the route that I was not too worried about hiking with a bunch of unknowns. But when I arrived at the trailhead, I was a bit taken aback by the clothing some of the team members had chosen to wear for the trip: sneakers, tracksuits, shorts. The rest of the team looked better prepared, dressed in several layers of shirts, nylon pants, waterproof hiking boots, hats and gloves. Oh no, I thought, what have I gotten myself into?

One individual was responsible for organizing the group, so the others saw him as the leader of the pack. We started walking up the mountain on snow-free trails, an unusual sight for me as I'd only ever done this route in the winter. Traveling through unfamiliar territory, in lock step with the people in front of me, I recognized at one point that we were off course. I knew we'd missed a left turn. I ran up ahead to get the attention of our "leader" and let him know we needed to change direction.

As we walked back towards the correct route, we headed straight into a thick fog. The bare dirt and rocks turned to patches of icy snow. My new friend with the sneakers was doing pretty poorly, but once I coached her on some better strategies for crossing the snow, her spirits lifted considerably. As the snowfields grew longer and more consistent, the organizer passed out traction devices to other members of the group.

We slogged ahead for hours in a cloud, chit-chatting about miscellaneous things to keep ourselves from feeling too lousy about what was supposed to be an easy and straightforward climb. It reminded me how much of mountaineering is pure drudgery, and to normal people, it is not that fun. Since I'd done so many trips like this before, I understood that the misery is only temporary, and that current discomfort leads to future joy. As social media sharing becomes more and more popular, people who are new to the outdoors are lulled into a false sense of what getting those cool shots actually entails. The mountains aren't always as beautiful, fun and accessible as they are portrayed online.

I took a moment to think about why I'm drawn to mountaineering. The drudgery, to me, is an essential part of the pursuit of climbing mountains. It's the feeling of overcoming physical and mental challenges that make reaching the summit feel like such an achievement. It's also the opportunities to learn about myself along the trip: my decision-making skills, my ability to take care of myself and others, my willingness to push ahead through adversity and my wisdom to know when it's time to turn back. These things, which are not fun in the moment, help make mountaineering a thoroughly fulfilling hobby. I snapped back into the present moment and tried to share some positive insights with my team.

"Don't worry, we'll climb above the clouds and you'll see, it will be spectacular," I said with confidence in my voice but not in my heart. While I couldn't be certain of clearing skies, I had to have hope that all this work would end up with a great reward. I counted on breaking through the thick cloud layer like a winning marathon finisher, breaking through the tape with a hug, joyful grin. In time, we saw the sun poking through the edge of the clouds, and we emerged victorious, with the summit of the mountain in view. We took a break above the clouds and looked down at the earth below. It was covered in a giant, puffy blanket, through which only Mt. Rainier and Mt. Adams were tall enough to penetrate. It was incredible.

After a tough morning ascending the mountain, we made it to the summit and enjoyed panoramic views of the Cascades. I celebrated with snacks and a rest break, cheering on each person as they reached the top.

On the way down, everyone took to glissading pretty quickly. It's fun and easy to slide down the snow on your butt! However, the excitement of glissading distracted us from keeping an eye out for our trail junction, and we ended up far from the winter route yet again. The trip leader was way out of earshot, so I couldn't signal his mistake. I was worried that we'd end up at the wrong parking lot and have a lot of backtracking to do to return to our cars. I ran ahead, eventually grabbing the full group's attention and re-oriented us towards our route. We took a sharp left, following some snowfields and gullies as we approached the tree line.

Again, I found myself in a leadership role, pointing our group towards the trail we needed to be on. It became clear to me how astute one needs to be when taking charge of a group. Everyone follows your lead, so if you make a wrong turn and no one knows any better, everyone else makes a wrong turn too.

> PRO TIP
>
> Leaders make mistakes, too. Do a little planning ahead of time and pay attention as you hike. Never be afraid to ask questions about the route.

I look back today and wonder how this group's day would have turned out if I hadn't been there. Would they have made it to the top? Would they have gotten hopelessly bogged down in the trees after the errant glissade? I can't know for sure. But I started to realize that maybe I have more leadership skills than I'd imagined, and that it was about time to step up and use those skills to help others navigate their adventures safely.

In 2014, I volunteered as a hike leader for the Mazamas. I chose Silver Falls as my first hike lead since the route is straightforward, accessible in early spring and easy to get to from Portland as well as Corvallis (my home at the time). A few Corvallis friends came with me on this hike and we met up with a couple of new people and an experienced hike leader who would oversee my trip.

It was a completely ordinary hike. We all had a great time; the waterfalls were beautiful and there were no major issues to problem solve. It was the type of day that could make anyone feel like a successful leader. I was glad to get started with such an easy experience.

I enjoy sharing the outdoors with people who don't get out much on their own. I can only hope to spark an interest in hiking or capture someone's imagination to go further, climb higher and explore more obscure places in the future. It was not that long ago that I was the new person, making all the mistakes and blissfully unaware of what I didn't know. When I see someone doing those things, I think back to my own beginnings, remembering that everyone was new at something once.

With the Mazamas' blessing to add any hikes I wanted to their calendar, I aimed for leading one trip a month. During most months I met my goal. That June, I took a group to a rarely visited summit on the Old Cascades Crest. In July, I led a small group up Dome Rock, one of my favorite and more obscure highpoints. It's a long, hard hike up through dense forest to get to the top, but the expansive views from the summit and the pretty alpine rock garden make it worth the effort.

Not all of the highpoints I scheduled to hike garnered much attention, especially the ones that required a bit of driving to get to. In August, I put Bear Point on the calendar. It was a little further away from any major cities than my previous outings. When I showed up at the carpool spot, there was only one other hiker. The minimum number of people required to run an official trip is three, but since we were both there and wanted to go hiking, off we went!

Everyone else missed out because we stumbled into a patch of ripe huckleberries alongside the trail. Our grazing may have slowed the hike down, but it was time well spent. At the summit, we had close-up views of beautiful Mt. Jefferson all to ourselves.

In the fall, I took a full group of twelve up to McNeil Point, a popular viewpoint on the flanks of Mt. Hood. The fall colors were spectacular, and we were fortunate to have perfect weather, too!

I continued to lead hikes throughout the winter, mostly getting my fellow Corvallis residents outdoors, in the dreariest months of the year. But in the spring, I reached out to the Portlanders in the club. On Easter Sunday 2015, we took a walk along Opal Creek, where our lunch spot would also serve as the site for an Easter egg hunt. As my group sat, eating their sandwiches among the gorgeous old-growth trees, I poked around in a little clearing nearby, where I hid several plastic eggs with treats inside. I thought it would be a fun way to break up the walk and add a silly activity. If I was going to hike all year round, I was also going to share these seasonal opportunities with others. Some people take their hobbies very seriously; I much prefer to retain a child's playfulness and be open to experiencing the outdoors in a variety of different ways.

Later that summer, I decided to coordinate a string of hikes in Central Oregon that would begin from a convenient base camp in the area. I called it "Lavapalooza" due to the impressive lava flows nearby. The first hike in the series went to the top of Black Crater, an excellent viewpoint overlooking the lava flows.

Over the next several days, I led three more trips, including a hike to the top of Belknap Crater. While this hike is described in a popular hiking guidebook, there is no official trail to the top. I had hiked a route years before with some friends and was confident I could repeat it with a new group of people. Due to the open terrain and the sheer number of people who walk up this hill, the route is really easy to follow. The social trail is well-established, leading the way from the Pacific Crest Trail (PCT) to the summit. We also toured the lower and craggier Little Belknap Crater before heading back to camp.

PACIFIC CREST TRAIL (2,653 miles)

Long-distance hikers have walked from Mexico to Canada on the Pacific Crest Trail (PCT) since 1970. Recent books and movies have popularized this hike, causing a huge spike in the number of permits being issued to hikers looking to complete part or all of the trail. While only a handful of people walked the entire trail in the 1970s, it is estimated that over 1,000 people completed the PCT in 2018.

The following day, I led a loop hike over a mountaintop, near several small lakes. With seven people participating, this was the most popular hike of Lavapalooza. The route offered a nice variety of terrain features and included travel on both official and unofficial trails. I was excited to show off a place that not too many Portland hikers get to visit. I decided that part of my mission as a leader would be to challenge people to expand their comfort zones, taking them to locations that don't make the top-ten lists.

My personal interests did not always align with others, and I learned to compromise by showcasing some iconic destinations as well. In 2014, I organized a group of novice hikers for a winter climb of Mt. St. Helens. We'd spent a few months preparing for the trip. The ascent, which covers nearly 5,000 vertical feet in six miles, is a great achievement for an aspiring mountain climber, especially in the winter. The team went on training hikes together, we practiced snow-climbing skills, and we learned how to use an ice axe to stop a fall (self-arrest) in case of a slip. It would be a new and exciting experience for most of my team members.

We started hiking before dawn, trudging up the well-worn trail by headlamp. When the sun rose and we inched our way to the tree line, it looked like we were in for a day of perfect weather. With blue skies overhead and crunchy snow underfoot, there was nothing between us and the summit . . . except lots and lots of footsteps. But we were ready. The team forged ahead, one foot in front of the other, all the way to the top. We celebrated our accomplishment with lots of food, water, photos and smiles. The summit was only half the journey, though—we still had to make our way down safely.

Before heading back down, we reviewed the descent strategies we practiced earlier that month. The entire crew took quickly to plunge stepping and glissading. I smiled as each person sat down on the snow and shoved off, hooting and hollering until slowing to a halt at the bottom. We slid down as far as we could before standing back up and walking the rest of the way down the mountain. It felt good to have facilitated such a memorable experience for everyone. But I'd soon come to understand that things don't always go so smoothly.

ঌৎ

Hiking takes a backseat to other activities in most people's minds during the winter, so I made it my mission to entice people out who might not have envisioned hiking outside of the summer months. Since I began leading group hikes, I always made an effort to organize winter outings. When crowds flock to the ski slopes, I prefer to find quiet places in the woods. If I open just one person's eyes to the joys of winter hiking, then I consider my mission successful.

One of my favorite team outings that I organized is a winter trip to Crater Lake National Park. Crater Lake in the winter is no joke. The park averages forty-three feet of snow per year, with a record of seventy-three feet in the winter of 1932-1933. It is a beautiful park to visit on a clear winter day. But planning months in advance for a trip does not guarantee you'll hit the weather just right. The first three times I visited Crater Lake in the winter, the weather was so bad I could barely even see the lake. Skies were gray and the snow was deep and untracked. I wondered why people want to come to this awful place.

On December 13, 2014, I got really lucky. My group of seven drove to the park from our rental house an hour away, excited for a day of snowshoeing bliss. We began our trek from the upper parking lot at the edge of the lake. The temperature was just below freezing, and the snow sparkled in the bright sun. Aaron, who'd come on the trip last year, led our team along the road that contours around the edge of the lake. We traveled west, following old snowshoe tracks for about three miles. Watchman Peak loomed high above us; it was the most prominent feature around. And while I clearly advertised the hike as "relatively flat," the team quickly found out that even small elevation changes feel big.

We veered off the broad, flat road and angled up a steeper snow slope towards the Watchman viewpoint. There were some groans and grumbles about how hard it was, but eventually everyone made it to our destination. And once there, overlooking the impossibly blue and wide Crater Lake, everyone forgot about how tired they felt and immersed themselves in the magical moment. According to my journal:

I cringed as the complaints rolled in: "I thought you said this was flat!" Maybe I hadn't properly prepared my team for the short section of hillside leading to the Crater Lake viewpoint. But soon, all was well. As each person broke free of the trees and stood agape at the sparkling expanse of water, I knew I had successfully delivered a memorable experience. Sure, we were only halfway through the day, but here we could each rest and rally enough energy for the hike back.

Even I had forgotten how tiring the last stretch of walking is. Sure, I'd done this hike before, but memory is selective. I clearly recalled the long, gentle road walk and the panoramic view overlooking the lake. I could see each snow crystal, each tree branch, each ripple in the water. I remembered the stout, stone structure standing high above the edge of the crater. My brain had chosen to forget the agonizing last half mile of walking that made my legs and lungs burn. Perhaps I hadn't inadequately warned my team; instead, I had subconsciously prevented all of us from dreading the worst part of the day.

I'm going to have to find balance as a leader, learning to provide the right information, encouragement and support while also respecting individuals' independence and autonomy. It's what I would want from my leaders, too. I suppose I'll never get every last thing right for every person, but I will try to remain open to learning lessons from each outing in order to do a better job on the next one.

᪲

There are many reasons why I choose to lace up my shoes, load up a backpack and start walking. One reason is training. On intentional training outings, there is usually a physical or skills emphasis on the trip. If my goal is to build up my endurance to cover more miles in less time, I'll set out on a trail that will push my distance limits. If my goal is to be able to carry a full mountaineering pack and keep up with the team, I'll pick a shorter but steeper trail and load my pack to the brim. And if my goal is to be able to practice more technical skills in a safe learning environment, I'll join a team led by people who have more knowledge and experience than me.

In April 2007, that's just what I did. I was eager to learn how to travel on a rope team and to work on mountaineering skills I'd only read about in books. I was a student in the Mazamas' Basic Climbing Education Program (BCEP), under the tutelage of the great Monty Smith. Monty, as well as several assistant leaders, took our team of students on a practice "climb" to Illumination Saddle on Mt. Hood. While a rope is not necessary to make the ascent, the route is useful for practicing tying in, traveling as a team and using ice axes in the snow.

Seemingly simple tasks tested my patience. I struggled to move comfortably as a member of a rope team: not walking too fast or too slow, with respect to other people on the rope. To make matters worse, I had one useless hand that was thickly bandaged after a finger injury. I called it my manatee flipper. Monty helped me protect my flipper with a thick, insulated mitten and made sure I was given assistance on tasks that required two hands. He helped me feel like I was a valuable part of the team despite my injury. Although this climb was physically and mentally taxing, we reached our destination in good spirits. Under pretty blue skies, we sat down and enjoyed some food before returning to the parking lot.

Years later, I was on the teaching end of things. In order to devise a plan that would whip hikers into shape for a big trip, I thought back to my days of being a student in BCEP, when my class went on many training hikes as a group. As many as eighteen of us would resolutely march up a trail, like we did on our January 2007 ascent of Hamilton Mountain in the Columbia Gorge. I remembered cramming as much gear in my backpack as I could fit in order to get a good conditioning workout. Those hikes served not only as a way to get exercise, but also as a way to build camaraderie with the team, prepare us to pack well for winter hikes and get us used to being outside in less-than-optimal weather. I know that hiking is not all about physical stamina; it's important to develop those other skills too.

In 2013, I assembled a group of novice hikers who were interested in climbing South Sister, Oregon's third highest peak. The route to the summit is a well-traveled but difficult trip that involves 5,000 feet of elevation gain in just under six miles. The mountain is classified as "easy" to mountaineers and "very difficult" to hikers. The mixed messages sent through social media confuse many people attempting to hike this peak for the first time. Sure, you don't need any technical skills to scale this peak, but you do need a bit of mountain sense, good weather and some mental and physical endurance.

Living in Corvallis, it was difficult to simulate the challenges faced on this peak. I developed a series of training hikes that would help build my team's skills. We loaded up our backpacks with the ten essentials and headed out in search of the most challenging routes within a thirty-minute drive from town.

The first easy choice was Bald Hill, which is right in Corvallis. This hill is only 400 feet tall, but with some clever planning I was able to contrive a route that gained 800 feet in a total of six miles. It was a far cry from South Sister, but it was a good first chance to get everyone outside, moving together and figuring out how their gear worked (Considering that many hikers never carry the ten essentials, this seemed like a great place to start).

Next, we hiked at Chip Ross Park. Our route at Chip Ross provided a hike with more varied terrain, steeper trails and a greater elevation gain overall. Still, we were in the foothills of the Oregon Coast Range, not the taller and more rugged Cascades, so it would just have to do.

Our final training hike took place on Marys Peak, the only "mountain" near Corvallis. Despite its mountain status, casual visitors can drive to within a half mile of the summit. Looking at my options, I cobbled together a route that would ascend the north side of the mountain to the summit and descend via the east ridge and a connector trail. Compared with our hike at Chip Ross, we accumulated more elevation gain and more time on the trail. Still, it was nothing like South Sister. I crossed my fingers and hoped I'd done an okay job of getting my team prepared.

That year, our preparation was sufficient to get us up and down the mountain in a reasonable amount of time, with no major issues. However, in later years, I followed the same protocol with drastically different results. Most of the team moved well and had a great time, but one participant ascended very slowly. I should have recognized that she needed to turn back. But we persisted, guiding her along, all the way to the summit. I rationalized that we would be able to make up time on the way down, since the snow conditions were perfect for a rapid descent. But she could not get over her fear of sliding down the mountain. And so we descended, one slow step after another. I had to split up the team because it was taking so long; something I swore I would never do. Our agonizingly slow return hike became a safety issue and I regretted encouraging her to continue upwards even though, in hindsight, it was clear she was not ready. I learned that one size does not fit all, and that I need to find more rigorous training hikes to help people determine if they are up to the final task.

For four years in a row, I took teams to a steep snow slope near the Santiam Pass to practice snow skills before tackling one of the Pacific Northwest's best beginner climbs: Mt. St. Helens. This particular snow slope is one of the few places in Central Oregon that provides a safe, easily accessible place to practice self-arrest, glissading and climbing with an ice axe and crampons.

Every group I've worked with experiences different challenges and obstacles. In 2014, I had one participant who completely lost her head while coming down the snowfield, fearful of slipping and falling. We coached her down without incident, but I worried that she would not be able to handle our big climb up Mt. St. Helens. Much to my surprise, she rocked it and couldn't stop talking about how amazing it was. That year, I learned that people are full of surprises, and not always in a bad way.

In 2016, the snow conditions on the practice slope were much different, with barely enough snow to make for good skills practice, so we made do with what we had. There was one snow patch that was steep and deep enough to practice wearing crampons, and to get a sense of how to use an ice axe. This particular team's major deficit was its speed: what should have taken three or four hours took six. And when we finally went for our big hike up Mt. St. Helens, one individual's slow pace created a hazard for the entire group. In the mountains, speed is safety. The longer you're in the mountains, the more you're exposed to the elements. In retrospect, I wonder if I should have asked that person to sit out and keep training for the next climbing opportunity. But who can really predict the future? Some people do poorly in training and rise up on game day; others perform well in training and fall apart when it comes to the big climb.

Not every hike culminates in a life lesson, memorable experience or an amazing story. Many hikes are simply just walks in the woods, and there's nothing wrong with that. Hiking is such an integral part of my lifestyle that each trip doesn't need to be epic in order to be meaningful. When I go out on a hike, I'm choosing to take some time to be with my thoughts. Or perhaps I'm choosing to share that time with a friend or a group. I'm getting some physical activity and time in nature. I'm reducing stress. I'm hitting the reset button.

I know I've been to Indian Point in the Columbia River Gorge because it's on my spreadsheet, but do I recall the details? I can rebuild my memory based on the handful of pictures I took that day and the brief note that I wrote after returning. Otherwise, it's just a check mark in the book. Having no expectations going into a hike means that it can turn into anything. Maybe I'll have a life-changing experience. Maybe I'll challenge myself to my edge. Or maybe I'll just be present, live in the moment, and let it go.

It's on these hikes in particular that having a partner or group makes the time go by joyfully. Whether I'm hiking with friends or strangers, we end up growing closer by the end of the day. Being active outdoors with others is a great way to build relationships and create shared memories that last.

I've come a long way from being the new hiker in the group,

wearing the wrong shoes, carrying an ill-fitting backpack, packing too much extra gear and not knowing north from south. I am incredibly grateful for the people who welcomed me despite my lack of experience, taught me valuable lessons and encouraged me to keep showing up. Today, I feel honored that I am able to do the same for others who have more motivation than skill, and big outdoor goals they can't quite achieve on their own.

3

Going Solo

I had no intention of becoming a solo hiker. It happened by chance. In 2005, when I started getting interested in going outdoors and taking hikes, I asked everyone I knew to join me. But I had no takers. That left me with a choice: stay indoors or go it alone. Fortunately, I was stubborn enough to stick to my guns and go by myself.

In the fall of that year, I set out to hike Mt. Moosilauke, a 4,000-foot peak in New Hampshire's White Mountains. I had hiked in groups all summer and I longed for some alone time in nature. I had no idea it would be one of my most transformative experiences in the woods. I wrote about my trip as soon as I got home, and I can't communicate my thoughts any better today than I did in the moment. Here are some excerpts from my journal on October 15, 2005:

I needed to get away from it all and have my own adventure for a change. Much of my hiking earlier in the year was done alone, and I felt that I needed to get back to that. We all hike for different reasons, and for me, the feeling of being alone in the wild is one of the most desirable emotions achieved through hiking.

I hit the Glencliff Trail at 7:30 am during a brief respite from the rain. The trailhead was underwater; little did I know that this would be one of the driest spots of the hike. The path begins as a gentle, scenic foray through some woods and a beautiful pasture. Apple trees lined the way, producing a strong, delicious aroma. Combined with the sparkling fall colors and soft patter of raindrops, it excited all the senses.

After scaring away a small bunch of turkeys, I exited the pasture, encountered my first stream crossing and entered the woods. I was already feeling the weight of deadlines, responsibilities, and the other banalities of city life dropping from my shoulders. I felt awake and alive. Today would not be about peak-bagging, making good time, or hiking someone else's plan. Today would be about experiencing nature for myself and letting go of the nonsense that normally consumes my life.

I was captivated by all that surrounded me. I wandered along the trail, half in a dream, constantly smiling and looking up at the rain. I was warm and only used my jacket as a hood and cape over my backpack, so I could feel the raindrops on my bare arms and face. The raindrops were soothing.

There were times that I was completely aware of every inch of wildness that surrounded me, and there were times where I was so deep in thought that I may have been walking through outer space. My mind was gripped by feelings of complete peace and happiness; in that moment, nothing else mattered but the present. I am not a spiritual or religious person, but this was probably the closest I've ever been to a spiritual experience. I wanted to cast off my pack, lie down on the wet leaves and soak in every bit of the moment.

The last half-mile or so to the Moosilauke summit was wet and windy. The short spruce that lined sections of the trail provided a substantial amount of protection from the elements. Once I stepped out from behind that barrier, I felt the full effects of the weather. I felt a burst of energy and a new motive for hiking. My heart raced and my smile broadened as I swiftly walked past towering cairns to the bright-orange summit sign. I threw my hands up over my head, spun around dramatically and absorbed all of the awesome power of nature hurling itself at me. Now the moment was not about a solitary reflection on life but about a struggle between (wo)man and nature, face-to-face on a barren playing field.

Summiting those bare peaks was invigorating. I loved that I had Moosilauke completely to myself.

I anticipated a long, thoughtful descent through a mixture of terrain, and simple observations about life, friends, and nature. And although the way had been wet so far—I was completely soaked from the waist down—I had no idea what I would be in for during the second half of my adventure.

Approaching the Hurricane Trail, I noticed that the water levels seemed to be rising significantly. Rivers rushed by loudly and dramatically. Footing became less sure. Although the fall leaves are pretty, they cover up loose rocks, deep puddles of water and other surface features of the trail. I started to slow down to prevent ankle injury or any other stupid mistakes.

The trail soon became indistinguishable from the myriad streams in the area. There were some points where I had to stop and look around to assure myself that I was, indeed, following a trail. There were blazes on a few random trees and sparse bits of orange flagging along the way. These little trail reminders did wonders for my confidence, but they were few and far between. Several times, I remember pausing, laughing and wondering where I was supposed to go and how I would get there. There were streams, running alongside trails, that contained less water than the trails themselves. There were also flattened areas of forest that were completely flooded.

My socks were saturated. After a while, I figured it would just be easier to accept the fact that I was wet and splash right through the water. It made footing decisions infinitely easier.

My epic journey was coming to an end. It felt like a physically and mentally cleansing trek. The symbolism was hard to miss. As I entered the pasture and sloshed down the home stretch to the road, I was somewhat saddened that it was all over. I felt that I really accomplished something that day. My body and mind felt clear and refreshed. I promised myself that I'd leave more time for solo hiking as long as the weather permitted.

It has been great these past few months meeting so many new people and having wonderful new experiences, but ultimately, the one person I need to keep happy is myself. Having my own plans, my own moments and my own experiences are vital for my self-preservation. I hope that I get to feel like this again sometime soon.

Those early experiences of solo hiking had a profound impact, showing me how hiking is a necessary part of my life. I have always sought quiet spaces and time to be by myself because that's where I feel the most comfortable. Knowing that I can be by myself in the outdoors, surrounded by trees and flowers and sky, gives me a sense of freedom I've never felt in any other situation.

When I tell anyone that I'm going out for a hike alone, their immediate response is almost always: "be careful." The general perception of hiking alone, especially when a woman goes hiking alone, is that it is dangerous. It took a decade for my parents to change their opinions about my style of adventure. And I constantly wrangle with strangers, friends and family all questioning the reasonableness of solo hiking.

What shapes that perception? Hiking is just walking. Few would question the safety of taking a walk alone along most city streets and walkways. So, is it that hiking involves being further from medical help? Is it the extremely rare circumstance of a deadly animal encounter? Is it the fear of getting lost? Why are people so afraid of taking a walk in the woods by themselves? It's a fear I don't connect with or let stand in my way. While I may not convince you in this chapter to go take your first solo hike in the wilderness, I hope you will at least come to see how I arrived at my perspective and to share a glimpse in to the exciting and profound experiences I have had while hiking alone.

As I filtered my hiking spreadsheet containing the 366 hikes that I completed for this project, I calculated that I did over a third of the hikes solo. That's well over a hundred hikes (not including the ones I did that were not on my project list), and none of them were any more "dangerous" than the ones I'd done in groups. In fact, all of my major epics were hikes involving other people.

I believe we tend to have a false sense of security when hiking in groups. It is easy to shift responsibility to other people—

especially people who are more experienced—in group settings. When I hike alone, I know that I am my only lifeline. I know that my skills and judgment (and of course a bit of luck) are responsible for getting me back to my vehicle safely. I often feel safer, and that I make better decisions, when I hike alone.

In 2013, after a Mt. Hood climb was canceled at the trailhead due to bad weather, I had to come up with a backup plan on the fly. I drove south to the Ochoco Mountains in Central Oregon to hike up Lookout Mountain. I didn't have any hiking guidebooks in the car with me, but I vaguely remembered hiking Lookout Mountain from a particular trailhead several years earlier. I knew the mileage was a little on the longer side and that there would be little chance of seeing other people. It was an out-and-back hike on a single trail, so the risk of getting lost was low.

> ## DEFINITION
>
> Epic (n): a challenging and possibly dangerous adventure that pushes one to her limits. An epic is often characterized by one of the following: getting lost, hiking into inclement weather, getting injured, spending an unplanned night outdoors, or encountering unpredicted and dramatic obstacles. Often these hikes take longer than planned, end in the dark or prompt a traumatic response.

I unpacked all of my mountaineering gear and, unsure of what weather to expect, shoved a variety of clothing layers into my backpack: hat, mittens, long pants, raincoat, and puffy jacket. GORE-TEX trail shoes replaced the heavy-duty boots I'd packed for Mt. Hood. I wore long underwear beneath short pants, plus a long-sleeved shirt. The air was chilly on that May morning.

Leaving the trailhead at 9 am, I glanced quickly at a warning sign posted right up front: "Warning: Mountain Lion Area . . . Hiking alone is not recommended." That sign highlights one of the most overblown dangers of hiking solo—wild animals. It's kind of an understood safety rule that hiking alone is dangerous, whether you're in mountain lion country or not. In Oregon, there has been one presumed cougar attack in recorded history. One. Considering the thousands of people that hit the trails each day, I hardly consider fatal mountain lion encounters as a relevant risk factor on any of my hikes.

When it comes to assessing risk, I think about several factors. Let's take the Lookout Mountain scenario as an example. First, what are the potential hazards involved in my hike? Examples might include: hypothermia, animal attack, spraining an ankle, getting stuck after dark . . . The list goes on and on. Then I think about the likelihood of these things happening. My chances of getting hypothermia on a chilly day in May, for example, are pretty high. My chances of encountering a mountain lion, even if one has been sighted in the area within the past year, are extremely low. Even if I were lucky enough to see one on a solo hike, it would probably not be coming for me.

Next, what can I do to mitigate these hazards? I can carry extra clothing, drink warm liquids and turn around if it gets too cold or starts to rain. I feel very confident that I can reduce my risk of hypothermia to almost zero. There's not much I can do to alter my chances of encountering a mountain lion, besides staying home.

Lastly, I consider the consequences of each of these hazards. This is where the "solo" part of hiking has the most impact on risk assessment. If hypothermia sneaks up on me, if I break a leg, if I am attacked by an animal, then it will be more difficult or impossible for me to get help. This is where I need to acknowledge the risks I am taking and decide if the benefits of my hike outweigh the potential consequences.

To me, the risk of a deadly mountain lion encounter is not high enough for me to choose not to hike alone. As of February 2019, there have been twenty-six recorded fatal mountain lion attacks in the United States since 1890, and most of the victims were children. Bear attacks are more common but incredibly rare in Oregon. Most bear-attack victims are hunters who mistakenly approach a live bear that they think they have killed.

Sure, the consequences of a large-animal encounter are very high, but the odds of that happening are so impossibly low that it seems silly to use that possibility as a barrier to going out. Most hikers are injured or killed due to environmental factors, a lack of skill and/or poor decision-making. Since I am fairly confident that I can manage my body temperature, reduce my risk of injury and deal with small problems on my own as they arise, then taking a hike on my own makes sense. I am so passionate about my solo time in the woods that I cannot give it up for the extremely low chances of being killed by an animal. I did my hike. I saw no mountain lions. It was a glorious day.

⁂

I learned about finding my limits while solo hiking. On a visit to Grand Teton National Park in the summer of 2006, I hiked up to Amphitheater Lake, a gorgeous alpine lake surrounded by rocky cliffs. Inspired by the grandiose scenery, I decided to scramble up some of the rocks above the lake to get a better view. This was even before Instagram! I did it for myself! I had a fun time making it up to a cozy little perch with a panoramic view, but I soon realized that going down would be harder than going up. I did not have to call for a rescue, but I made a mental note on my careful down climb to check my enthusiasm before wandering into unknown vertical territory.

When I moved across the country and landed in Oregon, it was easy to prioritize solo hiking because I didn't know many people yet. Without friends to turn into hiking buddies, I thrived on solo hiking. It was freeing. I wasn't on anyone else's timetable; I didn't have to worry about the needs of a group; and I could go exactly where I wanted to go. I felt adequately prepared for the trips I went on, and I knew that if I ran into adverse circumstances that I had the wherewithal to figure it out. My parents didn't like the idea of me venturing out by myself, but I usually left my trip plans with someone. (This was before the days of social media check-ins and constant connectivity.) I had a cell phone but I hardly used it. I learned early on to develop my skills and confidence in the backcountry so I wouldn't miss out on hiking every time I couldn't find a partner.

This adeptness came in handy. In August 2006, I took one of many enjoyable Oregon solo hikes. As with every hike, I learned some valuable lessons. For starters, I ran out of water for the first time. I underestimated the intense August heat, and while I thought the Mt. Defiance trail didn't quite live up to its crazy-hard reputation, it gave me enough of a workout to get a sweat on. Traveling back down the mountain, in an effort to rehydrate, I remember stopping to eat some berries that I was pretty sure were edible (this is not advised). Luckily I'd made an accurate identification and didn't end up puking in the parking lot. After that hike, I took my water situation a bit more seriously.

Later that year, I upped my solo game by taking a one-night backpacking trip into Hells Canyon. I didn't have any backpacking gear, and I'd never done an overnighter on my own before. I borrowed some equipment from a friend, packed up my car and headed into the unknown. Again, some reflections from my journal:

My goal was to find McGraw Cabin by following the Reservoir Trail for two miles to Old McGraw Creek Route, which is now mostly destroyed and impossible to follow. I figured it would be easy enough to navigate just two miles to the cabin, located right near the creek.

Of course, I forgot the golden rule of hiking: Nothing is just that simple, and if something looks like it's right there, it really isn't.

I carried enough food and gear to last several nights, in case I decided to stay longer. Weather reports looked grim, so I was prepared for cold, rain and snow. All I had for navigation was a sketch map from a guidebook and a detailed description of the route. I set out along the Snake River, beginning a little before 10 am on a beautiful Thanksgiving morning. I'm not used to carrying a heavy pack, so every step felt like death.

Over the next two days, I negotiated a difficult off-trail route to the site of a cabin ruin, set my tent up in a snow flurry, fought with a leaky fuel canister, ate a cold Thanksgiving dinner, and nearly got myself trapped above impassible cliffs on my return hike. It was frustrating and challenging as much as it was victorious and educational. I don't think this trip sold me on solo backpacking, but I was grateful for the many lessons I was taught. Also, never do this. Always test out new gear before you head off into the wilderness by yourself, unless, like me, you like to learn things the hard way.

I continued to learn about my capacity to handle things on my own by taking solo road trips. Over the years, I've taken many memorable long drives, stopping along the way to camp, hike, see new cities and take on unexpected challenges.

While I was still teaching at the high school, holiday breaks were perfect opportunities for solo travel. I'd pack up my car with a week's worth of supplies and hit the road. In 2011, I trekked through the loneliest places in Eastern Oregon by myself. One stop took me to Jordan Craters, a remote volcanic landscape a hundred miles from anywhere. After exploring the single mile of signed and developed trail, I struck out on my own to get close to the strange lava formations. I followed a rough route description from my hiking book and took my time to negotiate the loose rock. I wandered from one interesting rock to the next until I grew tired of the unsteady footing, got back into my car, and searched for a place to camp. Being alone in a desolate landscape felt a little eerie, but it also felt empowering to be outside on my own terms.

Summer vacation was another convenient time to hit the road. In 2012, I plotted a driving route across Central Oregon. I snagged a limited-entry permit into the Pamelia Lake area so that I could hike to the top of Grizzly Peak. Hiking alone on a well-trod, easy-to-find trail didn't really feel like hiking alone. It was no less dangerous than taking a walk to the grocery store or strolling through a city park. This was a sharp contrast from my experience at Jordan Craters, and it illustrated the range of experiences I could have while hiking alone. Trail character, proximity to civilization, number of other people hiking, season, time or day, and many other factors contribute to how "alone" I feel while hiking.

Occasionally, hiking wouldn't be the primary reason for my road trips but would serve as a way to stretch my legs on the way to my planned destination. This was the case as I drove to Sacramento for a fitness workshop in 2018. It was March, and the mountains were buried in snow. I spent a little time researching low-elevation trailheads online and came across a hike description for Feather Falls. I made a slight detour off my Sacramento route to reach the trailhead and discovered that the extra driving was worth the trouble.

I camped at the trailhead the night before my hike to get an early start. I was the first one on the trail, which meant I got to spend twenty glorious minutes at the waterfall overlook by myself. It was a beautiful hike through a unique-to-me landscape, and I enjoyed every step of the eight-mile loop.

As I got closer to the trailhead, I began running into people starting their hikes. One older couple, who looked more suited for a trip to the mall than a half-day hike in the forest, asked me a few questions as I passed. "How long till the falls?" they asked. I thought about it. The maintained route was about four-and-a-half-miles long. And while the trail wasn't particularly strenuous, neither of them had a backpack, and the woman was wearing dress shoes with heels.

I told them that there was a small waterfall not far up the trail, but that they'd be in for an eight- to nine-mile hike to see Feather Falls. They nodded and thought about it for a moment. Soon after I started walking again, I heard their footsteps following behind me.

And the naysayers say hiking solo is dangerous. I'd say those two characters were in over their heads, not me.

No matter the reason for my traveling, I manage to make hiking part of my agenda. Traveling with my husband, Aaron, means I have a hiking buddy at my disposal. (But if he wants to do his own thing, that's okay too.) On a trip to Hawaii, he decided to go on an early morning SCUBA dive with a local tour group. That left me a few free hours to do whatever I wanted.

I had a few things in mind from the research I'd done back home. After dropping him off at the boat dock, I drove to Makena State Park to check out the beach and walk up a big red hill. It was much too early for the average beach-goer, so I had the place mostly to myself. I scrambled up a washed-out hillside to a trail leading up Pu'u Ola'I cinder cone, where I was treated to an idyllic view overlooking the ocean. I walked the circular rim of the cratered hill and then blasted back down to explore the beach. I took off my shoes, strolled across the warm sand and settled down to let the sun warm my face before I had to go retrieve Aaron.

Being unafraid of solo travel means that I've got more opportunities to play. Not having an activity partner is not a barrier to going hiking.

Solo winter hiking would prove to have its own challenges. Small errors can lead to bigger consequences in less time during the winter. Winter means short days, cold temperatures and avalanche danger. I respect these seasonal challenges and make different choices about where and when I venture out alone in the winter. In the beginning, I stuck with groups as much as I could once the snow started to fall. But over time, as I grew my skills and confidence, I started to learn about what risks I was comfortable managing as a solo hiker and ventured out on my own.

In December 2010, I hiked up Bald Butte in the Mt. Hood National Forest. When I arrived, I followed boot tracks on the snow-covered trail. In about a half-mile, they disappeared, leaving me feeling completely alone. This was a new route for me, and all I had for navigation were a few sentences describing the route in the back of a hiking book. I used the description in conjunction with a visual assessment of the landscape to make my way up to the summit. I got off-trail a little bit, but I made it to my destination. On the way back down, I could follow my tracks to the trailhead. It was a success.

But winter is not always so forgiving. In January 2011, I hiked steeply uphill in the Columbia River Gorge towards North Lake. The trail was snow-free at the base, but I encountered heavy snow cover at about 4,000 feet. I hadn't brought any snowshoes so my progress was frustratingly slow. In addition, the trail wasn't very clear, so I didn't feel particularly confident about my position.

Surprisingly, I crossed paths with another hiker who was wandering around—following his GPS—and aiming for the same location I was. But based on our brief interaction, I was not confident that he knew what he was doing with the device. I said "Good luck!" and retreated, following my footsteps back the way I came. Until I felt better prepared, with the right footwear, and improved my map and compass skills, I knew that I was safer turning around than blindly following a disoriented stranger.

In those early days, I mostly chose to hike solo in places where it would be easy to stay on-trail. Steins Pillar, a towering rock formation in the Ochoco National Forest, was one of those places. An easy two-mile trail leads to the base of the pillar, where I wandered around and explored it from every angle. Although the hike was short and straightforward, I loved being out there on my own. No need to turn every trip into an epic.

Most solo hikes aren't much different than hiking with others. On popular routes, there are almost always other people on the trail, so I don't usually feel like I'm alone. Nothing unusual or difficult happens along the way—it's just hiking. And these easy solo hikes can take place at any time of year.

This has been the case on many occasions: in January 2014, as I explored the trails of Cape Perpetua on the Oregon Coast; in February 2014 on Eula Ridge; at Spencer Butte in Eugene, Oregon, in March 2016; on a walk up Crescent Mountain, June 2016; on Mt. Garfield in the White Mountains in August 2005; on a jaunt up Salmon Butte in October 2009; on Fuji Mountain near Willamette Pass in November 2014 . . . The list goes on and on. But those humdrum, everyday hikes aren't nearly as fun to write about as the dramatic ones. In 2013, in preparation for leading a group hike up South Sister, I hiked to the top of the mountain alone to get my bearings and reacquaint myself with the terrain. It was beautiful. I made it to the summit in under four hours with just a few short breaks. It felt so nice to be able to walk at my own pace and stop only when I needed to stop. I moved so much more efficiently than I do when hiking with a group. At the summit, I enjoyed a leisurely rest and then circumnavigated the crater before heading back down. All was going quite well so far.

On the descent, clouds started rolling in. Whenever I could, I picked up my pace to a jog, using my poles to help propel me forward more quickly. When I hit a flat section of trail, the clouds had sunken down, brushing the tip of Mt. Bachelor nearby. These clouds were dark, gray and ominous. There was no time to waste; a storm was heading this way. I paused briefly enough to pull my raincoat out of my backpack and tie it around my waist. I didn't want to be digging around for it in the rain. Sprinting down to the parking lot, I balanced the risks of turning an ankle on the rocks with getting off the trail before the rain and lightning began. One minute after I got into my car, huge drops of water started pelting my windshield. My timing was perfect.

I did many solo scouting hikes like this. In January 2014, I hiked up Marys Peak the day before my planned group hike to find out the status of the trail at that time. On a winter day, I was surprised to find summer-like conditions. The trails were bone dry, the air was warm and there wasn't a speck of snow anywhere. I'd been up there in full-blown winter conditions, so I was a bit incredulous of my luck. When I returned to town, I let my team know that they could leave their snow gear at home the next day.

Because it was so close to home in Corvallis, Marys Peak was a convenient place to go on solo hikes, any time of day, any time of year. The previous year, I hiked the upper trail system in thick, autumn cloud cover. My treat for enduring the poor visibility, however, was a plethora of gorgeous mushrooms. They sprung from fallen logs in a multitude of colors, shapes and sizes. I was in a fairyland filled with fungi.

❧

There's no "season" for hiking, is there? Not to me, of course, but there are more and less popular times of the year to hit the trail, depending on the climate in your local climbing area. In the hot southwest deserts, winter is the most popular hiking season. In high mountain ranges that are snowed in much of the year, late summer is prime time for hiking. Other factors, such as the severity of bugs and the times of year when kids are out of school, also influence how popular hiking is in a specific area. In Central Oregon, the area I now call home, most people go hiking in the middle of summer, when tourists on vacation flock from all over. Fall is somewhat surprisingly one of the less popular times to hike.

> TIPS FOR FINDING SOLITUDE
>
> If your idea of solitude is seeing no other humans on your trip, here are some strategies for discovering your own quiet little piece of paradise:
>
> Hike off-season
> Hike in poor weather
> Hike off-trail
>
> There are plenty of reasons why people avoid doing these things. Before venturing out, be sure you leave the house prepared with the gear and skills you need to enjoy a solo adventure.

To be fair, autumn in the Central Oregon Cascades can provide a mixed bag. Trails are sometimes blocked by snow. Weather might be colder and wetter than usual. Days are shorter, meaning there are fewer hours to get in a long hike without a headlamp. And everyone's either rushing to get one last mountain bike ride in or getting their skis waxed for ski season. It's an odd time to be wandering around on the trails, which is why fall is one of my favorite seasons to take a hike.

What does fall have to offer, besides quieter trails? First, there are no bugs; the mosquitoes have long died off. The sometimes unbearably hot and dry climate has softened, providing cooler and more comfortable temperatures for being active outdoors. The colors pop under the sheen of moisture that suddenly seems to appear that time of year. There's a crispness in the air forecasting the coming winter. Change is palpable.

In late October 2013, I took a quick stroll along the Echo Basin Loop in the Willamette National Forest. I saw many different types of mushrooms and was shocked by the diversity of forms. Each variety of mushroom was much different than the next. I observed the colors, textures, shapes, sizes, growth patterns and density of each fungal display. Although I could not name or identify each one, I still appreciated the beauty and intrigue they brought to my simple forest stroll. The densely treed trail led to an opening in a meadow, where I turned my gaze upward. Steep hillsides surrounding the basin were colored red, orange and gold: the shades of fall. Alone in this surreal place, I felt so fortunate that I'd made the stop.

To truly find alone time, however, I also travel off-trail. This type of travel requires specific skills, most importantly navigation skills. I enjoy the challenges that come with getting off the beaten path. It feels more adventurous and demands more of my attention. There's nothing that helps me focus more when hiking alone than walking cross-country, because I know I won't have well-worn paths and directional signs to help me get back.

In July 2017, I set my sights on a couple of highpoints in the Three Sisters Wilderness that looked fairly easy to reach from the developed trail system. I started walking from a popular trailhead and followed the trail as close to my first destination as I could. Once I neared an access point towards the first summit, I carefully stepped off-trail, finding a durable path where my footprints would leave minimal impact and the main trail would be out of sight.

The reward for my efforts was an incredible view. With the warm sun overhead and plenty of time left in the day, I relaxed on the summit, eating my lunch, sipping on a big bottle of water and listening to the distant sounds of birds chattering. I reveled in the quiet, the aloneness. I couldn't help but feel a small sense of accomplishment for mapping out a goal, taking the steps to get there and realizing the outcome all on my own. If only it was always this easy.

I can attest that venturing off-trail is not often easy. In June 2012, I made a plan to hike to Red Butte, a little bump in the Willamette National Forest. My hiking book described a route that followed a trail for 95 percent of the distance, leading to a short and straightforward cross-country ramble to the top. June was really early in the year to be heading to high elevations. Less than a mile from the trailhead, I hit snow. I was able to follow boot prints for the next mile or so, but they eventually became erratic and sent me walking in circles. I managed to get back on track with my map and compass, but it was clear that with the slow progress I was making I would not find my butte.

In my frustration I took stock of where I was and spied a rocky highpoint to my left, across a lake. According to my map, it was Duffy Butte. I had no route description to go by, but I thought I could figure out a path on my own, so I veered off towards the ridge leading to the summit. I bumbled my way through scraggly trees and up piles of loose rock to the ridge I'd seen from down below. Since I was alone and off my planned route, I moved slowly and cautiously, taking care to find solid footing with each step—it wasn't an ideal time to take a tumble. Not sure which point was the true summit, I carefully traversed the ridge until I reached the other side. By walking the entire length of the ridge, I knew that I must have crossed the high point, and I could call it a summit hike. Up high on that ridge, I enjoyed views of the surrounding peaks, capped with wintry coats of snow. I felt a sense of accomplishment as I overlooked the landscape below. Although I had failed to accomplish my original plan, I found success in reaching a different summit.

As it turned out, the descent to the lake was much easier than the climb up the ridge. I chose a route down that was covered in deep snow. The jumbles of rock and brush were buried beneath the snowpack, leaving me a smooth surface to walk upon. Once I reached the trail again I followed my tracks back to the car. Not surprisingly, I got to enjoy a full day of hiking in peaceful solitude. I checked two boxes on that trip: hiking off-season and hiking off-trail.

It's easy for me to change plans on the fly when I'm hiking alone because there's no one else who needs to approve of my plan. If something catches my attention or if the terrain turns out to be not quite what I expected, I can modify my route or destination.

I was glad to have the freedom to do so on a hike to a waterfall in Oregon's Coast Range. From my notes on September 30, 2015:

The drive to the falls was the most harrowing part of the day, negotiating numerous unmarked forest roads with no cell service and hoping I had good-enough directions. Once I made it to the trailhead, it took less than an hour of walking to arrive at my planned destination. The falls were pretty, but I thought I should keep hiking since it took me so long just to drive there. I continued along the trail.

Soon, the path felt a bit more rugged and wild. In places, huge fallen tree stumps were covered in moss, creating tall green walls on the sides of the trail. I pushed through curtains of dangling lichen as if I was entering an ancient temple. Mushrooms sprouted from every possible surface. But I had yet to discover one final gem. I walked a bit further and caught a glimpse of the river through the thick trees. I continued until I found an easy way to get down to the river. And there I found paradise.

The flowing water had carved bowls, pools, potholes and cliffs into the bedrock beneath the river. I wandered around, walking from rock to rock, observing all of the shapes and patterns. The gentle flow of the water created a lovely background of white noise. No one else was around. I felt like I'd stumbled into a private sanctuary. It was true bliss. I scouted out a resting spot and there I sat, taking it all in, savoring the time and place, alone on the river.

Would I have gone there if I had been with a group? I'll never know for sure, but I can guess that we would have stuck with the original plan, hiking back from the waterfall instead of following my curiosity further.

In July 2014, I also let my imagination dictate my route plan in the moment. I hiked the short, steep trail to Middle Pyramid, one of a cluster of three highpoints in the Central Oregon Cascades. At the top I gazed out over the landscape to survey my options. I'd hoped to find a way to connect the three points together in one hike. South Pyramid looked like it was guarded by rocky cliffs and thick trees. However, the ridge between Middle and North Pyramid appeared to be easily passable. I decided to go for it.

Following the path of least resistance, I walked across the ridge in the direction of the blocky summit. At times, the ground angled steeply beneath my feet. I grabbed onto tree branches and rocks to help maintain my balance as I progressed towards the top. Periodic clearings in the trees gave me a better perspective on how far I had traveled. Once I reached the unmarked summit, I enjoyed unobstructed views of the wilderness, with Mt. Jefferson as a distant centerpiece. It was definitely worth the detour.

Some might argue that veering from your plan is not a safe thing to do, especially while hiking alone. I'd argue otherwise. Safety is never guaranteed in any activity, and I do what I can to mitigate risks. I carry my satellite messenger with me in case of emergency. It allows me to send friends and family check-in messages to indicate that I'm okay. It also provides a button that contacts Search and Rescue if I need assistance. I calculate my decisions based on perceived risk versus reward. If the rewards appear to outweigh the risks, then I'll choose to go. Making these risk calculations has become an integral part of my decision-making process on the trail. Every time I reach a decision point, I consider my options and make a conscious choice. When I'm hiking solo, there's no one to argue with, so making decisions is easy. In addition, traveling in a group carries its own risks; I notice myself mentally checking out far more often when I'm in a group than when I'm out alone.

It is up to each one of us to do our own personal risk assessment and make informed decisions based on our goals, knowledge and experience. A "go" decision for me might be a "no-go" decision for you, and vice versa. It helps that I've been doing this risk assessment exercise since the very beginning of my foray into hiking. From a February 2006 journal entry: "Today I had a pleasant, reflective, quiet day on Mt. Monadnock. It's the Wednesday of February vacation, and a beautiful, partly sunny day at that. I saw no one on the trails today."

COMMUNICATIONS DEVICES

Personal locator beacons (PLBs) and satellite phones/messengers are devices that can send and sometimes receive messages via satellite systems. They are more reliable than cell phones in backcountry areas that lack good cell signal.

There is a variety of devices on the market today with different features, and at different price points. These devices provide a connection to search-and-rescue services in an emergency.

There was no mention of fear, of hesitation, of difficulty. I simply took a nine-mile walk alone in the mountains as if it were the most natural thing in the world. Whether it was good luck, naiveté or both, I am grateful that I fell into solo hiking right at the get-go.

That attitude has stood the test of time. In 2013, I went on a camping trip with Aaron on Memorial Day weekend. We drove up into the high desert, where we were hit with a surprise snowstorm and deep snowdrifts in the mountain cliffs above our camp. Aaron decided to stay in camp and relax, but I got antsy and needed to take a walk. There was a trailhead at the edge of our campground, so I packed a light backpack and set off into the woods.

I didn't get far before hitting snow patches, and I lost the trail. I headed towards a boulder field and made a beeline for the top of the cliffs. The snow filled the gaps between the rocks and made the whole thing feel quite treacherous. I assessed the risks and dangers of continuing on and decided that it was not worth it to continue. So, without reaching the highpoint or any remarkable destination, I turned back and walked to camp. It was an easy decision to make. Since I was alone, I didn't have anyone pushing me to keep going or making me question my feelings about the route.

In Southern California I learned the hard way that it can sometimes be impossible to be alone. On a beautiful spring day in 2017, I pulled into the entrance of Santiago Oaks Regional Park and stopped at the following sign: "PARK FULL." I'd never seen such a thing! I talked to the parking lot booth attendant and he said I could park in the staff parking lot and see if someone left the park in the next ten minutes. I slouched back in my seat, waiting patiently for someone to exit the park. After some time passed, I walked back to the booth and the attendant waved me in.

During my brief two-mile hike I encountered several people walking and mountain biking on the trails. One fellow hiker sternly cautioned me to watch out for rattlesnakes. His warning induced the opposite reaction than he intended; I got excited. I'd only ever seen two rattlesnakes in the wild, and I had never encountered one when out hiking.

The trails were wide, gravel and well-traveled. There were huge signposts marking the trails at every junction. It was a far cry from my idea of a wilderness experience, but I enjoyed the opportunity to get away from the city. I loved seeing the yucca, cactus and other unfamiliar desert plants. As I circled back towards the parking lot, I was greeted with the shrieks and screams of groups of schoolchildren. No solitude. And I didn't even see a rattlesnake.

❧

Crowds are sometimes the worst things about hiking. I'm a solitary and introverted person. I enjoy quiet. I get giddy in wide, open spaces. I prefer to get lost in my own thoughts than to chat with other people I encounter on the trails. But as outdoor activities continue to get more popular and city populations expand each year, it gets harder and harder to escape the crowds. Some people feel safer among groups; I feel the complete opposite. Crowds, to me, bring noise, bad behavior, conflict and overuse.

In 2011, I visited Coyote Wall Loop—a beautiful hike on the cliffs above the Columbia River. At the time, I had no idea how popular these trails were for mountain bikers. The hike began nicely enough, but as I navigated the maze of roads and trails making up the middle part of the loop, I was constantly dodging people on bikes. They were traveling in huge packs and were racing downhill as I was walking up. While some cyclists were mindful of sharing the trail, I mostly felt terrified and anxious about colliding with a person on a bicycle. I hiked as quickly as I could to the upper plateau. But there, still, I encountered bikes.

I tried really hard to focus my attention on the delicate, purple grass widows and the dramatic views of the river gorge, but my overall experience was negative. I feel really strongly that mountain biking and hiking are not compatible activities because there are too many opportunities for user conflict. While the rules state that bikers must yield to hikers, I have found in practice that this is not always the case. And even when bikers do yield, it still creates a stressful experience. As a hiker, I feel like mountain bikers look at me like I'm in their way. Trails should be used for one or the other, but not both. I've never gone back there since.

Throughout this book, you'll notice that I gripe about crowds and praise solitude quite a bit. This is not to say that I'm against other people recreating in the outdoors. To the contrary, I'm thrilled that so many folks are finding happiness in our shared outdoor spaces. I just know myself; I find joy in being alone outside. It has taken me many years to find peace between these conflicting feelings. Nowadays, I work extra hard to plan hikes around popular use patterns so that I can be outdoors in a manner that makes me the most comfortable. If that means I can't go to the places everyone's talking about, that's just fine; I've made peace with that.

If time is short, it's easiest to pick a familiar trail close to home for a quick solo adventure. When I lived in Corvallis, I had my go-to parks on the edge of town: Fitton Green, Bald Hill, Peavy Arboretum. When I got tired of the same old hikes, I'd find a new trailhead, a new connector trail, or try a route I'd already done, but hike it in reverse.

On the days when I wanted to walk more and think less, I'd choose a familiar place. There is something soothing about hiking a known route. I don't need to pull out the map or question my navigation skills. I just walk, look around, breathe and think. Sometimes my mind ponders big questions and other times it weaves a path between silly little thoughts. It's nice to not be on high alert with every step.

Occasionally my desire to hike locally would force me out into less familiar parks for new experiences and views. On a delightful September day in 2015, I wandered the trails at Finley National Wildlife Refuge. Another day, I strolled the busy trails at Mt. Pisgah Arboretum. Both of those places were less than an hour's drive from my home at the time. Although they were close by, I had not spent much time in either park. By looking at online maps and reading local hiking books, I got curious about these places and set aside time to walk the trails. I am still amazed at how certain parks are able to fly under my radar, despite being quickly and easily accessible from home.

When I had a little more time on my hands, I sought out trips to the Oregon Coast. On a sunny day one May, I drove out to Beverly Beach to amble barefoot on the endless coastal sands. It was so peaceful, so refreshing. The salty sea breeze brushed past my nostrils as I strode across the beach. The water twinkled in the sunshine. To my right, the waves swirled and crashed onto shore. To my left, coastal trees grew close together, creating a green fortress above the striped sea cliffs. It was like walking through a painting, and there was hardly a soul in sight. I passed my intended turnaround point and just kept walking. Gulls swooped overhead. Thin clouds streaked across the sky. Sand grains squished underneath my feet. And I had the whole world in front of me. Surely nothing could be so glorious.

When it was time for me to head back, I took a sip of water, looked around and turned towards the parking area. But wait. That gentle sea breeze at my back now felt like hurricane-force wind blasting at my face. Each step was agonizingly more difficult than the one before. Ack! I thought I'd never make it back to my car in time. I moved slowly, becoming very cold and feeling every exposed patch of skin being abraded by flying sand.

After what felt like an endless march, the stairs leading off of the beach came into view. I lunged at them, desperate to get myself out of the maelstrom. I'd never felt so caught off guard before. I didn't have enough layers to stay warm, and I swore I'd never be so silly as to wear shorts to the Oregon coast again. Growing up in Rhode Island, where the local beaches were along warm, protected bays, that meant swimsuits, coolers and frozen lemonade. At the Oregon Coast, I had to forget my childhood memories and remember sunglasses, wind layers, hats and gloves!

MORE TIPS FOR FINDING SOLITUDE

The more curious you are and the more research you're willing to do, the more likely you'll be able to discover new and quiet places.

Avoid "top ten list" places
Read maps often
Meet the locals

Show some interest in a place. Take the time to start at the popular spots and get the lay of the land. Talk to people who live and work nearby. The more you inherently respect and value the lands you visit, the more places will reveal themselves to you.

When I moved to Bend, driving to the coast for a quick hike was no longer possible because it was much too far away. I had to find new "local" hiking trails, especially in snow-covered winter months. Luckily for me, I discovered the Tumalo Canal trail system, which is accessible all year round. In February 2018, the trails were lightly dusted with snow. The yellow grasses, neon green lichen and brown juniper bark looked brilliant next to the fluffy snow. I walked alone, savoring all the little things as I explored this local gem.

No one had ever mentioned this area to me before and it wasn't in any of the hiking books I had on my shelf; it took some creative investigation to stumble upon it. And yet, the information anyone would need to access the Tumalo Canal trails is available online. When most people search for hiking information on the internet, they click on the first link and read the "top ten" lists. As a result, most foot traffic is concentrated on a handful of popular trails.

If you're truly interested in finding solitude, it's not that hard to do. Steer clear of all the places you hear about through social media and spend a little more time perusing local maps. Better yet, get to know the area by hiking the popular trails first, becoming familiar with the lay of the land. There's nothing inherently wrong about going where the crowds are; there's a reason why they are so popular. Hiking the top-ten trails will help you develop a mental map of an area and begin to understand the topography and weather. Get curious about the places you notice from viewpoints: lakes, summits, rivers and other unique features. Figure out what they are and how to get there. Meet people who have hiked the area for a long time and develop relationships with them. Locals will rarely divulge their favorite places to a stranger, but if you become a friend, you've got a better shot at learning about some out-of-the-way treasures.

Hiking solo is simply one tool in my hiker toolbox. It serves as a way to escape the routine of daily life, a way to connect with the natural world, a way to meet my need for quiet, and a way to create space for my feelings. It is sometimes a necessity and other times a choice. Hiking alone fulfills my desire for solitude and helps me improve my outdoor skills. With no one to draw my attention away from the present, I am mindful of my movement, my thoughts and my environment. I challenge my physical skills, my navigational skills and my ability to handle unexpected scenarios. I learn to make better decisions and trust myself. It is so easy for me to defer to the knowledge and experience of others on group hikes, even when I'm the most skilled and trustworthy decision-maker on the team. Unaccompanied, I see more things. I think more deeply. I walk further. I honor my physical and mental state more honestly. I am my true self when I hike alone.

If only all of my hikes brought me the same joy I felt on July 28, 2012. As I wrote in my journal: "Solitude, flowers, views, sunshine, epic."

Solo hiking may not be for everyone, but it is essential for me.

4

The Long and Short of It

Aaron and I awoke slowly as the sun rose over our campsite on the Metolius River. We arrived there the previous day to enjoy some quiet time in the woods. One of Central Oregon's loveliest waterways, the Metolius River slowly rolled by, glistening in the morning light. After eating breakfast and packing up the car, I decided I wanted to take a walk. I knew there was a trail along the river and a fish hatchery nearby, so we made our way to the hatchery to start our lazy adventure.

We stepped out of the car and into the surprisingly warm March sun. Slowly wandering around the edges of the hatchery's tanks, we peered into the water to look for fish. We took turns tossing handfuls of fish food into the water and watched the feeding frenzy that ensued. After making a loop around all of the fish tanks, we turned towards the trail and walked along the river with no particular destination in mind. Our pace was relaxed. I didn't run a GPS track. I was not aiming for a highpoint. And I didn't try to push my speed or distance. Was this hiking? Years later, as I sat down to write this book, I agonized over whether or not to "count" this day. Yes, it was a hike. No, it wasn't a hike! Well, maybe...

Since starting my hiking journey in 2005, I had mostly assessed the value of my hikes by the number of miles walked and/or the number of peaks bagged. In my mind, a hike wasn't a hike if it was less than ten miles long. As I've racked up the miles and grown as a hiker, I've learned to respect each opportunity to get out and walk, regardless of how long or difficult the hike is.

When I describe this writing project to someone new, their first question is almost always "How do you decide what counts? Does it have to be a certain distance?" Now that everyone, it seems, is tracking steps or daily mileage on an electronic gadget, people assume that there must be a minimum distance requirement.

It has taken me some time and reflection to include short hikes in my personal definition of hiking. Looking back at my history, I see that I've taken many meaningful, satisfying and memorable hikes that didn't reach that initial (and completely arbitrary) ten-mile minimum.

In 2006, I drove across the country alone in search of a new place to live. Along the way I stopped to visit various parks and points of interest. One of these detours was Devils Tower National Monument in Wyoming. This volcanic butte rises 1,200 feet above the surrounding landscape, making it noticeable from quite a distance away. Its tall, gray walls are fractured into vertical pillars of stone. As I drove closer to the park's entrance, I became excited about exploring this rock formation more closely on foot.

I walked the one-and-a-third-mile trail encircling the massive rock tower. As I walked, I stared upward, mouth agape, at the impressive monolith. I couldn't believe people actually climbed up that thing! Today, I know I'm totally capable of completing some of the park's classic routes, but back before my climbing days, this looked like a brave feat. While short, this hike helped stir in me an emotional attachment to a unique geological feature—one that I couldn't have experienced any other way. Seeing a photo just doesn't create the same connection. I didn't appreciate short walks very much at the time, but eventually I would learn to value hiking no matter the distance I walked.

The Columbia River Gorge, dividing the states of Oregon and Washington, is an excellent location for discovering quick, little hikes. In 2007, I took my brother on a hiking tour of the Gorge, including a walk to Wahkeena and Multnomah Falls. You can see Multnomah Falls, Oregon's tallest, from your car on the highway. A short wander from the parking lot brings you to a viewpoint bridge at the base of the falls. A similar short viewpoint trail leads from a parking area to Wahkeena Falls. While we didn't rack up a lot of miles that day, we created a wealth of quality experiences together.

I repeated that trip with Aaron in 2013, since he hadn't really spent much time in the Columbia Gorge. The trails in the Gorge are designed so that visitors can do anything from a quick leg-stretcher of a hike to a multi-day backpacking trip. There are hikes for all abilities and interests. It was fun to be a tourist that day, stopping off at each pullout and point of interest in order to see the main sights and learn a little more about the geology and natural history of that beautiful place.

There always seems to be a short trail to any waterfall. In 2013, as I was researching some hiking locations for a guidebook, I hiked a mere two miles to see a pair of waterfalls in the Oregon Coast Range: Niagara (no, not the famous Niagara Falls) and Pheasant Creek Falls. Never mind that Aaron and I had to drive endless miles on confusing Forest Service roads to get there. Once we reached the parking area the hard work was over! A slippery but easy walk led us to lush, roaring waterfalls.

In 2016, we went full-tourist and booked a guided day trip to "Secret Falls" on the island of Kauai. The trip involved a mellow kayaking adventure to a take-out point, where we left the boats and hiked along a trail to a pool at the base of a gorgeous waterfall. The hike was short and very muddy. Since we were the first ones to the waterfall, Aaron and I got to swim and play in the water before the rest of the herd descended on the area. Several outfitters had permits to bring people to this "secret" spot, so we made sure we got on the very first trip of the day in order to see it in a natural and uncrowded state. Once the other groups arrived, we got out of the water, ate our snacks and packed up for the brief hike out. Every now and again it's nice to shake up the routine and join the crowds.

Not every short hike is quite so dramatic, of course, but each has its own charm. On an October hike to Linton Lake in Central Oregon, I enjoyed sitting by the edge of the lake, surrounded by golden grasses, watching the sunlight sparkle on the water's surface. It was my last opportunity to enjoy the trails off of the Old McKenzie Pass Highway before the snow gates were closed for the season. I felt it was a proper way to close out the summer, with one last glimpse of that majestic landscape.

Short hikes often provide convenient opportunities to stretch one's legs on a road trip. On January 1, 2014, Aaron and I were wrapping up a winter camping trip with a cabin stay at La Pine State Park in Central Oregon. Before loading into the car and heading home, we strolled along the river in the desert sun. We didn't walk far; we didn't have any particular destination or goal; we just wanted some time outdoors. We needed to absorb some of that high desert magic before returning to the wet side of the mountains. Trips like these likely began getting us thinking about what it would be like to live in Central Oregon, where we'd move just a few years later!

When Aaron and I arrived in Bend in June 2017, we took a short hike to celebrate. Less than two miles from our new home stands Pilot Butte, a 400-foot cinder cone right in the middle of town. We walked up the trail that spirals around the butte, admiring the views that have since become very familiar. From the summit we looked down to find our neighborhood, our street and our house. We watched streams of cars driving by on the roads below. We breathed in the fresh desert air and knew that we'd made the right choice in moving to Central Oregon.

In 2015, we took a vacation that covered a lot of ground; we explored hikes in Northern Nevada, Southwest Utah and Southern Idaho. It required a lot of driving in just two weeks. Between major stops, we found some quick and easy excuses to get out of the car. One of these quick stops was Hickman Bridge in Capitol Reef National Park.

We waited for the daytime sun to wane before getting started. I took my shoes off, grabbed an interpretive brochure for fifty cents, and we strolled up the trail. We paused at each numbered post so I could read the information in the brochure. It felt nice to move at such a relaxed pace. Knowing the walk was less than two miles round trip, I felt no rush to complete it. The sun fell low in the sky and the dimming light played with the colors and shadows of rocks and vegetation near the trail. I enjoyed this walk because it was unhurried and casual—a chill walk was just what I needed that day. It seems silly to take the time to describe the benefits of this type of hiking since I think many people see hiking this way, but to a recovering speed- and distance-focused hiker, it was a new concept to me.

Later, on that same road trip, we took another short walk at Shoshone Falls in Idaho. The waterfall was running very low, but the interpretive signs were informative and we learned about the local geology and history of the area. Mostly it felt good to be off my butt and on my feet. We made a number of these little stops on our trip. I enjoy the combination of movement, fresh air and education that these walks provide.

Taking short walks allows me to reflect on why hiking is so important. It allows me to clearly see all of the benefits that are not derived from the mere physicality of hiking. By removing the physical element, I am more able to appreciate the beauty, the quiet, the sense of exploration, and the company of my hiking partner(s).

I recall a camping trip with a friend in the Willamette National Forest, during which we took a short walk from our campsite to Independence Rock. It was just under a mile of walking on a gentle forest trail to a rock of no major significance, but it gave us the opportunity to move our bodies, spend time in nature and catch up with each other. Does that "count" as a hike for this project? I feel like it does.

It is on those short hikes that I ponder what makes a hike, a hike.

❦

On a chilly November day in 2013, Aaron and I drove out to the Oregon Coast to do some exploring. I don't know how far we walked, or how long we were out, or many of the details you might find in a hiking guide for that type of adventure. But we walked. It was outside. Isn't that a hike?

The Internet offers some definitions of hiking:

Merriam-Webster: "a long walk, especially for pleasure or exercise"

Cambridge Dictionary: "the activity of going for long walks in the countryside"

Wikipedia: "long, vigorous walk, usually on trails (footpaths), in the countryside"

Urban Dictionary: "walking where it's okay to pee"

We checked some of those boxes for sure. But others? Who defines "long"? Does that mean miles covered or time spent walking? What constitutes "countryside," and who uses that term anyways? It sounds British to me. Honestly, the best definition is the silly description from Urban Dictionary. Ultimately, I decided that I am the only one who is allowed to define hiking for me.

I'm calling our stroll on the Oregon Coast a hike. We were out for hours; we must have covered a decent amount of ground. While we had no particular destination, no heart rate monitors, and no summit to achieve, we enjoyed all the other benefits of hiking: nature time, physical activity, visual stimulation and the excitement of being in a novel environment. Oh, and it was okay to pee.

Earlier that summer, we had taken another short jaunt at the Oregon Coast. We were spending time with family, which meant that the pace was pretty slow and the activities were not very vigorous. Aaron knew I'd need to be walked, so we headed for the beach. While we were there we decided to hike to the top of Proposal Rock. There's no official trail there, but since enough people are motivated to do such a thing, a user path is well-beaten into the thick vegetation. We followed the tracks of those who came before us to stand atop the prominent rock. We could definitely pee there, in the privacy of the salal thicket, so I'm calling it a hike.

Short is relative, of course. A steep four-mile round-trip hike up a mountain might feel short to me, but it might not feel so short to someone else. Likewise, a ten-mile hike might feel long to me but would seem short to an ultramarathon runner. And at different times of life, the same hike might feel either short and easy or long and grueling. My six-year-old self definitely thought a mile was pretty long and that our favorite campground in Connecticut was an eternity away from our home in Rhode Island (the drive takes less than an hour). And there are definitely days when my forty-year-old self feels like a mile of walking is really far.

❦

Short hikes can provide an outlet during times of healing, physically or mentally. In 2008, I decided to take up skiing. Once I began feeling like I was getting the hang of it, I fell and tore my ACL. A few months later, I had surgery to repair the damaged ligament in my knee.

This injury completely devastated me. My hand surgery the year before was much easier to deal with than a knee surgery— at least I could walk while my finger was knitting itself back together. After tearing my ACL, I had two recovery periods: the rehab after the injury but before surgery, and then the rehab after the surgery. The injury occurred in March. Surgery took place in June. So that meant that I wouldn't have a real summer that year.

I fell into a depression. Hiking had become a huge part of my life and a source of well-being, of feeling grounded. What would I do now that my passion was taken away from me? I looked on with sadness as my friends headed out for trips: climbing, hiking, backpacking. I sat on the floor watching old movies while I did my rehab exercises. Squeeze quads. Relax. Squeeze quads. Relax. Slide the towel across the floor with my heel. It was a miracle the day I could walk to the mailbox without the assistance of hiking poles. I felt reduced to nothing.

In the months after my surgery I began to venture out onto the trails again. I chose easy trails on those first hikes. They were often short and, to my mind, not terribly interesting. But they got me back out into the world, and I cherished those opportunities. Sometimes I went out alone, fearful that my sluggish pace would turn off any hiking partner. Sometimes I felt confident enough to ask a friend to join me on an easy walk. On my recovery hikes I discovered new places, trails that were off my radar because they were previously "too short" to consider.

The Weldon Wagon Road in the Columbia River Gorge was one of those hikes. It was not particularly special, except for one thing: I got to be outside. I got to use my own two legs to propel myself across the landscape. Each step was a small victory. My knee was coming back.

That summer meant lots of resting and frequent, short hikes. Once I started feeling more like myself, I set out on longer and longer adventures. But by that point, I'd learned to appreciate the short ones, too. Twice that year I hiked Coffin Mountain in the Willamette National Forest. At only three miles round trip, it met my definition of short, but it was still pretty challenging, with 1,000 feet of elevation gain to the top. Although I discovered this hike during the summer when my mileage was limited by what my body was able to do, I loved it so much that I brought a group of friends back there in late November. Being injured forced me to value different qualities about hiking trails and, as a side effect, broadened my awareness of what opportunities were out there.

My friends were my greatest champions during my recovery. They were happy to spend time with me on the easy hikes I could do while my knee was healing. A small group of us took a trip to the coast later that fall for some easy walking, and I was reminded of how much diversity there is in Oregon. On the Weldon Wagon Road, I walked through a dry, dusty oak forest. At Clatsop Spit, I walked across a broad, sandy beach scattered with interesting bits of debris and dead things to look at: birds, seashells, jellyfish, driftwood. The sun glinted on the rolling waves as we casually strolled along. After our walk, we sat by the campfire telling stories, drinking beers and making s'mores. I learned to find pleasure again in the little things. I learned that my self-worth did not have to come from hiking the farthest, climbing the highest or setting a personal record. Instead, I could be satisfied with just spending time outdoors in good company. I had been so goal-oriented for so long that I had forgotten the reasons why I started hiking.

I was delivered another blow just two years later. While practicing lead climbing in a rock gym, I fell, slamming my heel into the climbing wall so hard that I actually saw stars, just like in the cartoons. My trip to urgent care led to a broken heel bone diagnosis, which would also require surgery. I felt a knot form in my chest. Again, I was going to lose another summer to injury. What could I do with only one good foot? Hiking was out.

I noticed a disturbing pattern of injury: every two years something on my body needed fixing. I had to face my reality; my foot was broken and I could not proceed with the active summer I had planned. With this injury and surgery, I was more mentally prepared than the last time. Although I was living alone, in a second-floor apartment, I was determined to remain as independent as I could while not being too stubborn to ask for help when I needed it.

The broken heel was in some ways more difficult than the ACL tear. The doctor told me to stay off of my injured foot completely for three months. That would mean a lot of hopping around on one leg, and a lot of atrophy to deal with after I could put my left leg on the ground again. I knew I'd lose a great deal of strength in my left leg while being completely dependent on the right.

After a month and a half of dragging myself around on crutches, I searched the internet for other mobility tools that would help me get some freedom back. Walking with crutches is miserable; they make other parts of your body hurt that were fine before you started using them. They force you to occupy your hands so you can no longer carry anything. I dreaded leaving the house for anything because I'd have to deal with the crutches. After some sleuthing, I discovered a piece of equipment that looked like it was designed just for someone like me.

The iWALKFree crutch was like nothing I'd ever seen before. This device basically gave me the use of my leg back. I strapped the metal bar to the front of my thigh and the back of my calf and rested my knee on the knee pad. The crutch allowed me to walk while keeping my foot completely off the ground. I called the crutch my "peg leg." After a quick weekend of camping with some friends to test out the crutch in the field, I decided to take off on a weeklong solo road trip with my new toy.

The longest hike I did on this device was a section of the Pacific Crest Trail at the Brown Mountain lava flow in Southern Oregon. That segment of the PCT cuts through a jumble of lava blocks. It is remarkably well-graded and comfortable to walk on, considering the rugged terrain it covers. I plodded along at a roughly one-mile-an-hour pace. It was quiet. It was beautiful. It was everything I needed. The months I'd spent holed up in my apartment, dreaming of being out in the summer sun, had made me appreciate this opportunity so much more than if I hadn't been injured. I was proud of myself for enduring a whole two miles on the trail. Instead of thinking about what I could have been doing had I not broken my foot, I focused on what amazing things I could do despite my injury. This mindset shift took some time, but it helped me get through my recovery phase without feeling as depressed as I had been after tearing my ACL.

I took many other memorable hikes along what I dubbed the "robo-hiker road trip." One stop was at Harris Beach State Park on the Oregon Coast. I saw a little brown sign announcing the park's entrance while driving, pulled into the parking area, and took off down the paved path that headed towards the beach. What at first seemed to be an ordinary access trail turned out to be a collage of colorful wildflowers. I whipped out my camera every thirty seconds to take pictures of each new flower I encountered. I walked slowly and inquisitively, inspecting each small splash of color decorating the side of the trail. When the path terminated at a pile of logs, I paused and looked at the ocean. It wasn't that far away, and with two good legs I could have easily scrambled over the pile and walked across the beach. But it would be difficult on my own, with this crutch.

ROAD TRIP PRO TIP

First, try saying that phrase five times fast!

Seriously, the next time you're on a road trip, keep your eyes peeled for little brown signs.

These signs point to scenic viewpoints, state parks, historical markers and other points of interest for the road warrior.

If you happen to be driving down Highway 101 on the Oregon Coast, there are hundreds of these signs pointing to all sorts of interesting stops.

And for the first time, I thought, "that's okay." I had found so much joy in my miniature wildflower hike that I didn't care that I couldn't make it to the ocean. I smiled, turned around, and slowly walked back up the trail to my car. With a clear mind and an insatiable curiosity for what I'd find next, I drove on to my next mystery destination.

After graduating from the peg leg three months after surgery, I finally got to walk on my own two feet again. I nearly hit the ground running. For the next phase of my recovery, I called on my friends again to accompany me into the mountains. I was on a mission to climb South Sister in October, just five months after I had broken my left heel, and I needed to get in shape.

Rooster Rock, with an elevation gain of 2,200 feet in just over three miles of hiking, was a good testing ground for my recovering body. It was a recovering body, not just a recovering foot, since a foot injury impacts every muscle, joint and tendon above it. The muscles in my left leg had withered away to nearly nothing, whereas the muscles in my right leg were strong from completely relying on them during recovery. And my back and shoulders were still a little messed up from being on crutches for so long. I was working hard to get everything back to a state of normalcy and balance.

I hiked with a bunch of patient friends. Sue, Karen and John, who'd been with me all the way on my road to recovery, accompanied me on the trek up Rooster Rock. We cruised it. I leaned heavily on my hiking poles the entire time. Despite having an initial revulsion to hiking poles, I'd learned after my previous knee injury that using poles was a key strategy to regaining strength and confidence in the mountains. My left foot fatigued much more quickly than the right, and I noticed my left ankle wanting to turn to the side, especially when going downhill. By using hiking poles, I could help stabilize my ankle and prevent a sprain or other injury from occurring. Those two extra points of contact helped keep some of the weight off of my foot and provided more balance overall. I could not have progressed as quickly as I did without the help of my poles.

The next day, however, I was tired and felt ready to dial it way back. My group of friends took me to McDowell Creek Falls, a small park with several waterfalls and a network of easy trails that's popular with families. We slowly meandered along the trails as I focused on taking care of my sore foot. Since I'd learned to enjoy these more relaxed outings, I relished the time we spent on those casual trails.

These were just two of several hikes I did prior to attempting South Sister. By gradually increasing the difficulty of the hikes during my recovery, I felt ready to tackle my goal. When the weather looked good, Sue and I drove down to Central Oregon to take a crack at it. I felt strong going uphill, and I almost made it off the mountain without a hitch, but the last two miles felt like agony. I relied heavily on my poles to take weight off of my newly healed foot. I found myself limping more than usual for a week after the hike, but it was worth it. I had proven to myself that I was not broken, that I could still get out and do the things that fulfill me. I learned to accept help, have patience with myself, and adjust my expectations.

In 2012, I broke the cycle of injury and had a completely

normal, affliction-free spring and summer. For years to follow, things rolled along quite nicely. I enjoyed having a body that gained strength and durability each year. And then I was taken down by a seemingly innocuous cut.

While on a road trip through Southern Utah, Aaron and I did a long, barefoot hike through a flooded slot canyon. We walked across sharp gravel, smooth stones, sand, and slickrock. We spent all day in a harsh environment, and I felt great the entire time. My feet held up on all the difficult terrain that I would not have wanted to walk across in wet shoes.

The next morning, I rolled out of my tent and tried to stand up. Searing pain from one of my feet sent me back down. What had happened? I looked at the bottom of my foot and saw a deep cut in my sole. Either a rock had sliced my foot or popped a blister open. Either way, I could barely walk. I got mad.

For the next several days, we had to drastically change our plans. I could no longer tackle big, challenging hikes—I could hardly stand up. I was so frustrated that such a small injury could have such a ripple effect on my activity level. I had felt whole for so long that it was difficult for me to create a new itinerary to match this new reality.

And so, with this small but imposing injury, we slowly ventured out into Snow Canyon State Park in Utah. There were lots of trails there that I had been excited to see, but we were limited to a handful of short trails to explore, accommodating my foot. Our mini adventures took us to a tiny slot canyon, a flower-speckled nature trail, and a natural amphitheater made of white slickrock. The park was simply gorgeous, and once I relaxed a little bit about my foot, I was able to enjoy it.

Injury is a great teacher. It forces a shift in perspective. It reminds me that, while I cannot always control how my body feels, I can control how my mind responds to it. Do I choose to be angry, frustrated and victimized? Or do I choose to be grateful, patient and appreciative for what I can do? Once I accepted the fact that I would have to adjust the length and speed of my hikes, then I was able to enjoy my modified trip.

Injuries happen to the heart, too. In 2017, my father-in-law passed away after a short hospitalization. It was a trying time for the family, especially for my husband. On our drive to the celebration of life we stopped on the Santiam Pass to do a short hike and clear our heads. I chose the Echo Basin trail, a short loop that doesn't see a lot of foot traffic. We needed a place to be alone.

The route was not well marked and was somewhat obscured by snow at the time. So, while it was short, it still had an element of adventure. We breathed in the damp air, admired the bright yellow skunk cabbage blooms and savored the quiet. It was a place my husband's dad would definitely have appreciated. There, we felt, we could honor his memory and connect with his spirit.

For the two of us, hiking is part of the healing process. Grief is an inexplicable thing; it presents itself in unpredictable ways. But out on the trail, we walked with our own thoughts and feelings tumbling around in our heads. We could share memories and emotions freely. The simple act of being out in nature was calming, soothing. Nature seems to have healing powers beyond scientific explanation. On the trail that day, we grieved in our own ways. I don't know what Aaron was thinking, but I do know that the simple act of walking in the forest brought some peace and comfort in that difficult time.

Just a year before, I was processing my mother's death in a similar way. I was about to embark on a day-long kayaking adventure with some friends and clients when I got the call. "Mom died last night," my dad whispered over the phone. I knew it was coming; she'd been diagnosed with aggressive cancer just a year and a half earlier. The last couple of weeks were particularly bad. I had recently visited her back home in Rhode Island and I could tell she had not long to live.

I went on the kayaking trip anyways. As I slowly paddled alongside one of my long-time clients, she asked how my mom was doing. "She died yesterday," I said. She looked befuddled that I was out on the water that day. But there was no place I would have rather been. On the quiet river, surrounded by people I cared about, enjoying a relaxing outdoor activity, I felt that I could sit comfortably with my emotions. Besides, my mom—ever the practical person—would not have wanted me to cancel a trip I'd already committed to and paid for.

For the months and years that followed, I would feel random pangs of grief about my mom's death. It was out on the trail that I could handle these emotions the best. Nature doesn't care if you burst out into tears, or if you need to sit down for a minute or ten. Nature provides a safe and beautiful place to feel, to be, to express yourself. Nature doesn't judge. For me, hiking has offered an outlet for me to be myself and feel all the feelings whenever, wherever, and however they rushed over me. It is always my default place to go when I need to deal with difficulty.

❧

When I first committed to completing this project, I wrote down a list of dates on which I needed to go hiking. These dates were all over the place, with many of them falling on weekdays. The benefit of not having a nine-to-five job meant that I could often squeeze in a weekday hike during a break in my schedule. These "squeeze-in" hikes ended up teaching me more about myself than I ever could have imagined.

One of my challenges was finding new parks and trails close to home that I could explore on those random calendar dates. I relied heavily on William Sullivan's hiking books as well as a book I had contributed to titled *Wild in the Willamette*. Between those two resources I found a number of interesting trails within an hour of home.

Many of those trails fell below my unofficial hike-length threshold of ten miles. These short, close-to-home hikes showcased a variety of geological and biological features that I would never have explored without the intent of completing *Hike366* driving my choices.

In September 2015, I ventured west of Corvallis to the Beazell Memorial Forest and Fort Hoskins Historical Park. In order to squeak out just under five miles of hiking, I explored trails in both parks. I really enjoyed the quiet, lush vegetation in the Beazell Forest. Not surprisingly, no one was out there; it was an out-of-the-way destination with very short trails. Fort Hoskins, on the other hand, probably would have been a great place to visit on any other day, but an active logging operation was loud, distracting and unpleasant. I quickly got irritated trying to read the interpretive signs and enjoy the environment while listening to the heavy machinery grinding away. The two parks were a study in contrast.

I had so much more to learn on my hiking project journey. By chance, I happened across an old hiking guidebook in a used bookstore. It had been written out by hand and was likely printed in small quantity. I had no idea how many copies existed in the world, but I was delighted to find one for myself. Concerned about the present-day accuracy of the book's information, I cross-checked it with more recently published information to make sure the trails and roads mentioned were still accessible.

One of the book's hikes took me to the forest outside of Eugene, where a short trail led to a lookout tower. The trail was brutally steep, but it led to an outstanding view over the trees. I explored a few other trails highlighted in the book and they each had their own charm. Many of the trails were hard to follow because they had fallen out of popularity and were obscured by brush and fallen trees. My map, compass and GPS were handy companions on these hikes. I felt like I was stepping back in time, traveling on some old-timer's favorite trails. It was a journey I doubt I would have gone on if not for the *Hike366* project.

When I was stuck for new ideas, I returned to familiar places near my house. Sometimes I'd mix things up by choosing a different trail, going at a different time of year or choosing an unusual time of day. On a winter morning in 2016, I saw a window of opportunity between my early morning appointments.

Although I'd been to Peavy Arboretum dozens of times, that day felt like a new experience. It was the first time I'd seen a fiery red sun rise up through the tree trunks. The first time I'd seen those exact shadows falling across the trail. Because I knew the trails well, I remembered each turn and hiked along without looking at a map or thinking about which way to go. My feet moved underneath my body effortlessly. I broke into a jog. I found myself entering a meditative state. As I got back in my car and drove to my next obligation, I felt refreshed and alive. That time in nature, however brief, was worthwhile.

On March 14, 2016, I had only an hour of free time to spare and I was determined not to skip that day's hike, wanting to keep my project on track. Peavy was again the natural choice for this "squeeze-in" hike. I started on the half-mile Woodland Trail and walked as long as I could, connecting up bits and pieces of gravel road and forest trail until I ran out of time. I stopped only briefly to admire some colorful fungi. I moved quickly, grateful that I'd chosen to get out and hike, if only for an hour.

ARE YOU BUSY?

We all live with certain demands on our time. But each of us can choose to make time for the things that are important. If you can fit in even thirty minutes to walk at a local park, you can gain the benefits of hiking.

Open up a map and take a look at where the green spaces and trails are near your home. Use these spaces for quick getaways as often as you can in between longer trips and vacations.

Quick hikes like those are always worth it. It's better to step out for a breath of fresh air when the opportunity presents itself than sit and "kill time" until the next appointment. If the *Hike366* project has taught me one thing, it's that hiking is meaningful no matter how many miles I do, how much elevation I gain or how rugged the terrain is. Even an easy walk in the park has its merits and joys. It's important for me to leave space in my life for those types of hikes as well as the long ones.

During the project, I began to fall into a routine of fitting in short hikes throughout the week. As a result, I observed an unusual shift in attitude. Upon looking at my jam-packed agenda one morning, I said, "I do NOT want to go hiking today." That feeling made me sick to my stomach. How had I turned a hobby that brought me so much joy into a chore I didn't want to do? Something wasn't right. In that moment of realization, I made the decision not to finish the *Hike366* project in one calendar year. I decided that if I did not want to hike on a certain day, I simply would not do it.

As soon as I made that choice I felt as if a huge weight had been lifted off my back. It was okay not to go for a hike. I did not have to stick to plan A. If it meant delaying the project an entire year, so be it. There was no rush to get it done. Up until that point, I felt like missing a day was a failure—I wanted so badly to succeed. But I realized that my first definition of success had left no wiggle room for life's circumstances. What was the point of the project, anyways? To do it quickly or to do it well? Ultimately, it was my project and my decision, so I chose to follow my heart and let myself complete it in my own time.

I made the same decision a few more times along the way, delaying the completion of the project again and again. With the freedom to make my own choices, I felt more motivated to plan ahead for the days I knew I'd be able to make time for hiking. One of those days arose in May 2016. I chose to get outside, filling in a gap on my hiking spreadsheet. My research drew me to Baskett Slough National Wildlife Refuge, a lazy forty-minute drive from home. It was an absolutely gorgeous spring day, and I was very excited to go hiking.

When I arrived I glanced at the trailhead map and mentally worked out a route through the refuge. I was immediately struck by the bright colors, crayon blue sky, and grasses as tall as I was. I walked blissfully through the unexpected paradise, until I suddenly noticed that the trail had disappeared under my feet. Either the route map at the trailhead was inaccurate or I'd made a wrong turn. I fumbled through the grass, avoiding the shoe-swallowing marshes, and used my compass to roughly navigate the loop I had planned. Eventually I made it back to the trail and fell back into my nature-induced reverie. It's easy for me to let my guard down on short hikes, but I was reminded to be diligent in map-reading and navigation no matter where my hikes take me!

I did not enjoy perfect weather on most of my "squeeze-in" hikes because their dates were mostly in the winter and spring. On a wretched day in January 2016, I drove out to Minto-Brown Island Park in Salem, Oregon. It was gloomy and wet. The swollen Willamette River had flooded half the trails. I was cold to the bone as I trudged along the soggy paths. I reminded myself that every hike isn't a winner, but it still feels good to get outside.

A few days later, I ended up just a few miles north at Willamette Mission State Park. Conditions were roughly the same: cold, gray, flooded trails. In fact, my boots got soaked within moments of leaving the parking lot, so I chose to go barefoot for the rest of the hike.

It was cold. It was January. Everything was gray and brown.

I walked quickly, heading towards the eerie house frames that I had seen on the park's website. They are an homage to the old mission that once stood there. When I arrived at a good viewpoint, I just stared across the river. And then, to my delight, a beaver poked its head up from beneath the water. After walking through the gloomy woods without seeing many signs of life, the beaver offered a flash of liveliness that brightened my mood. I watched the beaver swim for quite some time, until it occurred to me that my feet were getting cold. Of course, I was still barefoot. I headed back to my car, pledging that next time I would visit on a warmer day, with waterproof shoes.

On February 23, 2016, I had little time to spare. It was a designated hike day, and I was very motivated to figure out how to squeeze one in. So I had a crazy idea: I'd drive an hour to the coast, hike the beach as the sun was rising, and then get back to town before my workday started. I arrived in Newport, Oregon, just after six a.m. and took my shoes off in preparation for my beach hike. I have a rule: no shoes on the beach! As I stepped onto the sand, I noticed the full moon was crashing down towards the rippling ocean. What a beautiful sight! Looking over my other shoulder, the sun was rising over the bluffs in town. The sky flashed purple, pink, orange—it was glorious. I didn't know where to turn my head.

By seven a.m., the color was fading in the sky, and I turned my attention to some crows playing on the beach. I watched how the waves carved intricate channels into the soft sand. I noticed how the light reflected off the narrow pools of water trapped on the beach. I observed the seemingly out-of-place rocks, eroded by a long history of crashing waves. Before eight a.m., I found myself already back at the parking lot, hitting the road so I could make it to work on time.

What a whirlwind of a morning and a spectacular way to start the day! Nearly five miles of walking barefoot in the cold sand, and I was the only viewer of the morning's dance between sun and moon. I felt so lucky to have the opportunity to blast out to the coast so quickly on a weekday morning. Experiences like that made me grateful to have "Hike Day" scratched into my calendar.

Water continued to inspire me to take those last minute, "squeeze-in" hikes. On a gloomy winter day I visited McDowell Creek Falls. I'd been there once before in the summer and noted how low the waterfalls were. I hoped that a winter visit would yield more impressive falls, because winters in the Cascade foothills are far wetter than summers. The waterfalls were, indeed, incredible. I stopped to let the image of my surroundings settle into my memory. I left, taking very few pictures due to the rainy, damp conditions. I didn't have the right equipment or skill for that. On the drive back, I pondered the purpose of my being out there and the interference that photography has on my experience.

I hike for the sake of hiking, not for taking photos. For me, photography is a way to capture a snapshot of a moment so that I can relive it in my mind later. It's not my profession. I don't go hiking specifically to take a particular shot or spend an hour trying to frame the perfect composition. It's an incidental thing that I do, sometimes, while I'm out and about. The act of taking pictures, for me, detracts from experiencing the moment. I don't end up with all the killer photos that go viral on social media, but that's okay. What's more important to me is that I enjoy the experience for myself.

Despite my commitment to only hike on the days I wanted to, there was one day on my to-do list that I was not going to miss for anything. That day was February 29, 2016: leap day. If I didn't hike on that day, I'd set my project back by *four years*. In order to keep things moving forward, I chose to prioritize hiking on leap day and blocked out an afternoon to get outside. My mission: to go on an adventure somewhere I'd never been.

I settled on a combination of hikes: Abiqua Falls and Butte Creek Falls in Northwest Oregon. I'd seen lots of incredible pictures of Abiqua Falls online, but the short hike, sketchy road reports, and long drive always kept me away. Fortunately, the road to the trailhead was drivable for my little car and I made it to the parking area with no problem. I hiked down to the river on a wet, steep trail and turned towards the sound of the waterfall. Just around the corner, I arrived at a huge basalt amphitheater created over thousands of years by water pouring over the cliff's edge. It was as gorgeous as I'd imagined. The gray cloud cover made the scene ominous and dark. I enjoyed a few moments of quiet there by myself. Once I heard voices approaching behind me, I turned back and made the short trek back to the car.

Heading through a maze of forest roads, I reached my second destination and saw two small waterfalls. Altogether, my daily hike stats totaled two miles, but length was not what I was going for on that day. In the course of an afternoon, I saw three waterfalls that were new to me and enjoyed a little bit of solitude at each one. Leap day mission: accomplished.

After moving to Bend in 2016, I continued my quest to fill in the missing dates on the list. In February 2018, with snow covering the ground and a winter chill in the air, I drove to Shevlin Park to explore the north end of the area's trail system. I realized I'd only seen the trails on the popular south side of the park. The other side was much smaller and had fewer trails, so it never captured my imagination. With my journal imploring me to "take a hike today," I decided to take a chance on that small parcel of land. It wasn't a long adventure but it was pretty. The snowy landscape, the flowing river and the cold breeze created an experience I won't soon forget.

I quickly exhausted many local options for short, accessible trails to hike, so I enlisted my friend Sarah to share some ideas and join me on hikes I hadn't done yet. The first of these was Bessie Butte, a small cinder cone on the outskirts of town that has a one-mile trail to the top. It's almost identical to Pilot Butte, which I've walked on numerous occasions as it's located a few blocks from my house. For this reason, I never thought to venture out there. How different could two symmetrical buttes with mile-long summit trails be? We hiked to the top and back on a chilly, gray day. It wasn't spectacular but it was different, and I crossed another item off my to-do list.

Sarah and I would have many adventures together. On another crummy day in March we went to explore parts of the Oregon Badlands that were new to me, including a trail around Reynolds Pond. It was an absolutely gorgeous surprise, tucked in the otherwise desolate sandscape that is the Oregon Badlands Wilderness area. Located only twenty minutes from Bend, it's one of the few year-round accessible hiking spots in the area because of its low elevation; it doesn't get snowed in each fall like the surrounding mountains do.

The following month, we drove just a little bit further in the opposite direction and walked a lap around Suttle Lake. Perhaps the best discovery on that short hike was the lakeside restaurant and bar. After our three-mile hike, we stopped to grab a drink and have a chat while lounging on cozy couches near the fireplace inside. Sometimes, hiking is not entirely about roughing it.

Several of the last "squeeze-in" hikes I completed took place on a road trip covering four states and a couple thousand miles of driving in the spring of 2018. This trip was originally planned to be the grand finale of *Hike366*, but when I discovered a missing date in May, that plan was thwarted. On that trip, however, Aaron and I went on several hikes that are included in the project. One of these was a hike in Nevada's Cathedral Gorge State Park. My foot had been bothering me, so we ended up doing a few short hikes instead of one long one. Our casual stroll through Juniper Draw helped me take it easy on my foot while still completing a hike. It was stark and beautiful. I marveled at the badlands' cathedral-like formations that make the park so unique; the fluted spires and pillars that looked so fragile had, in fact, formed from ash deposited tens of millions of years ago. My foot was aching by the end of the four-mile hike, but it was worth it. We were checking boxes left and right.

꽃

Almost as soon as I started going on regular hiking trips back in 2005, I was mostly interested in long, challenging hikes. "Long" is as relative a term as "short." My fitness level, my mental state, the amount of elevation gain and the difficulty of the terrain all factor into how long a hike feels. Once the mileage entered the double digits, I typically started considering the hike "long."

No one would argue the difficulty of the Presidential Traverse. At twenty-four miles and almost 10,000 feet of elevation gain, this hike is a butt-kicker in just about every sense. Weather can play a huge factor in the likelihood of success completing this route, since many of the miles traverse above the tree line in some of New Hampshire's most inhospitable terrain. The route crosses over the tops of ten summits, and the trail surface changes from dirt to roots to rocks and back again.

I decided to join a group of strangers for this epic trek on May 27, 2006. We left the parking lot at 4:30 am to give us a head start on daylight. We ascended through the fog and clouds and ticked off one mountaintop after another. The group took several breaks and rested much longer than I would have hoped, considering the amount of ground we'd have to cover in a day. But I stayed with the group all the way to the tenth summit. As they sat down for yet another rest break, I decided I needed to go my own way. My body wanted to call it quits, but I still had a ways to go to get to the road.

Mentally I felt like I was fighting a losing battle, and I quickly entered a downward spiral, feeling worse and worse. In my journal, I wrote extensively about this hike. I even divided it up into sections: summary, physical progress, mental progress, people, and trail conditions. Here's an excerpt from the "mental progress" section:

Once I began to feel bodily aches and pains, my mental state started to deteriorate. I felt tears well up a couple of times, but I managed to press ahead, just at a slower pace. I stayed in the back and tried to forget about the rest of the group so I could focus on myself.

Each climb became more agonizing. Time moved in slow motion. I had waves of positive and negative thoughts as the day progressed. At the last peak, Webster, I knew it was over, and I just wanted to get out.

The descent was very steep and the trail was littered with rocks and roots that made for tricky footing. JC took the lead and I followed, but even he was going slow. Each step was painful. I had a mental breakdown and couldn't stop crying. I kept pace with JC, but I made sure he was just out of sight until I could get a handle on my tears.

I felt really stupid for crying and thought to myself, "Think of something funny." Nothing came. But the fact that it had come to this made me start to laugh—uncontrollable fits of laughter, the kind you can't hold in. Once I started, I couldn't stop! But hey, I thought it was surely better than crying.

The team kept taking more and more breaks. I thought, "We'll never finish at this pace." Each time we stopped it was harder for me to get going again. I told the leader I would go ahead and meet them at the end. Now it was just me and the trail.

I promised myself I'd be out before sunset, so I needed to take a tough mental stance. I started by giving myself pep talks, both in my head and out loud. Then I started talking trash to the trail: "Is that all you got?" "Bring it on; you won't beat me!" "This stream crossing is a piece of cake!"

The more I talked, the faster I went and the better my body felt. I felt good and strong, so I kept talking the whole way down. At some points I sang aloud, doing whatever I could to keep my legs moving and the pain away. The sun dropped lower and lower. But as I walked I noticed hints that the end was near.

It felt so good to reach the road, even though I knew I still had to walk to the car. I burst from the woods with a big smile on my face, hands raised over my head in victory. As the sun set, I quickly walked to the lot to get my car. I threw my hands on the roof of the car and felt tears pooling in my eyes again. This hike pushed me to my absolute limit.

I don't remember how long it took the rest of the group to arrive, Five minutes? Thirty minutes? It didn't matter. I was so deliriously blissed out and proud of my accomplishment. The Presidential Traverse was neither the first nor the last of my long, epic day-hikes, but it was one of the most memorable. To this day, I can still feel the burning in my legs and the strain on my emotions when I think about this hike.

Sometimes the absolute mileage isn't the only factor that classifies a hike as long. In 2005, I did a nine-mile hike along a ridgeline in New Hampshire's White Mountains. My hiking partner—an avid cyclist—walked quickly uphill on his strong legs. His fast pace made the whole hike feel much harder and longer than it would have been on my own. But, being a nice person, he slowed down to hike with me instead of leaving me in the dust. Somehow, his downhill muscles weren't as well-conditioned as mine, so I got my chance to race ahead on the last leg of the trip, regaining some semblance of confidence in my hiking ability.

That didn't happen the next time I visited the range. I joined a group of what I would call "elite hikers." Those folks had climbed actual mountains, in places like Alaska, Washington and Colorado. They'd completed ultramarathons. They were in peak physical and mental condition. And me? I'm not sure why they let me tag along.

We set out to complete a traverse of the range. Our plan was to walk over the tops of four 4,000-foot peaks over eighteen miles, with an unknown (to me) amount of elevation gain. Let's just say it was a lot. We moved at such a quick pace that I didn't have time to take in much of the scenery around me. The mountains passed by in a blur. I was so focused on keeping up with the team that my mind blocked out other sensory stimuli. We stopped for breaks at each peak, some longer than others. One member of our team lost his camera somewhere between two of the highpoints, so the rest of us got to hang out for a bit while he ran back to retrieve it. I was silently overjoyed. A rest.

I stayed with the pack of elite hikers as long as I could. They knew I was struggling. A couple of people took turns hanging out in the back of the pack, chatting with me and giving mini pep talks as we went. Those chats were actually quite helpful! I felt supported by my team, although I knew they were rushing me along for the safety of the group. There was only so much sunlight in the day, and I was dragging the hike out longer than it needed to be.

We reached the last summit just before sunset and still had miles to go. I put on my headlamp and let the others go ahead of me. The group did wait for me at all river crossings and trail junctions, which I greatly appreciated. But I'm glad they didn't stop more often, because I felt like a wreck. One hiker kept by my side for the last mile, encouraging me to keep walking and distracting me with silly stories. At the end of the day, I could not have been happier to see the parking lot. I had stepped far outside my comfort zone but really enjoyed meeting that group of people. I hoped I would get to hike with them again, and I became determined to improve my stamina so I could keep up with the team in the future.

When I moved to Oregon, I couldn't find anything like those long ridge traverses in New England. I quickly learned that the hiking would be very different in the west. I had to challenge myself in other ways to remain interested in hiking. Just across the Columbia River in Southern Washington is the Klickitat Rail Trail. This walking path follows an old railroad along a creek. In April 2011, my friend Sue joined me for an as-long-as-we-felt-like-it walk on the thirty-one-mile trail.

It was an absolutely gorgeous spring day. The sky was blue. Marmots dashed between boulders near the slowly moving creek. Early spring wildflowers brought small bursts of color to the greening slopes. As we walked and talked through this idyllic landscape, the miles just ticked away. At about the nine-mile mark, the trail took on a new character. There were junked cars and trash everywhere. The weedy canyon seemed to close in on us. We decided to turn around. In comparison to my epic on the rugged Franconia Traverse, those eighteen miles on a gentle railroad grade felt like nothing. Yes, hiking in the Northwest would be different.

With some effort, it was possible to piece together long and difficult hikes in Oregon. One of my favorites is Tanner Butte, in the Columbia River Gorge. The hike to the summit gains about

4,000 feet in roughly twenty miles, round trip. While the hike starts from a developed trailhead, it finishes via an unofficial route to the upper viewpoint. Actually, it's one of the more official off-trail routes I've ever seen. A sign at the base of the route states, "Please find scramble route to summit. Trail not maintained."

In the fall of 2006, I started the long trek to the top of Tanner Butte by headlamp before sunrise. I was alone, of course, because no one I knew would be up for that sort of thing. It was a cool, damp fall day. I walked quickly through the dense forest and paused often to admire the view of the surrounding trees nearby, because everything else was shrouded in fog. As I walked along the obviously low-use trail, my pants and socks got soaked from brushing up against wet vegetation. The trail was sometimes difficult to see because of drooping branches and leaves. The final bit of the hike up to the summit was the best part. Hiking out of the trees and into alpine territory, my heart raced in anticipation of the view. The view never came, but I sat and ate my lunch as I watched the clouds dance along the treetops. I took off my socks and shoes, dried my feet, and put on clean socks. I wrapped a fleece neck gaiter around my feet and stuck them in a large zipper bag, where they were warm and comfy. I basked in the accomplishment of reaching the summit far earlier than expected and enjoyed the occasional glimpse through the clouds, imagining the breathtaking vistas one would see on a clear day.

The whole hike back provided wonderful photo opportunities, since I was no longer concerned about time. I stopped to admire mushrooms, fall foliage, and the mist rolling through the trees. I felt grateful for early starts and the fortitude to get out for a long day hike by myself.

When I could find friends who were ready for a big adventure, I was happy to take them up on it. In November 2011, Sue and I raced up Table Mountain on the Washington side of the Gorge. In just over two hours, we made it 3,200 vertical feet to the summit, where we enjoyed lunch with a view. It was an unseasonably beautiful fall day, with not a speck of snow anywhere. I was grateful for the lack of moisture on the ground, which made scrambling up the long, rocky slope fun and easy.

I could always count on Sue to endure a long, arduous day of hiking. The month prior, we set out on the Yocum Ridge Trail with the intention of hiking as far up as we could before we could take no more. We hiked a total of sixteen miles. At our halfway point, we stopped along the trail for lunch. With a view of snow-capped Mt. Hood under blue skies, I couldn't have asked for a lovelier rest spot. It was a magnificent sight, its ice-covered rocks gleaming in the autumn sun. Long hikes provide opportunities to push myself and develop a better sense of what I'm capable of. They are also much more fun than running on a treadmill or doing something strictly for "exercise." I'll take my physical training with a side of mountainous majesty, thank you very much.

For me, long hikes almost always equate to climbing something. Whether or not it's a technical climb is not important to me. What is important is that there's a summit involved, and hopefully some off-trail scrambling as well. There's some perfect ratio of physical challenge, mental challenge, skill and scenery that comes together to make my favorite kind of hike.

One of these mountain climbs took place in spring 2013 in California's Death Valley National Park. Aaron and I set our sights on the park's highpoint: Telescope Peak. At 11,049 feet, the mountain summit provides a bird's-eye view of Badwater Basin, the lowest point in North America.

The trail to the summit was long and mellow. There was much less snow than I was hoping for on the route. (Yes, snow in the California desert.) When I started doing research for this trip, I was stunned to find photos of people climbing this peak using crampons and ice axes. The prospect of hiking from the heat of the desert basin into full winter conditions excited me. We hiked through a few small snow patches along the trail, but there was nothing too challenging about it.

It can be difficult to plan a hike to an unfamiliar area based on weather and snow conditions from previous years. There's just too much variability from year to year. Nevertheless, we had a beautiful and enjoyable hike. At the summit, we met one solo hiker who had lots of great tips for places to check out across Death Valley. It's always nice to meet a kindred spirit on a mountaintop.

In July of that same year, I took Aaron up Diamond Peak in Central Oregon. Diamond Peak has a little of everything: a long walk in, some off-trail navigation, some Class 2 scrambling, and a summit. For a new mountaineer, it's a perfect place to go practice basic climbing skills.

The mosquitoes were ferocious, which only helped us walk

faster. The off-trail route was fairly well-marked and easy to follow on the way up—not so much on the way down. The upper ridge has some interesting rock and snow features to negotiate, making it feel like a bit more than just a hike. I was not-so-secretly hoping to turn Aaron into a mountain climber.

YOSEMITE DECIMAL SYSTEM (YDS)

The YDS is a subjective and imperfect system of classifying the difficulty of a hiking or climbing route. It gives outdoor explorers an idea of what kind of terrain and exposure to expect on a route.

Class 1: hiking, usually on a trail
Class 2: hiking, may involve off-trail travel and/or occasional use of hands
Class 3: hiking, scrambling, with frequent use of hands and feet, a fall would cause injury but probably not kill you
Class 4: scrambling, with frequent use of hands and feet, significant exposure, a fall would likely cause serious injury or death, some teams will use a rope and protection
Class 5: technical climbing where a fall would likely be fatal, most teams will choose to use a rope and protection

Later we tackled another peak in Central Oregon: Cowhorn Mountain. Patches of snow on the trail made it a bit more difficult to get to. Again, we followed an unofficial path from the well-maintained trail to the summit. We zigzagged from hot, snow-free scree to shaded, snow-covered boulders and back again. It felt much more treacherous and exposed than our romp up Diamond Peak. Nonetheless, we made it to the tiny summit and celebrated with snacks, water and selfies. Cowhorn was a perfect warm up for the truly epic summit we'd be climbing later that winter in southeast Oregon.

A long winter hike in the high desert of Southeast Oregon is no joke. Temperatures drop well below freezing. Daylight is short. There are no maintained trails. There are no other people.

No services. It's just you and the great, wide open. Mother Nature is not on your side.

Somehow I'd convinced Aaron that a summit-seeking adventure in the wild high desert was a good idea. I'd researched routes to a remote peak using books and the Internet, mapping out a few landmarks that would keep us on track for our journey. I anticipated between ten to fourteen miles of hiking with a 4,000-foot elevation gain.

We started walking cross-country from a rough dirt road, the mountain hidden behind some other land features. As we climbed higher and got a good look at our destination, we alternated between following an old Jeep track and walking straight across the sagebrush desert. The hillside got steeper and steeper as we hiked. Nearing what appeared to be the summit, we hit some snow. Luckily, deer had broken trail ahead of us. The snow was hard-packed from the wind, and kicking steps into unbroken snow was much harder than following the deer prints. We paused briefly behind a tall rock to put on a wind-proof layer before stepping out into who knew what next, which turned out to be a great idea. The wind picked up, and we soon found that we were nowhere near the summit.

Ahead, we saw a rock pile that looked higher than the one we were standing on. Then another. A long, gentle ridge stretched out for what felt like forever (but in reality was close to half a mile). The bitter cold and steady wind helped put some pep in our step as we raced for the official highpoint. After several false summits we finally topped out on our destination, Pueblo Mountain, and were treated with big views across the isolated desert range. As if on cue, two bighorn sheep crossed the same broad plateau that we had just come from. There are so many reasons why I enjoy these long, challenging hikes. Surprise cameos from rarely sighted wildlife ranks high among them!

As it turned out, hiking up Pueblo Mountain would be a warm up to what we'd encounter on a road trip a couple years later. While planning a visit to Great Basin National Park in Nevada, I decided to look into hiking the park's highpoint, Wheeler Peak. A tough but easily accessible hike in the summer, this mountain would prove to be a much greater challenge in the spring. At 13,065 feet, it is the second highest peak in the state and is capped by snow until summer. We arrived in the park in mid-April, when the road to the trailhead was still gated due to snow, doubling the amount of miles and elevation gain for this trek.

> TRAIL LINGO
>
> **Bushwhacking:** Hiking off-trail. Also called "hiking cross-country." The term presumably derives from hiking through a forested landscape with a thick understory, where hikers would have to "whack" their way through the "bush."

"We can do it," I told Aaron. It was sixteen miles and 5,300 feet of elevation gain. And so we gave it a go. We hiked up the road, found the trail, bushwhacked through the snow to the lake and then started up the snow couloir leading to the summit ridge. A park ranger had suggested that route when we stopped in to the visitor center the previous day. It looked like fun, so we geared up to climb the snow. It turned out to be wickedly fun for me and a bit terrifying for Aaron. Once we reached the top of the couloir, we just had to place one foot in front of the other to make it to the lonely summit.

That was one of the hardest hikes we'd ever done together. The combination of the hike's length, the high altitude, the snow conditions and the cold, dry air made each step feel more impossible than the one before. But we made it. We'd prepared well. We'd each pushed through some tough moments. And for what reward? The summit was windless, warm and sunny. We could see for miles across the desert basin and range landscape, mountain ranges stretching out in all directions. We were alone; no one else had dared to make the trek that day. And after the hike, we knew we were more capable than we'd thought.

Back at home, I began compiling lists of winter-accessible hikes that were long and difficult but not avalanche prone. Getting caught in an avalanche was one of my greatest fears related to winter hiking. I chose to avoid avalanche terrain altogether in order to feel safe when exploring in the snow. One of the mountains on my list was Paulina Peak. In the summer, you can hike up a short but steep trail that reaches the summit in just about two miles. You can even drive up the road to the top. But once the area's lower snow gates close for the winter, it takes a minimum of six miles of walking to reach the top.

In November 2017, I planned my ascent for just after the gate closed but before the snow got deep enough for snowmobile travel. I hate snowshoeing with those machines nearby. They're loud and emit noxious fumes that make it difficult to breathe.

On that glorious winter day, everything lined up: great weather, a well-prepared team, blue skies, and just enough snow to be pretty at the trailhead and snowshoe-able near the summit. The hike uphill was grueling since we had to do some route finding and break trail in fresh snow. We were rewarded with clear views from the top, which overlooked the sparkling blue Paulina Lake. With gravity on our side, the hike back down was quite pleasant. It was a superb way to kick off a new season of winter hiking.

Not all long hikes are planned. In 2009 I hiked to Paradise Park on Mt. Hood with a friend. We knew we were in for a twelve-mile hike, but we took a wrong turn on our way back to the trailhead. While we probably only tacked on another mile or two of walking, those extra steps felt so difficult! Knowing that I'd made a mistake put me into an irritated state of mind, and that affected how I felt physically. That was not the first time I'd made a misstep, nor would it be the last, but it's interesting how hard a mile feels when it's in the wrong direction.

One of my most memorable long hikes was the Belknap Range Traverse in Southern New Hampshire. I planned the trip as the grand finale for this project. May 10 stood alone as the last item remaining on my spreadsheet—the only calendar date on which I had never gone hiking. It was also the day that I flew into Logan Airport from the West Coast on a red-eye flight. My dad picked me up from the airport and we drove two hours north to the Belknap trailhead. I groggily shoved a bacon and egg sandwich in my face at a local Dunkin' Donuts (now known officially as just "Dunkin.") It wasn't the best breakfast before a long hike, but it would have to do.

Since the route traversed a mountain range, the starting trailhead and the ending trailhead were many miles away from each other. We parked at the endpoint and called an Uber to shuttle us back to the start. What a modern way to take a hike!

My brain felt pretty foggy and sleep-deprived as we walked up a steep gravel road at the start of the route. But once I fell into a rhythm, things became clear. We walked for nearly eight hours, tagging ten summits along the way. The trails were a mixture of roads, dirt, boulders, slabs, and roots. It was a classic New England hike. The views, the highpoints, the scenery, the solitude and the company all made this hike one of my favorite trips of the project. I was delighted to finish up with my dad right where it all began, in my homeland.

Long hikes have always appealed to me. Whether it's the physical difficulty, the mental challenge, the time immersed outdoors, or some combination of those factors, these hikes fill my soul. But I've learned to value the short hikes just as much. Distance is not a defining factor anymore; all time spent moving outdoors is amazing and wonderful. There's room for every length of hike in my life!

5

For the Sake of Climbing

Trembling in my climbing shoes, staring up the rock wall at loose boulders, I wondered what decisions had gotten me to this point. I briefly looked down at the rope dangling between my legs, my belayer out of sight. A breeze blew past my face. I stood on my toes, a couple hundred feet above the ground, with no one else around us for miles. But I couldn't think about that. We had to get to the top so we could get out of there. Turning my gaze upwards once more, I took a breath and kept climbing.

CLIMBING LINGO

"On belay!"

Belaying is a method of securing your climbing partner with a rope. There are many different belaying devices and techniques. The belay system ensures that the rope protects the climber in case of a fall.

It seemed like a good idea at the time. I had only been leading rock climbs for the last year, but I had my mind set on doing *this* climb. It was in one of my favorite climbing areas, Tieton River Rocks in Central Washington. This multi-pitch route didn't have a great reputation and, as far as I could tell, didn't see many ascents. The rock often crumbled with the touch of a hand, giving me an unsettling feeling while climbing. The loose rock on this geological feature, plus its distance from other good climbs in the Tieton area, kept most people away. But the moderate grade of difficulty, relatively easy access, and alpine-like character appealed to me. I originally wanted to learn how to rock climb in order to be self-sufficient in the mountains. The challenges on this particular route were just what I was looking for: interesting route finding, difficult gear placements, varied rock texture and quality, and solitude. I savored the opportunity to have no one to guide me. Although I was climbing with a partner, I took full responsibility for making the climb work. I did the route research and prepared myself mentally to lead each pitch in order to get to the top.

The hike to the base of this climb is just over a mile. Once we reached the start of the route, we unpacked our rope, put on our safety gear, and started to scale the rock. The climb demands more mental focus and skill than physical strength. The rocks are loose. The ledges are covered in dirt and moss. This is not a manicured route, scrubbed clean by thousands of ascents. It is raw, mysterious and exciting. I used a few psychological tactics to get myself through the most difficult parts of the climb. I assessed the rock critically, speaking aloud as I found useful holds and ledges: "Left foot here. Right hand there." It helped me home in on the task at hand, pulling my mind away from distracting thoughts.

I knew, rationally, that the climbing was well within my technical ability, but occasionally throughout the ascent I lost my grip on all rational thought. When I started to feel butterflies in my stomach, I would sing to myself. "Sweet Caroline. Ba ba ba...." Those soothing verses reduced my anxiety, allowing me to flow up the rock. With a patient and competent partner accompanying me, we finished the climb, topped out, and I was swallowed up by a wave of joy.

To some folks, hiking is a means to an end. Those people call themselves "climbers." A hike, in their minds, is just an annoying obstacle between the car and the start of the climb. I entered the climbing community in 2007 upon signing up for the Mazamas' Basic Climbing Education Program (BCEP). My goal in taking the course was to expand on my hiking skills and learn techniques for getting to mountaintops that proved too difficult to simply walk up. I found, upon moving to Oregon, that many of the Cascades' high peaks required these skills. But I had no intention on leaving my beloved hiking days behind. I saw climbing as just another skill on the continuum of ways to move through the outdoors.

The stories that follow are collected from over a decade of climbing trips. Some were mountaineering adventures, meaning we used technical gear when a formidable obstacle was encountered along a hike (usually just before the mountain's summit). Some were rock-climbing trips, which required a little bit of hiking to access a developed climbing area, such as Smith Rock (Oregon), Yosemite (California), and City of Rocks (Idaho).

Within the rock-climbing category, there are sport climbs and traditional climbs. In sport climbing, someone drills bolts into the rock so future climbers can ascend the wall and clip their ropes into the bolts, creating a safety system in case of a fall. Sport climbing has been a necessary training tool for me, helping to build skills and confidence on the rock, but it is not my passion.

Traditional (trad) climbing, on the other hand, immediately drew my interest and curiosity. This method of climbing requires the lead climber to place removable gear, like nuts and cams, along the climbing route for protection. There are no bolts pre-placed along the route as in sport climbing. Climbers often travel in pairs and use a rope clipped into the gear to cushion potential falls. The second climber acts as a belayer, managing the rope as the lead climber advances on the route, prepared to catch any falls. Some trad climbs also require climbers to build anchors at the top of each pitch using the gear they carry or features they find on the rock. That is what I expected to need to know how to do in the mountains, so I wanted to learn these skills.

On my trad-climbing journey, I have met many great climbing partners. The best partners have more experience than I do, are mindful of safety, enjoy teaching climbing skills and are fun to be around.

Even with supportive partners, rock climbing has not always been an easy romp for me. My mind has always been my biggest obstacle. And a negative mindset has halted me on many climbs. After moving to a new town and putting climbing on hold for a year, I met up with some friends in October 2012 back at Smith Rock's Lower Gorge. While the park is known internationally for its sport climbing, this particular area contains mostly trad climbs. For this reason, it is usually less crowded than the other walls. I had an okay time following my partner's leads, but once it was my turn to take the lead, I fell apart. Rock climbing is as much a mental challenge as a physical one. Thoughts of falling, of injury, of failure, of disappointment all create mental barriers that draw energy away from completing the task at hand.

Facing that climb, looking at the bits of metal dangling from my harness, and berating myself about how afraid I was, I bailed. "Nope, bring me down!" I yelled at my partner after struggling up a difficult route for an agonizingly long period of time. He lowered me, finished leading it, and set up a top rope so I could try again. When using a top rope, there's very little consequence for taking a fall. Theoretically, that should have helped me push past my self-imposed barriers and fly up the climb. But I didn't. The damage had already been done. I was in such a bad headspace that I still had trouble completing the route.

I've had a difficult relationship with climbing. Sometimes, I feel like it brings the greatest joys and the most wondrous experiences. Other times, I feel like it brings out the worst in me. It exacerbates my nervousness, my fear, my lack of self-confidence. But it is through difficulties that I learn to look deeply inside myself, facing the unpleasant feelings that I desperately try to push down when I question my ability to complete a route. And with each climb, whether I reach the top or not, I learn to become a better version of myself.

Despite my internal struggles with rock climbing, I just can't seem to walk away from it. In May 2013, I volunteered to assist the Mazamas' Advanced Rock course at a climbing weekend at Smith Rock. I was paired up with a student and we set off into the Lower Gorge. She was a strong climber, much stronger than myself, but hesitant on lead. She gingerly placed gear, proceeding up a few of the easiest climbs in the area. It was illuminating to see the rock through a new leader's eyes, and a reminder of how much I do know about climbing. Her trepidation helped me tap into some of my own confidence. I was able to offer encouragement, advice and support as she went through many of the same mind-games I played with myself.

In March 2018, I headed into the main area of the park, the one that's packed with groups, classes, vacationers and weekend warriors. I'd be leading the climbs that day, and my partner wanted to tackle some easy sport climbs so she could get back into the groove of climbing outside. We were a perfect match. I led the routes comfortably. I practiced some new skills from the classes I'd recently taken. I cheered my partner on. I felt the sun on my face and smiled as I gazed out over the Crooked River. This is why I hike. This is why I climb.

In the beginning, I never thought I'd be a climber. "Ok, climb!" Those words echoed meaninglessly in my head as I was tied into a rope for the first time. It was spring 2006 in Rumney, New Hampshire. My then-boyfriend had taken me out with his climbing friends to introduce me to the sport. I looked up at the wall, looked down at my feet, felt my heart race in my chest and timidly took the first step. "What do I do? How does this work? What happens if I fall?" I was nearly paralyzed by fear.

I think I made it to the top of that climb, but when I came down, I said I was done for the day. Climbing was not for me; it just felt bad. I didn't know anything about ropes, harnesses or safety systems. I liked hiking well enough, so why wouldn't I just walk up the backside of the rock face? There was an easier way up! Climbing was SO STUPID.

But a few short years later, I found myself climbing in iconic places, like Yosemite National Park, and having a great time. How things had changed! After taking some courses and meeting climbing partners who supported me in learning how to climb,

I became hooked. For me, the right education, the right people and the right environment were all necessary to usher me into a new and scary outdoor activity.

Since the beginning of my climbing journey, I was intrigued by the thought of multi-pitch climbing, where the length of the rock climb surpasses the length of the rope. To me, climbing was a natural extension of hiking; it was a way to get from point A to B. I wasn't interested in climbing just for the sake of doing something hard, I wanted to get somewhere. There's nothing quite like the feeling of knowing I just scaled hundreds of feet of rock to stand atop a panoramic viewpoint. I loved getting to highpoints, and multi-pitch climbing was just one more strategy to do that.

I drove to Yosemite in March 2010 to meet a couple of friends who had already been climbing and camping there the previous week. I met them with just enough time to climb one route—Nutcracker. It is a five-pitch climb with an overall rating of 5.8. I led the second and easiest pitch, a 5.4, which served as my first outdoor lead that spring. It was a safe and easy first climb of the season, leaving me feeling completely exhilarated by the time I reached the top.

YDS FOR ROCK CLIMBING

The Yosemite Decimal System (YDS) is further broken down for rock climbers.

Class 5 routes range from 5.0 to 5.15.

Roughly, these ratings can be thought of as such:

5.0-5.7: easy
5.8-5.10: intermediate
5.11-5.12: difficult
5.13-5.15: elite

Of course, these ratings are subjective, and climbs on different types of rock or climbs that require different styles of movement, even if they have the same rating, will feel quite distinct.

My passion for multi-pitch climbing took me on the road again in 2012, this time to the endless granite formations of Idaho's City of Rocks. A large group of Mazamas was going to be stationed there for about a week, so my friend Tom and I drove out together to climb. We did a mixture of sport and trad climbing, single and multi-pitch. Plus, I took a day off to "just" go hiking by myself. When my social bucket gets too full, I need time in solitude to reset the balance.

At City of Rocks I learned that slab climbing is nothing like crack climbing. A 5.8 slab, for example, felt much harder to me than a 5.8 hand crack. Ratings are so subjective that it's always hard to trust the numbers. I had so much more experience climbing cracks, where I could securely place my hands and feet inside as I moved up the wall, than climbing slabs. Therefore, I was comfortable on that type of terrain. On a slab, I had to learn to trust that my climbing shoes would stick to the tiny granite crystals underfoot as I gingerly brushed my hands against the slanted rock in front of me for balance.

The two climbs that really stand out to me from that trip are the ones with the most alpine feel: Sinocranium and Lost Arrow Spire. The five pitches of bolted slab on Sinocranium pulled both ends of my mouth up into a smile with every step. The climbing felt good; it was fun and well within my physical ability. After building up my confidence climbing some other slabs, I was able to relax and enjoy the delightful climbing on that route. Lost Arrow Spire, a traditional route with a single bolt and a few old pitons (metal spikes hammered into cracks in the rocks) on it for protection, had a great position overlooking the nearby rock formations and a fun summit. The top of the spire had just enough room for a handful of people to stand comfortably, and the rock was so steep that there was no way to get to the top besides climbing it. There's a certain sense of pride and accomplishment I feel when I stand on top of a highpoint. Climbing Lost Arrow brought me that sense of joy.

Since there was a large number of climbers in the Mazamas group, many of whom I'd met before, I had the opportunity to climb with people who weren't my regular climbing partners. Each new person gave me an opportunity to learn from his or her unique strategies and styles, and to practice my communication skills.

Climbing differs from hiking in one big way: it takes two (or more) people. It also requires a level of cooperation and attentiveness that differs from what's required when hiking on a trail. Poor communication or a lack of skill can turn an easy climb dangerous very quickly. As a result, my relationship with my climbing partner forms an essential component of the experience. To me, this has its pros and cons. As much as I love climbing, I can't run out and do it by myself. Instead, it forces me to develop my interpersonal skills, something contrary to my introverted nature.

Our trip to the City of Rocks was not the first time I'd climbed on granite. In spring 2011, I joined my friend Tom in Leavenworth, Washington, for a couple of days of climbing. I had one particularly exciting experience in Leavenworth that had nothing to do with the technicality of climbing rock walls. One afternoon, I was top roping a crack that my partner had just led. Partway up, I reached my hand into the crack to make my next move and heard a frantic squeaking sound. I quickly retracted my hand, peering inside to find a bat! It was wedged into the crack, its tiny bat claws clasped beneath its chin. I could see its wings folded up, and it was baring bright white teeth. Fortunately, I had my camera on my harness and was able to document this unexpected wildlife encounter.

Many climbs in developed climbing areas do not require much hiking to approach them. Joshua Tree National Park is a climber's dream. Most of the routes are adjacent to the parking areas, which means you can practically belay from the back of your car. Despite this fact, I included Joshua Tree on the Hike366 list because my partner and I chose to hike from one climbing area to another rather than moving the car from lot to lot. Some of the reasons I climb are the same as the reasons I hike: spending time outdoors, taking on physical challenges and enjoying nature's scenery, just to name a few.

But climbing in areas with easy approaches has a much different vibe than climbing in more remote places. I suppose the same is true of popular hiking areas versus unpopular, out-of-the-way areas. The day we visited Joshua Tree, it was crawling with climbers. They were everywhere. *We* were everywhere. This was not a trip for solitude and quiet reflection. It was an opportunity to see a new place, test my skills and enjoy warm sunshine in March. Just as I'd learned to appreciate short hikes as well as long hikes, I had to learn to enjoy climbing in popular areas as well as the more distant alpine environments.

Often, I traveled far from home to explore various climbing areas. In 2011, I spent a weekend at Frenchman Coulee in central Washington State. It was a far cry from the perfect granite slabs at Yosemite, Joshua Tree and City of Rocks. There, I faced walls of basalt columns that provided a wide array of traditional and sport climbing opportunities. Since the weekend was planned for students of the Mazamas' Advanced Rock program to practice leading on traditional gear, we stuck to trad routes primarily.

On the first day, I was paired with a student who did not seem ready to take the lead. I had to practice lots of patience because he chose to carry too much gear and stopped for long rests while trying to place protection on the rock wall. He wasn't receptive to feedback and I didn't really know how to help him, even though I was fairly certain what strategy I'd take to lead that climb. I had a frustrating day. Again, I was reminded of how much I knew about climbing, despite how unconfident I often felt while I was leading.

Crushed by that experience, I resolved to have a better time the next day. I joined a group with a skilled instructor and a couple of students and we played all day. We ditched the trad for sport, and we each took turns putting up routes that challenged us on lead. The other instructor was a much bolder leader than me, so I got to top rope some incredibly fun 5.10s. One climb in particular, called Easy Off, played into my strengths and was a ton of fun from bottom to top. It's interesting how some challenges are frustrating while others are rewarding. Is it the challenge itself or my ability to handle it in the moment?

Challenge as reward arose as a theme in climbing and hiking trips throughout my lifetime. At Madrone Wall in Oregon I was faced with my greatest technical challenge at the time: leading a 5.10 crack. I was notorious for not pushing myself on lead; it was just too far outside my comfort zone. But my climbing partner that day was a good friend, and an excellent and safe climber who tested the limits every time we went out. I was drawn towards that particular route, so I geared up and began.

I only focused on the fear. I was in over my head, I thought. Plunk. I placed a piece of gear. Then I took another step and, plunk, placed another piece of gear. "Take!" I yelled, letting my belayer know I was going to rest and put my weight on the rope.

"Ok, climbing," and up I'd go again. I repeated this slow and methodical procedure until I got all the way to the top of the route. Although I completed it, I did it in probably the worst style ever. I felt just like that guy who I got annoyed climbing with at Frenchman Coulee. But did that matter? I did it. I persevered despite the difficulty. Why? Why was I able to climb that route when I've bailed out on other ones? Those are the questions that I wonder about every time I go climbing.

Rock climbing continues to teach me critical life lessons. Lessons on how to focus in the face of difficulties, filter out unnecessary noise, and face my fears head on. It teaches me to trust others, to build relationships and to communicate well with the people in my life. And when those people are braver, more experienced and more skilled than me, I can really come up against some personal challenges.

In October 2012, I met a group of strong climber friends for a romp at The Zoo. The Zoo was just being developed at the time and was one of the lesser-known areas at Smith Rock. Most of the climbing was too difficult for me, so I spent much of the day just watching. I didn't have any desire to get on something that I thought I would fail at in front of a group. I didn't ask anyone if there were other routes that were easy, that I wouldn't have to struggle on. Despite being in a group of excellent and supportive climbers, I simply could not stomach the thought of failure, of not being good enough. That was the beginning of my falling out with rock climbing, and it would take a few years for me to get back into it.

But rocks aren't the only challenges in the mountains.

Mount Hood, at an elevation of 11,249 feet, is the tallest mountain in Oregon. Its snowcapped, pointed summit is easily recognizable from the Portland metro area. I'd heard it was a dangerous mountain; people die up there. In February 2007, soon after arriving in my new Portland, Oregon home, I was invited on a second date: climbing Mt. Hood. My eyes widened. Surely I wasn't ready? But my new friend wouldn't have asked if he thought I would be a liability, right? I rolled the idea around in my head for a bit and then accepted his offer.

LAYERING FOR WINTER OUTINGS

Winter can be a great time of year to take a hike. And wearing proper clothing can mean the difference between a good day and a bad one. Take note that wearing all of these layers all of the time won't be necessary. As you walk, your body will sweat and generate heat. Choose clothing that is easy to unzip, remove, and adjust as you warm up.

Next-to-skin layer: wear synthetic or wool fabrics that wick moisture away from your skin

Insulating layer: choose wool, fleece, down or other materials that help keep you warm

Barrier layer: above all else, carry a wind- and rain/snow-proof shell that provides a barrier between your body and the elements

Hats and gloves: bring multiple layers for head and hands to protect these sensitive areas from cold and wet

It was the dead of winter. I read as much about the mountain as I could, and I prepared for worst-case scenarios: getting lost, injured or even killed. In my backpack, I carried the ten essentials plus a sleeping bag and an emergency bivy sack, which was basically a step up from a flimsy emergency blanket, but it would offer a barrier between myself and the weather. If anything went wrong on Mt. Hood, it could get bad quickly, so the overnight gear felt totally appropriate for this day trip. I wore fleece pants and packed lots of layers for my upper body, head and hands. We pulled into the parking area in the wee hours of morning and started walking up the mountain at 3 am. Light from the full moon illuminated the snow, so we left our headlamps in our packs.

The air was warmer than I anticipated, so I actually had to remove some layers. As we climbed higher, the wind picked up. A couple of climbers ahead of us were headed down the mountain, citing the high winds as the reason for their retreat. We smiled and kept moving up the snowy slope. It was exhilarating. I rationalized that the wind was blowing because we were on a mountain, a fact that did not deter our team! As I plunged my ice ax into the snow with each big gust, the adrenaline kept pumping. I was having the alpine experience I'd been looking for.

As my partner chose to climb the line up and over Hogsback ridge and through the Old Chute, I followed closely behind. He carried a rope and ice screws, but we easily ascended to the summit without the use of any technical gear. Success, or so I thought. I climbed the big, bad mountain. But when I turned back to look at the route below us, all I saw was a thick cloak of white. For the first time, I realized the gravity of our situation. We still had to get off the mountain, and I could barely see my hand in front of my face.

We down-climbed through the Old Chute, with my partner leading right in front of me. I carefully placed my foot into each step we'd kicked into the crusty snow on our way up. After retreating down the Hogsback, a wind-sculpted ridge of snow below the summit slopes, we reached the broader mountainside and lost all sense of direction. I had a moment of panic: I couldn't see the ski resort; I couldn't tell up from down; I felt completely disoriented. I clutched my compass, feeling my heart race in my chest.

The wind was blowing and temperatures hovered below freezing. Wet snow careened sideways into my body and face, coating exposed skin and clothing with ice crystals. We walked into the unknown, visions of being swallowed by a crevasse plaguing my mind. At that point in time, I imagined huge crevasses lurking beneath the surface of every snow field. Unbeknownst to me, that was the least of my worries. Still, I couldn't do it anymore. I couldn't walk one more step.

"We have to stop," I said. I was confident that if we could hunker down and ride out the storm, we could eventually find our way back. It was impossible to navigate in the whiteout conditions. My partner agreed, and we fruitlessly sought to get out of the wind. The terrain was open and exposed, with little chance of finding a rock wall or cave anywhere nearby. We had both packed sleeping bags, but only I had an emergency shelter. We got into our sleeping bags and then crammed together inside the bivy sack. It was tight, but it would have to do. We comforted each other with stories and jokes, waiting for a break in the wind. I'd never been colder. I shivered as the storm roared on, soaking my bag through.

Sometime early the next morning, the clouds broke. My cell phone finally picked up a signal and we called 911. We were both cold and scared and tired but basically fine. My biggest fear was that my friends and family were worried about my safety, and I'd had no way of communicating with them to let them know I was OK. That feeling made me sick to my stomach. Once we checked in with Search and Rescue, they gave us some information on how to get back to the trailhead and we packed up to go. We easily hiked out to the car under clear skies.

That night, the mountain taught me a big lesson. Reaching the top is not an accomplishment if you're unable to return. I had no clue how difficult it would be to navigate in a storm in that type of environment. While I was prepared to ride out a night on the mountain, it never should have come to that. The team that turned around in the high winds made the right choice; we were foolish to continue on.

I vowed to come back and do it right the next time. I signed up for the Mazamas' Basic Climbing Education Program (BCEP) as soon as I could. I'd asked around for recommended leaders to train under and several people recommended Monty Smith. I was accepted into his group, and in the spring of 2007 I began my quest to become a smarter and safer mountaineer.

Monty was larger than life. He was outgoing, strong, intelligent, and he had a passion for the mountains. He was impossibly fit and a really nice guy to boot. I was excited to follow in his footsteps on my second Mt. Hood climb. I was sure we'd make better decisions and have a pleasant experience.

I was one member of a group of twelve climbers, so our pace was slow. Many of us were newly minted BCEP grads, taking our classroom knowledge to the field for the first time. I patiently waited as we tied into our rope teams. It was a bluebird day in June; I couldn't have asked for nicer weather. I felt like I was on an entirely different mountain than the one I had climbed in February.

Mt. Hood lay in front of me, her gleaming white flanks topped by ice-encrusted rocks that guarded the summit. I walked uphill in lockstep with my teammates, taking breaks when they did, and ever so slowly creeping towards the top. It took us eight hours to reach the summit. I turned around and saw, for the first time, the view from the top. Below me, the base of the mountain was covered in a puffy blanket of clouds. Above the clouds I saw the other Cascades volcanoes: Rainier, Adams, St. Helens, Jefferson. Hood was a giant among giants. The thought of attaining such a view compelled me to keep climbing higher on every subsequent trip I took. I cherished that novel perspective and celebrated my growth as a climber.

The rest of the day was as unmemorable as any other. We walked down the mountain without incident and I'd achieved my goal of climbing Mt. Hood in a responsible way. I felt relieved to have that terrifying overnight experience behind me, but I was glad that my mishap on Mt. Hood in February hadn't turned me away from the mountains forever. Instead, it encouraged me to seek out skilled instruction and to take a step back to assess my decision-making skills. I couldn't change what happened in the past, but I could make different choices that would affect my future.

Mountaineering involves utilizing skills that are built over time; book learning only goes so far. But as a fresh BCEP graduate, it was nearly impossible for me to get on any Mazamas club climbs. I was a nobody. I hadn't developed an extensive "climbing resume" yet. So the only trip leader who trusted me was my mentor, Monty. To my surprise, he accepted me onto two of his climbs that summer: Fisher Chimneys on Mt. Shuksan, and the Blue Glacier on Mt. Olympus. Both were technical routes in Washington and both would require multiple days of hiking, camping and climbing. These climbs would put me far outside my comfort zone.

First came Shuksan. As a new climber I had no idea what I was getting into, which was probably for the better. I made the long drive into the North Cascades from Portland and joined a large team of climbers with varying abilities on an attempt of a difficult route. It took us longer than planned to reach the summit, and I walked in fear nearly the entire time. While I've spent plenty of time in the mountains, Shuksan felt like a really intimidating one. The Fisher Chimneys route was one of the most complicated adventures I'd ever done. We moved from trail, to rock, to snow, back to rock again, and so forth. I shuffled across ledges that felt small and exposed, all while wearing a heavy backpack that threw me off balance. I crossed glaciers on a rope team, pausing to catch my breath near yawning cracks in the ice. The wind blew, the snow crunched beneath my feet. This was serious, and I was scared.

My hesitation and inexperience both played a role in why we moved so slowly. I felt like a burden on the team. Since the climb had taken us longer than expected, we were behind schedule on the way down. Navigation errors on the descent slowed us down even more and before we knew it, night had fallen. It was impossible to negotiate the steep heather slopes in the dark, so we stopped, sharing an impromptu mountain sleepover until dawn. As told in my notes:

I was so tired of walking. My legs had never felt so fatigued. When we lost the trail for the umpteenth time after dark, I sat down in defeat. Surely we wouldn't get off this mountain tonight. At 1:30 in the morning someone finally made the decision to stay put and stop trying to navigate in the pitch black. We were all sliding around in the brush and it was only a matter of time before someone got hurt. I dug around in my pack to find something, anything to help me get through the night. Since this was an organized climb, I didn't pack as much emergency gear as I would have if it would have been a private climb. That was dumb.

I put all my clothes on, shoved my feet and lower legs into a large black garbage bag and lay back on my pack. In my makeshift shelter I shivered all night long. Feeling grateful that it was not raining or windy or even very cold, I knew this uncomfortable feeling would pass and we'd be on our way at sunrise.

Once morning came, we hustled out of there, back to our first camp. My legs had next to no energy left, but we still had to break camp and hike a couple of miles back to our cars. I drifted towards the back of the group in order to walk slowly, at a pace I could manage. By the time I reached the parking lot, I collapsed in a heap.

That experience exposed my weaknesses as a new climber. Although I was relatively strong and good at following directions, I was not very efficient at moving quickly over 3rd- and 4th-class terrain, changing in and out of crampons, and moving on a rope system. I learned that these inefficiencies slowed the whole team down. And with such a large team, every little slowdown added up to a big impact. Someday I'd like to return to Fisher Chimneys. Now that I've accumulated so much more knowledge and experience, I think I would actually enjoy the route. Any takers?

My next big climb with Monty was Mt. Olympus, the highpoint of the Olympic Mountains in Washington. This route was longer but less complicated than Mt. Shuksan's Fisher Chimneys. It took us four days from start to finish. On days one and two we covered the eighteen-mile hike into base camp. Day three we climbed the mountain. Day four we hiked the entire eighteen miles back out to the car.

This was my first major backpacking trip, so I struggled to figure out what to bring and how to fit it all into my pack. I'd need a tent, at least four days of food, climbing gear, a sleeping bag, rain protection, etc. It was a lot! I pared my equipment list down as much as I could and dangled lots of gear off the clips and straps on the outside of my pack. It was heavy, cumbersome and soul-sucking once I loaded it onto my back. The next four days of hiking and climbing delivered one lesson after the next.

One of the greatest takeaways from my Mt. Olympus adventure was learning how to take care of my feet. For nearly a week after the climb I felt like my feet were ground hamburger. They were painful, swollen and blistered after only four days of hiking; this was surely not sustainable. Following that trip, I paid much closer attention to how my shoes and boots fit. I spent more time and money on acquiring new footwear, and I got rid of any uncomfortable or ill-fitting shoes in my house. In order to be able to keep hiking and climbing, I had to take care of my foot health.

With each climbing trip, both my confidence and humility grew. I felt better equipped to handle mountain conditions, but I also came to understand my place on the totem pole. The mountains were indifferent to my objectively meaningless pursuit of walking up them. Stormy weather, rockfall, stream crossings, crevasses and waning daylight provided hurdles I had to learn to navigate. All those things were going to present themselves whether I wanted them to or not. I had chosen to put myself in the mountains' environment, time and time again. If I wanted to climb mountains, I needed to accept the risks and understand how to mitigate them. I also had to accept the fact that accidents happen, and we can't always predict and prepare for everything.

In 2009, I joined Mazamas leader John Godino on a trip to Mt. Cruiser, also in the Olympic Mountains. Mt. Cruiser involved an eight-mile hike into camp and then climbing the mountain the next day. It was rated 5.0, the "easiest" rating in rock climbing.

The fun for me came not from the technical difficulty of the climb but from the route finding and the variety of terrain obstacles we encountered along the way. We did some rock scrambling, climbing over several ups and downs, chimneys, ramps and other interesting features. It was a great adventure climb!

On this climb I rose up to take more of a leadership role. I was more comfortable scrambling without a rope than some of the other people on the climb, so a few of us worked together to scout the route ahead while John set up ropes for the others to follow behind us. I loved having the freedom and responsibility. I felt like I had some skills to offer my team.

Others might chase grades and look for the hardest routes they can do, but this type of experience is what I had been searching for all along. Routes uncrowded by people. Unique locations. Endless views. I took pleasure in simply being there, in learning how to read the mountain landscape and solving problems to access the highpoints.

Each year I scanned the Mazamas' climbing schedule in search of mountains I'd never heard of before. Why? The popular mountains tended to attract the largest crowds. On my continual quest for solitude and unique experiences, I preferred to seek out the unfamiliar. That was how I got myself accepted onto an Austera Peak climb with Mazamas leader Preston Corless. Before I applied to join the team, I had to look up Austera online, where I learned that it was in the North Cascades. The route involves a classic mixture of glacier travel, technically easy rock climbing, navigation challenges and remote beauty. I was interested in all of that!

That time I was, by far, the least competent member of the team. Fortunately, I was in really good hands. Each of my teammates was a stellar person in addition to being a competent climber. They took me in as one of their own, coached me when I was struggling and reminded me of the skills I hadn't practiced in a while. I felt totally supported and motivated to do my best.

The mountains left me in a state of awe. The relentlessly steep approach to the peak was physically and mentally draining. But once we got deep into the North Cascades, I was rewarded with jaw-dropping views in every direction. I couldn't see a road, a town or any sign of human development anywhere. It was incredible. There I felt at home.

It took us a day to hike into base camp and a day to climb Austera. I was completely exhausted when we returned to camp, and went to bed before the sun went down. Our camp was positioned at the base of El Dorado Peak, which was our secondary objective on the trip. The next morning, half of the team slept in while the other half bolted up to summit El Dorado. I was in the latter group. I'd seen photos of El Dorado, which inspired me to get up early the next morning and climb. The photos were all taken at the same place: a knife-edge ridge leading to the top. I was really excited to get on that ridge.

We climbed, steeply, up a boulder field to the snow. The wind picked up as we made the final ascent. It was less dramatic than I had pictured—I wasn't sure if that meant I had gotten accustomed to that type of terrain or I had built the mountain up to be something that it wasn't. Regardless, it felt wonderful to sit on the summit, and I smiled as my partners stood above me with the map, trying to identify all of the peaks in sight. This took them a long while because we were surrounded by so many. I could have sat there all day.

I returned to the North Cascades with another Mazamas group in 2012. This time our objective was Inspiration Peak. It is a formidable mountain. A multi-pitch 5.8 rock climb to the summit is guarded by a heavily crevassed glacier. To get to the summit we'd have to endure a brutal approach by means of a very steep climber's trail through thick forest and gullies filled with boulders and snow, and other route-finding challenges.

Our team of four got off to a very casual start, which concerned me. We had to climb over 6,000 vertical feet in the course of six miles to get to our first camping opportunity on day one. Considering that the first couple of miles were on a flat, old roadbed, I knew we were in for a lot of steep hiking in the second half of the approach. Our packs were heavily loaded with all our mountaineering equipment: sleeping gear, rock gear, snow gear, food, water, etc. And it was hot. Despite all those factors, our leader seemed to be in no hurry, so we got in line and started walking into the forest.

As the day wore on I began to have my first real inklings of doubt. I thought about what decisions I'd make if I were in charge of this outing, and how they'd be different from the ones that our leader was making. We raced the sunset down a nasty gully before reaching flatter, easier ground where we could make our camp. We were still far from the glacier and the start of the climbing route. I made dinner and went to bed in anticipation of an early start the next morning to catch up on lost time. We had to stretch out the day as long as we could in order to reach our objective.

I woke up before the sun, hurrying to scarf down my breakfast and pack my bag for the day. Knowing the challenges of the route ahead, I thought we'd start walking before dawn to allow for a greater chance of success. The anticipation was nerve-racking and exciting. I peered around camp, noting that only one other climber was awake and two (including our leader) were still sleeping. The day before, one climber decided he would spend the day in camp to rest up for the hike out instead of climbing to the top of the mountain, so it made sense that he was still in his tent. But our leader? Why wasn't he up and going? My mind raced.

Well after sunrise, I looked over miserably as our cheerful leader sat up in his sleeping bag, sipping coffee. "What's going on?" I thought. "Sun's up. Let's go!" When we finally left camp, our team of three moved slowly through the complex labyrinth of snow, rock and ice. It took us two hours to get to the foot of the glacier. It looked like the navigation from there was going to get considerably more complicated. Our leader took off his pack and started putting on his crampons.

I paused and did a little math in my head. We did not have enough daylight left to make it across the glacier, climb up the rock face, rappel back down and recross the glacier. There was no way I wanted to cross the glacier in the dark. "Is there anything else we can climb from here?" I asked. While our leader was still intent on carrying out our original plan, my fellow climber shared my doubts. Fortunately, we were able to convince him to change our itinerary and we set our sights on West McMillan Spire instead. It would involve no technical climbing and no glacier, so we could do it in a reasonable amount of time. I was back on board.

> ## CLIMBING LINGO
>
> Rappel: to lower oneself by using a rope attached to an anchor.
>
> This is the preferred method of descending a technical rock, ice or snow slope.

The rest of the day was delightful. We glided across the snow, danced up the rock and sat on the spire's tiny summit with smiles on our faces. I felt relieved that we adjusted our goal based on our situation, but I wondered how things might have ended differently had I not said anything. Where would we be if I didn't hold my ground, refusing to carry out plan A? In that moment, my trust in leadership was shaken. It was an important lesson in listening to myself and being willing to put myself in an uncomfortable position in order to challenge authority. Perhaps that was what I was there to learn.

The mountains are powerful classrooms. The decisions made there can actually affect life and limb. The stakes are high. There is no room for complacency. And while I'd worked so hard to be a good follower all these years, I knew it was time for me to step up and become a better leader.

After my experience in the North Cascades I found that I was reluctant to trust any leaders I didn't know. I also noticed they were reluctant to trust me. Mountaineering is an endeavor that demands a great deal of skill, strength and decision-making capabilities. Many people, and rightfully so, prefer to climb with people they know versus people they don't, experienced or not. My list of past climbs did not seem to make strangers feel good about taking me. Personal connections were more valuable than lists of climbs done in getting accepted on a climb. I had moved away from Portland, where the Mazamas were based, so I was less connected to the group. Therefore, the only Mazamas climb

I was accepted on that year was led by my friend and climbing mentor Eugene. We shared a mutual trust, and I was really pumped to join his team in taking on another difficult peak in northern Washington—Luna Peak.

It has been said that Luna Peak has one of the best views in the North Cascades, but few people ever see it because the rugged, long approach to the top lacks the technical objectives that typically attract climbers. It takes a seriously determined person to put in that much work to get someplace without a mind-blowing rock or ice climb to top off the effort. While this may sound counter-intuitive to a non-climber, it's important to note that some challenges are more generally accepted as "fun" than others. An easy walk from a road up to the base of a multi-pitch climb on solid rock will always attract more climbers than a long, strenuous hike into a remote location with bad rock. I was one of seven adventure-seekers who set out to ascend the remote and lonely Luna Peak on Eugene's trip.

We found adventure right away, on the way to the trailhead. Our team piled into a boat that shuttled us across Ross Lake to the start of our hike. We spent the rest of the afternoon ambling along a beautiful trail to our forest camp. The next day, the fun began.

"Type 2 fun" is defined in Urban Dictionary as "an activity that is fun only after you have stopped doing it." When I use the word "fun" for the duration of this trip description, this is the definition I mean.

A short hike along the trail outside our camp led us to a cairn marking the start of the off-trail route. From there we thrashed around in thick vegetation in search of a specific log (mentioned in the route description) that bridged a nearby creek, which we had to cross to complete the remainder of our approach hike. The word "creek" doesn't conjure up quite the right image for the raging beast we encountered. Deep water thrashed and churned and rushed in front of us. We could not simply take our shoes off and shuffle across the creek bed. We needed to find that log or we weren't getting to the other side.

Once we located the log, most of us scooted across it on our butts to avoid falling into the torrent below. On the other side, we dropped any heavy gear that we wouldn't need for the remainder of the climb. We'd pick up our gear cache on the return trip.

Continuing through the forest, we encountered several

hazards: another creek crossing, thick brush, challenging navigation and an eruption of angry bees. Yes, *bees* flew up out of their ground nests and stung each of us as we passed by. I was stung four times, on my elbow, knee, hand and wrist. Since there was nothing I could do but keep walking, I pressed ahead with my team.

Many hours later we collapsed in exhaustion at a flat camp beneath Luna Peak. Gray clouds swirled overhead, putting our summit day at risk of being thwarted by thunderstorms. We all snoozed a bit, chatted about our options over cups of tea, and tried to get a few hours of good sleep that night.

In the morning, one of the other climbers woke us all up by exclaiming: "The stars are out!" We rushed out of our bivy sacks, knowing that clear skies meant we had a window of time in which we could make a bid for the summit. We moved uphill, slowly, as we adjusted our bodies to the alpine environment. My bee stings had swollen dramatically, making it difficult to use my left hand or bend my arm. Since much of our day would be spent scrambling over steep terrain requiring the use of both hands and feet, this would prove to be a bit of a problem. The summit route follows a rock-filled gully, crosses a steep heather slope and ascends a ridge scattered with boulders. Each section has its own beauty, charm and challenges. I continued climbing in spite of my swollen body parts, eager to see what was around the next corner.

The views of the mountain range surrounding us were breathtaking. I kept looking behind me to enjoy each cloud-free moment. As we neared the false summit, clouds poured in around us. The true summit lay just a few minutes walk away, along a sketchy ridge that popped in and out of view. We decided to skip that final ridge walk and enjoy our summit treats right where we were to avoid putting the team at risk for no good reason. I snacked on a Luna Bar, which I thought was apropos for this particular summit.

As the day wore on, the swelling in my joints increased and continued to restrict my movement. I had no choice but to keep walking, so that's what I did. We reached camp, dallied a little bit and then gathered all our strength for the hike back through the forest. We knew there had to be an easier way than the path we took coming up, so we kept our eyes peeled for cairns.

NAVIGATIONAL CAIRNS

Cairns are stacks of rocks built in nature that either serve a functional purpose or an artistic purpose. Navigational cairns are put in place as route markers. These cairns are essential to identifying routes across barren landscapes that cannot be marked in other ways. They are also less intrusive than colored plastic flagging or paint on trees.

There is much controversy over building cairns for no particular reason. What do you think?

Working as a team, we scouted a much better route on the return, making it appreciably less painful than we had anticipated. What a relief! We practically ran back to camp once we found the trail again.

There is something special about managing challenges with others when you're climbing in the mountains. Our team was supportive, inclusive and focused on good problem-solving strategies. We helped each other overcome obstacles, stayed positive and openly discussed various options throughout the trip. The group dynamic on Luna Peak was starkly different than the one on my Inspiration Peak trip. I'd stumbled across another element of mountaineering exploration that sparked my curiosity: the behavior of groups in adverse conditions. I needed to learn more.

In 2009, I headed to the North Cascades with a partner to attempt the East Ridge of Forbidden Peak. I was excited for the prospect of a real mountaineering objective, with bushwhacking, snowfield crossings, rock climbing, rappelling and the feeling of heading into the unknown. The approach to camp followed a rugged climbers' trail, which was predictably challenging. We lumbered uphill with our heavy packs, crashing through trees, crossing fast-moving streams, and scrambling over fallen logs. When we reached the first backcountry camping area and found it full, we kept going, into the misty clouds and onto a snowfield in Boston Basin. There, amid many impressive-looking North Cascades peaks, we settled in for the night.

Early the next morning, we saw no mountains. The clouds were dark, thick and low. We dozed in camp until late morning, when we got a brief break in the weather. There was no time to make a summit attempt so late in the day, so we wandered around, scouting the route and clambering over rock slabs. We ate lightly, since we'd only packed food for two days, and got a decent night's rest.

The next morning, we awoke early and hurried up the scramble to the ridge. Once we reached the top and got a view over the other side, we had to think fast—there were storm clouds heading right for us. It was time to hunker down. Huddled under our space blankets, we avoided getting drenched in the thunderstorm as it came down on top of us. Half an hour later, we emerged from our shelters to find the route soaking wet and us, again, behind schedule.

The right thing to do was to turn back, so we did. Back at base camp, we spent a couple of hours letting our gear dry out in the now blazing sun. All that was left was the short scramble back to the car and we could move on to another climbing area. We packed up and began heading down to the parking lot.

Nature had more lessons to teach us on the hike out. The forecast had predicted warm, clear days for the duration of our trip, so in order to keep my pack weight down, I didn't pack any rain gear. Partway through our descent, lightning and rain tore through the sky yet again, turning our hike into a jog. We just needed to get back to the trailhead! As I quickly picked my way down the mountain, I was stopped in my tracks by a deafening rumble. It sounded like I was on the tarmac next to a jet preparing for takeoff. I had no idea what was making that sound. Fear pulsed through my body with every heartbeat. What was happening?

As we approached the last stream crossing, I found my answer. Looking ahead, I saw trees and boulders hurtling down what was earlier a gentle mountain stream. A flash flood was happening right in front of my eyes. There was no way we were getting across that stream. Deflated and scared, I turned to my partner to discuss our options. We needed to make camp—right away.

We backtracked a little bit, setting up our tent on a steep hillside because there were no flat spots anywhere. We spent an uncomfortable night eating the last scraps of our food: chocolate energy gel spread on crackers. I don't know how much sleep I got that night since my head was filled with worst-case-scenario narratives: What if the whole mountain comes down on top of us? What if the stream isn't passable in the morning? How will we get out?

The next morning, all had returned to normal. The sky was clear and blue. Birds chirped cheerily. Water slowly trickled down the mountain. The danger was gone. We packed up our soaking wet gear and clothes, and made an easy descent to the car.

I breathed a sigh of relief when we reached the parking lot, and I quickly inhaled some food that we'd stashed for the latter part of our trip. But the mountain wasn't done with us yet. Our final obstacle: The flash flood had washed out the only road leading out of the woods. If I have learned one thing in my years of exploring the outdoors it is this: No matter how meticulous your plan A is, you'd better have plans B through E on hand, and be ready to abandon all of them when something you could never have predicted occurs. And you'd better have a smile on your face through it all!

When your climbing objective is closer to home, it's easier to assess the weather and other conditions before deciding to climb. In March 2010, my friend Matt had his eye on the Cooper Spur route on the north side of Mt. Hood. I did a little research to learn more about the route and checked the weather, and then we made our plan. Since it was late winter, there was a ton of snow on the mountain and we had to start our ascent at the relatively low elevation of 4,000 feet. Mt. Hood tops out at over 11,000 feet, so that meant we had a lot of climbing to do.

We got a very early start, heading up an icy ski trail lit by our headlamps. We slipped and slid our way up the trail to better snow conditions near the spur itself. Along the way, we noticed two headlamps bobbing up the mountain behind us; another team had the same plan. We joined forces and continued walking uphill.

It was just us and the mountain. Once we left the shelter of the trees, we were surrounded by bare snow slopes. In the distance, early morning light started pouring over neighboring peaks. Only the wind made a sound. There, on Mt. Hood, I felt a comforting sense of solitude.

Around 6:30 am, we geared up with harnesses, helmets, crampons and extra-warm layers in anticipation of the climb ahead of us. As this is a classic Cascades volcano, the snow-covered ridge would get steeper and steeper all the way to the top. From our vantage point it didn't look terribly treacherous, but my research indicated that we'd have to make some technical decisions at a point called the "Chimneys." We felt ready, so we started up.

In order to conserve energy, we walked single file. The person in front did the hard work of kicking steps into the snow, while each subsequent team member had the much easier job of reinforcing the steps made by the previous climber. I stayed close to the back of the group to take advantage of the well-packed steps in front of me. The snow conditions were perfect. The points on my crampons and the tip of my ice ax plunged nicely into the Styrofoam-textured snow.

At the Chimneys, our groups split up. We went left, while the other team went right. The angle was quite steep where we were, but the snow was so good that I never felt unsafe. All the climbing gear we brought sat securely in our backpacks as we made our way up through the rocks and snow. We rejoined the other team higher up the mountain, and together we hiked up the last ramp of snow to the summit. We hadn't seen another soul on the north side of the mountain all day.

As we crested the summit ridge, we emerged into what felt like a circus. There were people everywhere. Looking down the south side of the mountain, I noticed the ski lift, the parking lot full of shiny cars, and a line of people filing up the standard climbing route. The day's solitude was shattered by the sudden appearance of people, noise, man-made objects, and clutter.

That experience reminded me of my personal values. Why do I choose to spend time in the mountains? Certainly I do it to challenge myself and to see beautiful places. But part of that beauty involves more nature and fewer people. I don't enjoy being around swarms of other visitors in the mountains; that detracts from my experience. I'm incredibly glad to have ascended the Cooper Spur route, but it felt somewhat bittersweet to emerge from that joyous journey into a mass of humanity at the summit. At that moment, I decided to leave Mt. Hood be—I had other objectives that suited me better.

However, I am a sucker for invites. In my many years of outdoor exploration, I have almost always been the planner. Planning a trip takes quite a bit of work. It's work that I enjoy doing, but at the end of the day, it's work. When a friend proposes a trip and they've done the research and planning, it's easy for me to say "Yes!" In August 2012, I was invited on a climb up Sahale Peak. This involved a straightforward glacier crossing and some low 5th-class rock. I could even lead all of it! There was just one catch: My friend wanted to bring his eight-year-old boy.

I said yes. Climbing with a kid would probably turn out to be extremely taxing, but I figured I would do my best to enjoy the trip. I would be in the North Cascades, one of the most magical places in the Pacific Northwest, so I could deal with a little whining.

Who was I kidding? I couldn't handle it. I frequently had to leave my friend and his kid behind in order to preserve my sanity. At least when I'm struggling to enjoy myself in the mountains I keep it to myself. There's no uncertainty about how an eight-year-old feels. The incessant whining, complaining, sitting down in protest wore at me. Ultimately, however, it was a great trip. We made it to the summit. I discovered the most scenic toilet at our high camp in the mountains. I got to spend time with my friend. And I spent two days living in a picture-perfect landscape. What I learned: I'll take on additional challenges for friends, especially when they organize the trip.

The year prior, that same friend had invited me on a multi-day trip into Canada's Valhalla Provincial Park, where I was one of a team of seven people. On that trip we tackled several peaks from a single base camp, mostly splitting into smaller teams to move more efficiently. But we moved as one group on our first objective: Midgard Peak via the north ridge.

That was truly an old-school mountaineering trip. The only

route information we had came from an old climbing book, which stated: "Climb the north ridge." In contrast to modern route descriptions, this information was paltry. Today, I can go online and get play-by-play details, with photos, hand-drawn maps and written descriptions of the moves for a sixty-foot rock climb. But for a half-day outing with many route-finding challenges, I could find no useful advice. We put our heads together to make a plan, and then started walking.

The hike turned into a scramble over grassy ledges, wet rock, and snow. We brought some basic rock-protection gear, helmets and harnesses in case we needed them. We reached the summit without the aid of climbing equipment, but wisely decided to set up a rope for the trip down to protect against any slips on the exposed rock. On our way back to camp we scouted the next day's climbing route. It felt great to be part of a competent team. Although our experience levels were quite mixed, we worked together and communicated well as a group. Outings like these helped build my confidence as a leader.

In the fall of 2011, I joined a group of five for an ascent of the west ridge of Mt. Washington in the Oregon Cascades. The west ridge is rarely climbed, and for good reason. The rock is very loose. Protection is sparse. And there's a perfectly good route to the summit going up the north ridge. Why bother with the more rotten side of the mountain? My friend got it in his head that he wanted to do it, and he managed to wrangle a few others into doing it too.

We started hiking towards the mountain before the sun rose, taking little time to reach the climber's trail. But getting to the base of the rock from there was arduous work; the whole mountain is a crumbling, shifting pile of rocks. Once we reached the technical part of the route, it took us two hours to climb the first pitch. There was hardly any solid rock to be found for protection, so we were slow in finding a safe passage for the group. After everyone ascended the first pitch, we split up into two teams. I led my team of three on a pair of half ropes up five or six more pitches to reach the summit. The climb had awesome exposure and lots of mountain views. From the summit, we could see the plume of smoke rising from the Pole Creek Fire to the southeast.

By the time we were ready to rappel, it was 6 pm and the light was fading fast. We ripped through four rappels, barreled down steep scree and followed a faint climber's trail into the darkness of night. We hiked along the final stretch of trail by headlamp, making it back to camp sixteen hours after we started. Some highlights from my journal:

I froze my ass off belaying for an hour on the first pitch.
The rope drag was horrible.
I was glad to reach the belay alive.
Loose rock. DO NOT REPEAT.

Maybe someday I'll learn to say "no" to my friends' wacky ideas. But it's not always possible to know just how insane the scheme is until you try to put it into action.

Wacky ideas like our ascent of Mt. Washington are often born from lists. My friend Rick is a list guy. Mt. Thomson, a bump of rock in the Washington Cascades, was on one of Rick's lists. He invited me to lead him up there in 2014 since I had the rock skills to do so. But at that point, I hadn't touched any real rock in two years. Regardless, I said, "Okay."

Mt. Thomson's west ridge is no harder than 5.6, which is technically quite easy. But when you add in the route finding, the difficulties of placing traditional climbing gear, and the physical endurance needed to hike into a remote mountain, the objective becomes a greater challenge than it first seems. After an arduous hike in, a night of bad sleep, and an interesting approach the following morning, we reached the basin below the rock climb only to discover that the mountain was hidden behind clouds. Not wanting to climb into a foggy abyss, we took off our packs and sat on a rock to contemplate our options. We decided to wait for the clouds to clear, and if they hung around for a certain period of time, we'd call off the climb and return to camp. While waiting for the clouds to depart, I pulled out my marked photo of the climb and studied it closely. As if on cue, the curtain of clouds slowly rose, revealing the mountain I had so clearly envisioned from the photo. We made a run for the base of the route, and I racked up my rock gear.

Then I got stuck. I could not make the first move to get onto the ridge. There was an unprotected, airy step that I just didn't like. As time passed, a second team of two climbers appeared behind us, waiting for me to make my move so they could get on with their climb. I stepped up; I stepped down. I shook my head. I gave myself a pep talk. I tried all the tricks I'd used in the past. I knew I could have done it five years ago, but at that moment, I felt washed up. Lead climbing demands a great deal of mental focus and self-trust. In my break from outdoor lead climbing, I had lost the confidence that I once had. I kept looking down at the air below me, fearing a fall, a mistake, an injury.

"Hey, can I borrow that cam for the first move?" I asked the other climbers. I noticed that they had a particular piece of gear that I'd neglected to carry with me. Once I placed that cam in the rock, I felt safe enough to make the scary move. With renewed peace of mind, I took a breath and stepped onto the ridge. "I'm climbing!" I thought. Game on.

We made it to the summit in an inefficient but safe manner as I slowly dusted off my leading skills. It felt really good to be out there, despite the head games I was playing with myself. Rick believed in me, and I didn't want to let him down. And I truly wanted to stay connected to the rock climbing community. I did not want to abandon the skills I'd worked so hard to develop.

The next year, Rick headed south and east to knock out climbs on the Sierra Club's Desert Peaks Section Peaks List. He noted a few climbs that required some technical rock skills, including North Guardian Angel. "Where's that?" I asked. His response: Zion National Park. I'd never been there, scared away by reports of huge crowds. But once the seed was planted, I decided to plan a road trip. I'd travel well over 2,000 miles in two weeks to visit four national parks, several lesser-known local parks, and a handful of curious roadside attractions along the way. One stop on the trip was Zion, where I hiked for a couple of days with Aaron, then teamed up with Rick for the North Guardian Angel climb.

The three of us set out at the same time from the Wildcat Trailhead. When we reached the base of the magnificent slickrock mountain, Aaron turned back to do his own thing while Rick and I forged ahead. We put on our harnesses and started scrambling up the 3rd-class portion of the climb. My approach shoes felt sticky on the coarse sandstone. The rock is gorgeous. Eventually, the slope becomes steeper and ventures into 4th-class territory. In that "do-not-fall" terrain, I felt it was time to rope up. So that's what we did.

I really enjoyed climbing that route, and I loved that there was no one else on it. Since the climbing was easy, we moved quickly, only slowing down to sling giant Ponderosa pines for rope anchors. The views from the top of the peak were hard to beat. And while we couldn't see any other humans, we could hear voices rising up from the Subway, a popular canyoneering route down below us.

Easy rock, fun partner, blissful solitude, adventurous route finding. To me, those are the elements of a good trip. I'm glad that sometimes my friends stumble across these curious destinations and know that I'm the right person to ask to come along.

It's hard to explain why I like doing what I do to someone who is not a climber. Something about the adventure keeps drawing me back. The unknown has a magnetic pull—it entices me to get out and explore every time. Besides, it's better than staying home and watching television or surfing the Internet.

Climbing mirrors life, and the lessons I've taken from the mountains have made me better equipped to deal with life's obstacles everywhere. I've learned that the easiest path to the top is not always the most rewarding, and that overcoming difficulty is an inherent part of being human.

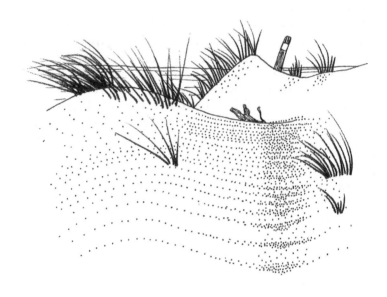

6

In the Rain, Snow, Heat and Cold

I pulled my jacket close around my face. The wind blew with a fervor, as if it was making a conscious effort to sand down every surface in its wake. This was, after all, the Oregon Coast. Sand was everywhere. I knew that because I could feel it in my boots, my clothes, my eyelids and my hair. As I turned to walk up the beach towards a towering sand dune, I felt a huge force shove me from behind.

"Thanks for the push," I muttered into the wind. I marched ahead with one goal in mind: hike to the top of Cape Kiwanda. It is only 240 vertical feet above the beach; it's not climbing a mountain. But I'd already spent a few hours out in the elements, and I was feeling it. As I reached the base of the dune, I realized I had an advantage: The wind was actually propelling me uphill. On top of the hill, the ocean revealed itself to me. Huge waves pounded the shoreline far below. I wanted a closer look. I ran down the backside of the dune, wind still at my back. The scenery was dramatic, stunning and somehow serene. Cape Kiwanda's picturesque cliffs seemed to glow beneath the dark, swirling storm clouds. Each red, yellow and brown band stood out spectacularly in the filtered light. Amid the maelstrom, no one else was there to see it.

On the return trip up the hill I realized that the wind was suddenly my enemy. Sand drilled straight into my face; I dropped my head to look towards my feet. And what I saw there, sharply sculpted sand formations, gave me a new appreciation for wind. When the breeze stopped and the dune returned to normal, all of those gorgeous sand fins would vanish. Although my toes were numb, my cheeks were red and my body was battered, I found myself appreciating the very thing that was making my experience difficult.

Do an internet search for hiking photos and you'll see a common thread among all the photos. The sun is shining. The people are smiling. The views are postcard-perfect. But in order to hike throughout the year, it's essential to learn how to manage your comfort and safety in the elements. Weather is variable and only somewhat predictable. Temperatures can range wildly from month to month and day to day. As a year-round hiker, I have been outdoors in every weather condition imaginable, from snow to rain to wind to sun to hail. And while I would often prefer to be outdoors on those sunny, perfect days, there is a certain character-building aspect related to hiking in difficult conditions that has made me a smarter and more resilient hiker.

> ## HYPOTHERMIA
>
> Hypothermia is a condition that occurs when body temperature drops below 95° F. Early signs and symptoms include:
>
> - Shivering
> - Clumsiness
> - Cold, pale skin
>
> As hypothermia progresses, more serious signs and symptoms include:
>
> - Confusion
> - Fatigue
> - Lack of shivering
> - Loss of consciousness
>
> Know the early signs of hypothermia and how to prevent it from occurring.

One of the first obstacles I learned how to deal with was rain. Rain tends to keep all but the most determined hiker at home. On a cool, spring day in 2006, I set off on a memorable overnight trip to Ethan Pond in New Hamsphire with one of my best hiking buddies, Lindsay. We hiked in the rain, we crossed swelling streams, we crashed through brush to see raging waterfalls, and we lived to tell the story. I remember the sound of the roaring falls and how awesome the power of the rain felt. I remember carefully trying to keep my feet dry until it was all but pointless. And how opening up zip-top bags, adjusting zippers and using my camera became impossible due to the hypothermia that was setting in.

Despite all of that, at the end of the trip all I could think about was how much I loved hiking in the rain. There are few people on the trails in weather like that, and the forest has an entirely different character. There is so much to see and explore when the conditions are less than perfect. If I limited my outdoor adventures to good-weather days, I would miss out on plenty of memorable experiences. It's also helpful to have some brave hiking partners who enjoy doing crazy hikes as well.

About a month after that experience, I went hiking in another part of New Hampshire's White Mountains. The forecast called for rain, and lots of it. Half of my team bailed due to the predicted weather, which was unfortunate. The mountains were socked in with clouds, but not a drop of moisture fell all day. That was an important lesson: forecasts are not always accurate.

When a rainy forecast does come through, it can make things difficult. In 2009, I attempted a thru-hike of the 100-Mile Wilderness in Maine with my dad. I had already moved to the West Coast, so we planned this well in advance. I set aside a ten-day period in June, which should have given us plenty of time to complete the trip. What I didn't anticipate is how grueling this trail would be in the pouring rain.

For the entire month before our trip, the area had received much more rain than usual. All the creeks were overflowing, the trails were mud bogs and the rock slabs were slick with moisture. Every step with my heavy backpack was agony. Before the end of day one, it began raining. We didn't reach our planned campsite, putting us behind schedule already.

It got worse. Each morning we woke up and put on our soaking wet clothes, since nothing would dry in the humidity. The bugs were ferocious. And due to our discomfort and lack of physical stamina, we moved more slowly than we needed to in order to make it to the end of the trail. By nightfall on day three, we decided to bail out at the nearest road.

It was a failure by definition, but I don't see how it could have ended any other way. Had we continued to slog ahead behind schedule, we would have run out of food. We would have been completely waterlogged and suffering from foot blisters, making it difficult or impossible to walk. I would have missed my flight back home. I'm pretty sure we wouldn't still be talking to each other today. While we failed to execute our plan, we made the right decision to leave. The rain may have thwarted that trip, but I learned about my lack of backpacking skills and the challenges of hiking for days in the rain, rebounded and kept getting out there.

Overnighting in the rain takes a real sense of commitment and preparation, but day trips are way more manageable in adverse weather. Rainfall, flooded trails, slippery terrain, and teamwork snags came into play on many of my hikes. Rain nearly foiled a visit to Nestucca Spit on the Oregon Coast. I organized that trip as a Mazamas outing and hoped some people would show up despite the weather. To my surprise, I attracted a small group of people who were willing to venture out. Most of the day was quite lovely, but our big surprise would come on the return hike. I'd decided to take us on a loop, hiking down the beach to the end of the spit, turning inland and walking through the forest to get back to the trailhead.

The forest got us. The inland trails were so flooded that the water was deeper than the height of our boots. I decided to take my socks and shoes off and walk barefoot in the icy water. A couple others employed this strategy too. The rest tried to keep their feet dry by walking on the side of the trail in the tall grass. They were not successful. But when there's a brewpub at the end of the hike and a bag with dry clothes in the car, what's the big deal anyways?

I would continue to have many wet adventures on the Oregon Coast. The Oregon Coast is an interesting place. It's not a place to put on a bikini and spread out your towel for a day of sunbathing. Growing up in Rhode Island, that's what I thought the beach was for. Building sand castles. Splashing in the waves. Running around in a bathing suit (unless the people were packed in sardine-tight). But in Oregon, the place where ocean meets land is different. It's not the beach. It's the *coast*. There are beaches, yes, but the atmosphere among beach-goers is quite different. People are often decked out in fleece, rubber boots, and jackets. There are sneaker waves and killer logs and other death traps. The coast is a beautifully forbidding place. And it really hits its stride during storm season.

I like taking trips to the coast with my husband because he's up for anything. In fact, one of our first dates was a day trip to the coast. It was a gray December day. Storms brewed over the ocean, bringing rain and high wind. But we visited the aquarium, took a lighthouse tour, walked on the beach and reveled in the ferocity of the weather. It was an early sign that he was a keeper.

In fall 2013, I saw wretched storms forecast for the area, so Aaron and I booked a hotel and made a dash for Newport, Oregon. We took several short walks while we were there, walking downtown and visiting some scenic natural areas.

The wind was absolutely ripping. I could hardly stand up when it gusted. Watching the wind blow across the puddles on the ground, I wondered if I'd ever seen anything move that fast. I dressed head to toe in rain gear and covered up as much exposed skin as I could. It was all worth it to see the immense waves crashing on the rocks, to feel the wind blasting at my face and to experience nature at its rawest.

The Washington Coast gave us the same dramatic welcome. On a memorable trip to Leadbetter Point in November 2015, Aaron and I hiked in a torrential rain- and windstorm. In just four miles of walking, we became soaked through, despite being completely decked out in rain gear. Most of the hike was, thankfully, under cover of protective trees in the forest. Once we stepped out onto the beach, however, we faced the brunt of the storm. It was so bad that we couldn't help but laugh. The wind practically blew us off our feet and the rain seeped between all the seams and gaps in our layers. Knowing we were only a couple miles from the car at the furthest point of the hike, we continued hiking and dreamed of dry clothing and warm heaters.

The coast does not have a monopoly on rain. On Table Mountain in the Columbia River Gorge, I found myself hiking blindly through wind and rain on a miserable day in September. It was no walk on the beach. The large boulder fields are difficult enough to walk over when they are dry; in the rain, they became slippery and unstable. The forecast predicted a chance of rain in the morning with clear skies by 11 am. So much for forecasts; it rained all day. I could hardly see through my rain-splotched glasses. We got pretty close to the actual summit but couldn't be certain how close because of the poor visibility and torrent of rain. After snapping a quick selfie, we rushed back down the mountain. I was never so happy to feel my raincoat snag against blackberry bushes, an indication that we were mere minutes from the car.

I got the rainy glasses treatment again on a seven-mile-loop hike at North Bank Ranch in Southern Oregon. I didn't have to hike over any boulders, but I did slide around on steep, muddy trails. The scenery was gorgeous, at least what I could see of it. Grass-covered hills rolled across the landscape between pockets of oak forest. Broken down, rusted farm equipment dotted the old road that comprised one portion of the route. But the best part of the trip was the solitude; no one else had ventured out there that day. I had the entire place to myself, and that is what keeps me going back out in bad weather: the peace and quiet.

My relationship with rain helps me get out year round and was particularly beneficial when I hiked in Oregon's wet Willamette Valley. During the spring and fall, or "shoulder seasons" (the months just before and after peak summer travel time), the region always receives a lot of rain. Those times of year can be so pleasant that I wish more people would come to realize the beauty of hiking in the rain.

Autumn in the Willamette Valley is also a great time of year to see waterfalls, because that is when they start to swell from the frequent rainstorms. On a rainy November day in 2006, I visited Silver Falls State Park near Salem, Oregon. I was excited to see ten waterfalls in one hike. Each one was more spectacular than the one before; I was awestruck. I'd never walked behind a waterfall before. Face to face with a flowing wall of water, I wondered what other natural wonders I had yet to experience.

Combine all of that flowing water with colorful fall foliage and you've got a sight to behold. Moisture brings out vibrant colors, not only in the reds and golds of deciduous leaves but in everything else too: bright-green lichen, deep-brown bark, waxy winter berries, and midnight-blue puddles.

There are countless other times that I've been drawn to hiking around waterfalls on a rainy day, but they didn't quite make the official *Hike366* list. However, there are so many other great reasons to get out in the rain, like . . .

Thunderstorms.

❧

Thunderstorms are frightening. They are powerful. They can sneak up on you and ruin your day. But when they're not right on top of you and there's no imminent threat of being struck by lightning, it is incredible to be in the presence of thunderstorms.

On a trip to Black Crater with Aaron, I had not prepared for rain. It was June and the weather was reliably warm and dry, but we heard thunder and rain while camped in our tent the evening before our hike. I was concerned since I hadn't packed any rain gear. Aaron, on the other hand, had a rain shell in his backpack. The next day, I improvised by grabbing the tarp from under our tent and using it as a makeshift poncho. I was as ready as I could be, given the circumstances.

We hiked with the impending threat of rain all day. As the trail emerged from the forest and up into barren cinder, we were amazed that we hadn't been rained on yet. Dark-gray rain clouds were present in every direction, except for directly overhead. We kept hiking, knowing that we could be hammered by rainfall at any moment.

> **PRO TIP**
>
> No matter where you are or what the forecast says, in the Pacific Northwest, always pack rain gear.

Those views, though. As I looked out over the snow-capped mountains with dark clouds behind them, I stopped in my tracks to enjoy the beauty. I was glad that we'd made the decision to hike that day, giving ourselves the opportunity to be in that place at that particular time. The air smelled different. The colors looked different. The wind and clouds added some drama to an already stunning setting. As I stood atop the summit of Black Crater, tarp pulled across my shoulders, a breeze blew by. The tarp lifted up like a cape, and I felt like a superhero standing there. We had not *conquered* the mountain; we had proceeded with caution, listening to what it had to tell us, humble enough to know that the conditions might not be right to continue. We were prepared to turn around at any time; reaching the summit was a lucky bonus.

Always go, but always listen.

With the right gear and mindset, hiking in the rain can be enjoyable and memorable. Later that year, in Corvallis, I had somehow convinced two other people into going out for a hike up Marys Peak. It was almost Christmas. It was cold, and the rain was coming down so hard it was challenging just driving to the trailhead. We showed up completely bedecked in rain gear. I was not surprised that ours was the only car in the parking lot at 10 am on a weekend; the weather had kept other hikers away.

TYPE 1 FUN

This is what most normal humans think of
when they say, "This is so much fun!" Examples
include enjoying drinks with friends, playing
on a playground, going on a guided rafting trip,
watching your favorite sports team win a game, etc.

TYPE 2 FUN

These activities are not at all fun while you're
doing them, but after they're over you look back on
them with fond memories. This is also known as
"climber's amnesia." Examples include mountain
climbing, running an ultramarathon, childbirth,
and doing a polar plunge.

Mountaineers are very used to this type of fun.
Climbing a mountain is nearly always miserable.
but once you get back to the car it's nice to say, "oh
I just did that!"

The rain was unrelenting all day, and a stream of water flowed down the trail. We moved quickly to stay warm and keep our spirits up. We were having type 2 fun. As we approached the final section of dense forest before the meadow, I could hear the wind whistling in the trees. We practically sprinted to the top of the mountain, pausing only briefly to snap a summit selfie before retreating back to the trees. Looking back at that photo, I see that we all had genuine smiles on our faces. We had a real human experience and emerged tougher on the other side.

On a chilly November day in 2014, I led a Mazamas group to the summit of Maxwell Butte. Gray clouds filled the air and it rained and rained. As we hiked, we fell into a rhythm and chatted with each other to keep our spirits up. There were some grumbles along the way, but the overall experience was positive. The folks on that hike would join me on future outings, which told me that it couldn't have been all that bad. I learned that a random group of humans recreating together on a nasty day can actually be quite enjoyable! It takes a certain type of person to deal with discomfort for multiple hours on end, and to be okay with it. I think it says a lot about a person's character. To me, lousy weather hikes make the good-weather days feel especially incredible.

I'll admit that sometimes the rain makes me grumpy. In 2016, Aaron and I took a two-week vacation to Hawaii. We spent a week on Maui and a week on Kauai. Friends had told me that Kauai was a hiker's paradise and that I couldn't go all the way to Hawaii without stopping there. I was somewhat dismayed when I arrived to find that the weather and landscape felt a lot like Western Oregon. It rained nearly every day. The forests were thick and lush, with waterfalls everywhere. There were people everywhere, too. I could have easily done the same kind of hiking back home, and for much cheaper.

The worst day I had on our island getaway was on a hike to Awa'awapuhi Ridge. The air was heavy with moisture at the trailhead and it rained the entire duration of the hike. Thick clouds blocked any chance of a view from the supposedly epic viewpoint we hiked to. I complained loudly on this hike. When I wasn't busy whining about the damp and mud, I paused to appreciate the diversity of the native plant life. The forest was alive with a wide spectrum of colors, textures, shapes and sizes. At least the wildflowers were different than Oregon's.

So I do let the weather get to me sometimes, but I really try not to. Most days, the rain is one small component of the experience; it does not dominate the day.

Rain plus cold is a recipe for hypothermia, as I learned on my trip to Ethan Pond in New Hampshire many years ago. But sometimes a hike can be cold despite the shining sun. In January 2013, I took a trip to the Oregon Coast with my friend Sue. We headed for one of my favorite hikes at the Oregon Dunes. The trail started through a dense coastal forest, continued through open sand dunes, dipped down into a thicket of shrubs and then burst out onto a sandy ocean beach. I was not expecting what was in the thicket. From my journal:

As we reached the far edge of the dunes, the sand turned into mud. Soon, water covered the thick mud and it became impossible to keep our feet dry. Rather than walk around in wet shoes, we took our shoes and socks off and continued through the water barefoot. It was so cold! At times my feet actually punched through thin icebergs floating on the water.

With the warm sun beaming down overhead I had forgotten just how cold the water in January could be. As we walked further, the water got deeper and deeper. We rolled our pant legs up to keep them dry. Walking in wet clothes in these cold temperatures would be dangerous. That wasn't worth the risk. Although it was temporarily uncomfortable, I knew it would be over soon. Or, would it?

Eventually, the water got so deep that we had to strip down to our underwear and shove our pants in our backpacks. I was afraid that we would have to turn back and lose all that progress we'd gained, without ever reaching the ocean. I looked back at Sue, and she wasn't complaining yet, so I kept moving forward. We could hear the waves close by; we just needed to get there!

At last, the trail emerged onto a boardwalk leading to the sand we'd been dreaming of. It felt so good to sit down by the ocean and let my feet dry up (and warm up) in the sun.

❧

Hiking in the cold, like hiking in the rain, requires additional planning. The most obvious difference between taking a stroll on a sunny summer day and stepping out into the freezing cold is the amount of clothing you need to wear. Sure, hiking in the cold means packing extra layers, but it doesn't always mean wearing them all. And, depending on the ground surface, it may also require the addition of snowshoes, crampons or other traction devices to keep you from slipping. The biggest factor that comes into play when hiking in the cold, in my opinion, is mindset. Approaching a hike on a cold day with an air of curiosity and patience helps foster a better and safer experience than setting your expectations for everything to be perfect and pleasant. Since I hate being cold, this is a skill I've had to develop over time. I've learned the difference between uncomfortable and unsafe, and I take precautions to manage my safety while providing the most comfort I can during cold-weather hikes.

The cold also creates unique environmental phenomena. On Marys Peak in November 2014, I noticed large swaths of trail broken up by frost heaves. The autumn rains that saturated the ground were turned into ice by subfreezing temperatures. Thin, strong ice crystals burst out of the earth, causing the soil to buckle and break open. They were quite spectacular! I was hiking in a small group and we all stopped at once to touch and photograph the miniature ice sculptures. You can only find such splendid acts of nature in the dead of winter.

One of my coldest and earliest hikes took place on a snowy, windy January day in 2006. I met up with a very determined hiking partner and we attempted an ascent of the Cannon Mountain Trail in New Hampshire. This grueling steep trail is hard enough in good summer conditions, but we decided to give it a go in single-digit weather with summit wind gusts reaching 60 miles per hour.

We needed crampons to help our boots stick to the slick, icy trail. To combat the frigid conditions we covered up in many layers. Despite the inhospitable weather, we pushed ahead. It was on that trip that I discovered the value of wearing ski goggles in such extreme wind and cold. I had neglected to pack mine that day, and the sideways-blowing snow had two negative effects on my experience. First, my glasses kept getting coated in moisture, making it nearly impossible to see. I took them off during the most exposed sections of trail, making it again very difficult to see but in a different way. Second, my face was really, really cold. I had a balaclava covering most of my face, but the goggles would have helped keep my whole face protected. I learned my lesson for the next time. Winter weather is a brutal, but effective, teacher.

Several years later, Aaron and I took a camping trip during Thanksgiving weekend at the Hart Mountain National Antelope Refuge in Eastern Oregon. That was the coldest camping trip I've ever endured to this day. Daytime high temperatures remained below freezing, and the lowest temperature we saw on our thermometer during the day was minus twenty-six degrees Fahrenheit. Making food was a challenge because everything was either frozen solid or barely fluid, including my eggs and pancake batter!

PRO TIP

Set a **turnaround time** to prevent returning to the trailhead after dark. To calculate a turnaround time, you need to estimate how long it will take you to walk the distance from your destination back to your car. You also need to know what time the sun sets.

For example, let's say sunset is at 5 pm. The return hike is four miles. At an average rate of 2 mph, I would need two hours to hike back. My turnaround time is 3 pm. If I want to add some extra padding in case of unexpected obstacles or a slower walking speed, I'll set the turnaround time to 2:30 pm.

The cold slowed down our usual camp routine, so we got a late morning start on our hike up Warner Peak. We had to walk five and a half miles in the snow, uphill and off trail, in order to arrive at the summit. It was touch and go; I was afraid that our progress was too slow to make it back to camp before sunset. We knew it was going to get significantly colder after the sun went down, and we were having enough trouble staying warm in the sunshine. Aaron expressed his concerns about the time, so I did some quick mental math. I chose a turnaround time that ensured we wouldn't get stuck after dark, and we kept walking. I did a little happy dance when we made it to the top before the time was up. Descending the mountain was much faster than going up, and we reached our camp just after the peak sunset colors faded. It was a close one.

The next morning, as we were packing up, we both took off our down jackets and looked at each other as if to say, "Ugh, it's really warming up out here!" The temperature: eighteen degrees. How quickly one adapts to life below freezing.

It's important to find the right partners to hike with in the cold. Not everyone is willing and able to do that. Real outdoor-adventure types are usually busy skiing or snowboarding, and casual hikers are not likely to go outside at all in the winter. Aaron has been a good cold-weather hiker from the start. In December 2013, we went on a couple of snowshoeing adventures at Crater Lake National Park. The sun was out, but the air was cold. We ventured off trail, making our way up to a couple of highpoints along the rim. There was hardly a sign of human activity anywhere. I love experiencing solitude in a national park; it feels like it should be an impossible feat. Huffing and puffing up a steep snow slope, layered up in the bitter cold, inching closer to a glorious viewpoint overlooking the lake, we knew it was worth the extra effort to get there.

The next December, Aaron and I embarked on an overnight trip to Warner Mountain Lookout in the Willamette National Forest with a couple of friends. The four of us snowshoed about three miles to reach our destination: a wooden cube sitting atop a tall metal staircase. For the next two days and nights we alternated between stoking the fire in the wood stove and bundling up to stretch our legs outside in the snow. There weren't any marked trails around, so we used the snowy roads as pathways to adventure. We moved quickly to generate heat and didn't venture too far from home base. But even those brief journeys out of our shelter brought great joy. The only sounds were the crunch of snow beneath our feet, the soft exhale of air, the occasional peep from a bird. Winter was at once harsh and soothing, stark and beautiful. It was easy to be there surrounded by friends who also appreciated winter's beauty. No one had to convince the others that it would be a good idea to take a hike, we all just knew.

Sometimes hiking gear fails spectacularly in the cold. I usually store my water in a bladder with a hose that leads right to my face. But when it's very cold, the water in the narrow hose freezes rapidly. I know that, and yet I let it happen on the trip to Warner Mountain Lookout.

I decided to deal with my frozen water situation by taking the bladder out of my pack and shoving it into my down jacket. My body heat melted the water in the hose and mouthpiece in a relatively short period of time. And the waist belt on my pack helped keep the bladder in place while walking, so I left it in there as we hiked.

There are other strategies to keep water from freezing in water-bladder hoses. First, I usually blow all the water out of the hose when I'm finished drinking. Then I stick the end of the hose inside my jacket to keep the mouthpiece from freezing. These two techniques work most of the time, but it's smart to have a backup water bottle in your pack as well. Carrying water bottles with wide mouths is the simplest way to preserve precious liquid water.

There's a lot to learn about hiking in the cold, and I get to teach people about this every time I lead a group in the winter. In 2016, I organized a small team of Cascades Mountaineers (a Central Oregon hiking club) on an outing to Lookout Mountain in the Ochocos. I picked that particular hike because I knew the trailhead would be accessible, even if the upper mountain was snowed in. However, I was not prepared for the amount of snow we encountered or how much the deep snow would slow us down. It was also very cold, which not everyone was prepared for. We shared gear and tips for retaining heat. I was glad I brought extra chemical hand warmers to pass around. On days like that, a thermos of hot tea or soup goes a long way to raise morale. We didn't make it all the way to the summit, but everyone learned a bit about winter hiking preparation.

The ten essentials list, which many hikers are familiar with, is an especially important guide for winter hiking. Carrying enough insulating layers for the entire body is key to ensuring safety and comfort during winter outings. That means bringing multiple pairs of gloves, hats and socks in addition to warm pants and jackets. Since my hands get cold easily, I carry no less than three pairs of gloves and mittens on winter day hikes. I also have several pieces of clothing that help retain heat around my head and neck, like buffs, ear warmers, neck gaiters and wool hats. My favorite winter hat has earflaps and a pair of dangling strings that can be tied to secure the hat tightly around my head.

The margins of safety and comfort are narrower in the cold. Frozen water, hypothermia, broken gear, injuries and other issues can become serious very quickly. I have learned to prepare adequately for cold weather with additional supplies that would not be needed in the summer. I usually have more than enough warm layers and some kind of shelter in case I get mired down for a period of time. Hiking in the cold can be absolutely miserable with the wrong gear and inadequate skill. But when you head out prepared, it is a magical time to be outdoors.

❧

I always chuckle a little when people talk about "going snowshoeing." What does that mean? Hiking with snowshoes on your feet? Just because there's snow on the ground doesn't mean you need snowshoes. And, in many cases, snow conditions are not consistent from the start of the hike to the end. To me, snowshoes are one of many possible additions to my hiking gear in the winter; they do not define an activity than hiking. Actually, snowshoes have come in handy in nearly every month of the year, depending on where I am!

A great example of off-season snowshoeing is my adventure with Aaron on Crescent Mountain in May 2014. Early May is shoulder season for the foothills of the Oregon Cascades. Conditions are not very consistent year to year. There may be deep snow, patchy snow or no snow. Most people wait until later in the spring or well into summer to tackle this mountain, wanting to be sure the trails are completely clear. I enjoy shoulder-season hiking for just that reason: Solitude is almost guaranteed.

The trailhead was snow-free, but I wasn't sure how much snow we'd encounter beyond that. Aaron and I strapped our snowshoes onto our packs, in case we needed them later, and started walking. The approach hike was pretty. The gently graded trail weaved through an evergreen forest dominated by Douglas fir. In spring, tiny fairy slipper orchids bloom along the trail. We crossed a bridge over a bubbling creek and started climbing uphill.

Once we reached the meadows, we were greeted by thick clouds enclosing the area. Eventually, we hit some consistent patches of snow and put our snowshoes on. When we re-entered the woods, the snow thinned out, revealing large areas of dirt in the trail ahead. We stubbornly kept our snowshoes on, anticipating more regular snow coverage. It never came. After "snowshoeing" in the dirt for quite some time, we admitted defeat and put them back on our packs. We sat on the summit in a thick gray cloud, eating our lunch and hoping the sky would clear out for a view. Not to happen.

As you can see, snowshoes are simply another tool in the toolkit when there's enough snow on the ground.

Snowshoes can even come in handy in the city. In the winter of 2016-2017, Bend was hit with one snowstorm after another, leaving a substantial snowpack that covered city parks and sidewalks for months. In January 2017, I snowshoed from my house to the top of Pilot Butte. Since few people had shoveled their sidewalks, snowshoes were essential in helping me get through the feet of snow piled up outside of businesses and residences. Without them, I would have sunk into the thigh-deep snow. Once I was on the Butte trails, I was again glad to have snowshoes for both traction and flotation. On most days of the year, hiking up Pilot Butte doesn't require extra care or equipment, but that winter made a walk up the hill feel like an expedition.

> ## BREAKING TRAIL
>
> Definition: walking in snow where no one has walked before you.
>
> This is much more strenuous than walking behind someone else or walking on a groomed path. If you want to raise your body temperature, get a good workout, and make some friends, offer to break trail for your group.
>
> Bonus: you get views of a winter wonderland, not someone else's butt.

Other places are famously buried in snow all winter long. Crater Lake National Park, Oregon's only national park, receives an average of forty-three feet of snow each year. If you want to get anywhere outside the parking lot in the winter, snowshoes or cross-country skis are necessary. In the winters of 2013-2015, I brought small groups of people there for a weekend of exploring on snowshoes. In 2013 and 2014 the weather was perfect. The snow was powdery and glittery and delightful.

In 2015, however, things took a turn. A massive storm had overtaken the park, leaving many areas closed due to high avalanche danger. In lieu of our usual day of hiking to spots with gorgeous views of the lake, we hiked in constant snowfall around a low-elevation campground near the park's south entrance. Despite the difficulties and lack of visibility, our group had an incredible time. It made me happy to see smiles on everyone's faces as we walked through the wet, heavy snow. We took turns breaking trail, which was the most difficult part of the outing. If you're a skier bombing downhill, then fresh powder creates the best conditions you could hope for. But when you're snowshoeing, fresh powder increases the workload tenfold. The person in the front of the line has to use much more energy than the people following behind. Whoever is last has the lightest workload. By frequently rotating places in line, we kept our morale up and enjoyed the adventure. We didn't let the snow keep us indoors!

It's a little harder to stay excited while hiking *alone* in the snow. On January 16, 2017, I set out for the summit of Gray Butte, a prominent highpoint near Smith Rock. That date was on my calendar as a hike day, and that peak had been on my to-do list for a while. Every single time I went climbing or hiking at Smith Rock I would stare up at that prominent highpoint. It was such an obvious destination, and I thought the snow would make things more interesting than walking up a dry, dusty forest road.

And it would have, but I chose a particularly dreary day. The color of the sky matched the color on the ground; it was all gray. I felt as if I was in a sensory deprivation chamber. The air was cold and there were no signs of humans anywhere. I trudged through the snow, very mindful of how alone I was, heading step by step towards the summit. Once I arrived, I was in a swirl of gray, with the hum of electricity filling the air. There were radio towers and buildings full of gadgets and antennae atop the butte, the collective bane of every summiter's existence. With no views, no one to share the moment with and no particular sense of joy in my achievement, I headed back down the way I came. It was a "check the box" kind of day, and a huge disappointment. I'd been looking forward to that summit for years, but it was terribly anticlimactic. As much as I enjoy solitude, sometimes being alone isn't fulfilling.

Those gray days are much more memorable in the company of others. In 2010 I did a quick overnight on Lookout Mountain in the Mt. Hood National Forest with a couple of friends. We hiked steeply uphill for miles in order to reach a ridge-top campsite. After setting up our tents in the snow, my friend pulled a colorful object out of his backpack. "Is that a kite?" I asked. Sure enough, I looked up into the cloudy sky to see a kite soaring and diving in the air. After an hour or so of kite antics, we cracked open some beers, told stories, ate dinner and enjoyed each other's company. That was a much different experience than the glum moodiness of my hike up Gray Butte.

In February 2016, Aaron and I snowshoed into a backcountry lodge in Canada in similarly gray conditions. It was a long, slow, uphill battle through the snow. What made it worse was watching cross-country skiers glide right by us with barely a water bottle attached to their backs. We'd decided to forego the costly snowmobile gear shuttle and carry our own stuff. (Self-sufficiency and all.) But we envied their light loads as we slogged along with overnight packs on our tired backs. Although we didn't receive any awards for schlepping our supplies up to the lodge, we knew that if anything had gone wrong along the way, we would have been prepared to handle it ourselves. You just have to be a little tougher to negotiate winter conditions.

There are several summer hikes I've gone back to in winter just to experience the seasonal differences. In March 2014, I took Aaron to Henline Mountain and Henline Falls in the Willamette National Forest. At the trailhead there was no snow on the ground, but as we climbed we soon ran into patches of snow. Then continuous snow. The trail became difficult to follow because it was not marked for winter travel, eventually disappearing entirely in front of our eyes. Having been there once before in similar circumstances, I had an idea of where we needed to go.

As we made the final climb up to the summit, we emerged from the trees to a viewpoint overlooking a cloudy sky with very small patches of blue. On a clear day we'd enjoy lovely vistas, but that day we simply had to appreciate the journey, not the destination.

WINTER TRAILS VS. SUMMER TRAILS

Most trails are designed for hiking in the good weather or, here in the Pacific Northwest, in the summer months. I consider these trails summer trails.

Winter trails are specifically designed for use in the winter, meaning they are accessible from parking lots that are cleared of snow and marked with trail markers high up in the trees.

Summer trails may be hiked off-season, with a few caveats: you might not be able to drive all the way to the trailhead and you might not be able to see the trail markers. Advanced planning and navigation skills may be required.

On a particularly beautiful day in February 2015, my friends and I took advantage of the low snowpack and hiked a delightful summer trail up Coffin Mountain. Remarkably, the trailhead was clear of snow. At over 4,700 feet of elevation, that's nearly unheard of for that time of year. We packed Yaktrax and hiking poles in preparation of dealing with some slipperiness and possibly deep snowbanks along our way.

The hike took us through a mixture of forest and meadows and made for a very pleasant outing. There was minimal route finding involved since the snow coverage was rather light. We appreciated the warm sun lighting up our faces and helping us stay comfortable in the cold air. On our hike we hit two summits: Bachelor and Coffin Mountain. Both provided clear views of majestic Mt. Jefferson and the valleys surrounding us.

Fall provides the best opportunity to get on summer trails while they're still accessible, as long as you arrive prepared for snow. In October 2016, I headed to the high country to sneak in one last fall hike before the snow gates closed on the Old McKenzie Highway in Central Oregon. My very snowy adventure ended up at Four-in-One Cone because my original destination was too ambitious for the conditions. I'd left my snowshoes at home to save weight, and it turned out there was a lot more snow on the trail than I had anticipated. Fifteen miles in that much snow without the right equipment was too much of a slog for me, so I settled for nine miles and a beautiful highpoint to boot.

Way back in 2009 I was already pushing the limits of fall hiking. In November of that year I started up the trail to Mt. Mitchell (which has since been closed to public access) in Southern Washington. I immediately saw there was snow on the trail. It was thick, heavy and sticky snow, and it didn't take long before the snow got deeper and deeper; I was glad I packed my snowshoes and poles. After about an hour of hiking I arrived at my first viewpoint, which was socked in. No one had been up there recently. I had to put in fresh tracks all the way up the trail. I stopped occasionally to catch my breath and admire the beautiful scenery. The way the snow clung to each leaf, branch, berry, and pine needle was picturesque. I hiked for hours through the ever-deepening snow towards the top of the mountain.

At last, the rocky summit of Mt. Mitchell stood before me. I scrambled up to the top and imagined the view—I couldn't see five feet in front of my face. I was completely surrounded by white. It was a little eerie, not having much sense of up, down, left, or right. The only thing visible was small portions of dark rock that stood out in the almost-entirely white expanse. This was not a tranquil walk over crunchy, autumn leaves; this felt much more like a winter hike. My experience on Mt. Mitchell illustrates the value of hiking all year long, as you can become more aware of seasonal changes and learn to be prepared for tough weather any day.

Getting back to where you started is always more straightforward than the trek up. The snow is already packed down, the route is clearly marked and, of course, downhill travel is easier than uphill—unless you're doing a loop hike.

In February 2013, I set off on one of many hikes up Marys Peak. Being only twenty minutes from my house, I considered it my local mountain. The trailheads were easy to reach any time of year, and I could be up and back in half a day or less. The notes section on my hike spreadsheet for that day simply says "icy as hell."

I planned on doing a circuit of the peak: hike up the north ridge, come down the east ridge, find the connector trail and circle back to hike the bottom half of the north ridge, ending up where I started. Marys Peak is a small bump in the coast range of Northern Oregon; it's not the Matterhorn or anything. I thought it would be a simple task.

But it wasn't that day. I neglected to pack any traction devices for my shoes, and I didn't have trekking poles, either. I don't know what I was thinking. As the terrain changed from dirt to mud to snow, my pace slowed. I carefully fumbled around on the icy snow, trying my best to step into previous travelers' footsteps in order to remain upright. A group of runners came up behind me and continued along up the trail in their running shoes. That was enough to shut me up about the slippery snow and keep me moving. Once I broke out of the trees and onto the road, I looked ahead at smooth, snowy, rolling meadows. It was beautiful! The summit structures were covered in rime ice. Rime is a treasure of winter hiking. Everything becomes more magical in the ice, even ugly buildings.

It was no small feat getting down to the east ridge trail from the summit area. I couldn't remember exactly where the trail came in and there were no signs to guide me. I looked at the map and made some guesses as to where to go. Of course, the hike would be a piece of cake in the summertime when I could see the ground. With the snow covering up any sign of the trail, route finding presented a challenge. To make matters worse, the ground felt like a skating rink and I had nothing to stop me if I slipped and fell. I didn't want to go for a long ride into a tree.

Using branches to hold onto for dear life (the "veggie belay" technique), I angled down the steep, icy slope towards any sign of a trail. It was terrifying. I'd never leave my Yaktrax at home again, I thought.

Yaktrax have taken me many places in winter that I would not have been able to go otherwise. One of those places is Smith Rock. In January 2017, my friend Sarah and I headed out to Smith Rock to hike up and over Misery Ridge. That hiking loop, and the park itself, is an extremely popular destination for both tourists and locals. But on that day, the parking lot was empty. Ice and snow covered the ground. A chilling breeze blew through the canyon. We sauntered past a warning sign that read: "ICY WINTER TRAIL CONDITIONS PARKWIDE." A grin spread across my face; I thought it was a great day to be there. We were about to have an adventure.

I'd been to Smith Rock dozens of times. But on that day, I saw the park in a way I never had before. We walked slowly up the steep, slippery Misery Ridge trail, taking care to find firm footing with every step. As we descended the backside, I admired the steep rock faces that were powdered with a dusting of snow. We watched birds in their flight formations glide across the sky. We enjoyed the silence and serenity of the park that day; no climbers dared scale the icy walls and no other hikers ventured out of the parking lot. It was a hike I still remember vividly.

❦

Most people never even consider hiking in the winter. They are either out skiing and snowboarding or they are indoors reading books and playing video games and eating soup. But not me. I enjoy winter hiking and introducing people to walking in the winter. In February 2011, I took a friend on a hike to Angels Rest in the Columbia River Gorge. Like the Misery Ridge Loop, Angels Rest is a very popular hike. People flood to the trail all summer long. The parking lot fills by 9 am and cars line the highway, parked on every available patch of land.

Hiking traffic comes to a screeching halt in the winter. At the trailhead, the path was completely free of snow. But as the trail ascended its many switchbacks, we began encountering ice and snow. With hiking poles in hand, we gently made our way up the trail. The last stretch to the summit viewpoint was the most treacherous. We walked mindfully across a narrow fin of boulders leading to a bench overlooking the Columbia River. As a cold winter breeze swept across my face, I admired the snow-capped peaks across the river. For those who brave the weather, winter hiking offers rewards unlike any other season.

The next winter, I took Aaron out on his first winter hiking trip. It was difficult to walk in the wet, heavy snow in our awkward snowshoes. We had a miserable day getting lost (ahem, temporarily misplaced) near the Santiam Pass on some poorly marked snowshoe trails. Despite that, he decided to give winter hiking a second chance the following day. I selected a summer trail for our outing and hoped that the trailhead would be accessible. As we drove up the road, we were met by an increasingly deep covering of winter snow. We cautiously drove until our low-clearance car couldn't go any further. From there we parked and set off on foot, hoping the "start" of the trail wouldn't be too far ahead.

The trail was very easy to follow, even under all of that snow. Aaron and I took turns breaking trail as we walked in and out of the trees. The desert forest was open and sunny, with views of the surrounding valleys and ridges exposed at points throughout the hike. Once we started getting views of big mountains ahead, I got excited about the prospect of reaching a summit. I wanted our trip to be a success, and I thought that reaching the top of Fields Peak was a good bet. There were several other peaks beyond that one on the connecting ridge, but hiking to all of those highpoints would make for a really long and exhausting day. After our soggy, meandering experience from the previous day, I hoped to provide Aaron a glimpse of the beauty and solitude of backcountry snowshoeing, getting him hooked for future trips.

It was hard work getting up to that summit, but we made it. The air was extremely cold. I had brought a thermos of chicken soup, which hit the spot in the bitter wind! We celebrated our ascent and then hurried back to the shelter of the trees. Aaron loved the freedom and speed of going downhill in his snowshoes. We made it back to the car in no time at all. He would go on many, many more winter adventures with me in the future.

☙

Aaron continued to be a reliable adventure buddy. In May 2013, we set out on a hike up Browder Ridge. What would normally be a very straightforward hike turned into a bit of a fiasco because of the snow. First, we got the car stuck in a snowbank less than a quarter mile from the trailhead. By the time we freed the car and got to the trailhead it was after 2 pm. We hiked on patchy snow for a while, then consistent snow, all the way to the summit. We navigated by map and compass when the trail became completely obscured by snow. It was 6 pm by the time we topped out, so we hurried to get down by nightfall.

That would be easier said than done. As the snow melted from the tree branches, the dripping water splashed onto the ground below. Those snow bombs effectively camouflaged our footprints; we couldn't simply follow our tracks back. Again, we pulled out the map and compass and did some navigation to remain on course. Finally, we emerged from the woods, hungry and ready to find a campsite for the night!

In February 2017, I went on a winter adventure with my friend Sandra. We decided to hike to two waterfalls and circle around a lake, making a circuit of nine miles. The route I envisioned was not well-marked for winter travel. While certain locations along the way were heavily visited, others had no signs of humans being there since the snow started falling. It ended up being quite an interesting day. We traversed slick, steep, icy snowbanks. We walked along flat trail sections following a gorgeous lakeshore. We tromped back and forth looking for obscured trail junctions. We stood in the freezing spray of rushing waterfalls. We enjoyed peace and quiet in frigid winter air. In the summer, it would have been a very simple hike, but in those conditions it felt as harrowing as any mountain climb. I loved it.

Most of the time, navigating summer trails in the winter is much less dramatic, and some trails are specifically built for snowshoeing. I first learned about groomed trails and winter travel on the West Coast in 2006 when some friends took me out to Trillium Lake in the Mt. Hood National Forest. The trails there were wide and well-packed, making snowshoeing a breeze. It was very different than walking on snow-covered summer trails.

Just outside of Bend, there's a huge network of winter trails. While most are marked for cross-country skiers or skate skiers, there is a small number of trails set aside for snowshoers. I have hiked on those snowshoe trails with small groups of friends, but I find the trails are designed for casual outings. There are no highpoints, no big climbs, no excitement.

Since most people seem to prefer cross-country skiing over snowshoeing, I decided to give that a try. In 2008 I joined friends for my first cross-country ski outing. We headed to Teacup Lake, again in the Mt. Hood National Forest. It is a very popular place for skiers, and we were not the only people out there on that December day. I got a few pointers from my pals and off we went.

> ## WINTER TRAIL MARKERS
>
> Trails are much harder to find in the winter without markers on the trees. In many Pacific Northwest forests, trails are marked with diamonds:
>
> Blue diamond = ski/snowshoe trail
> Orange diamond = snowmobile trail
>
> Color-coded markers help with navigation and prevent conflict with other trail users. Learn how your local trail systems are marked for winter travel.

I hated it. Sure, I knew I'd need to invest some time in learning the technique and getting the rhythm of the glide. But I didn't like that we were stuck on groomed trails, that my skis didn't perform well on even small changes in elevation, and that I couldn't wander off into the woods and explore. I felt trapped. We were forced to follow the madding crowd. It was the beginning and the end of my foray into cross-country skiing on groomed trails (until I discovered backcountry skis that allow me to ski off-trail—no, that might require writing another book).

I still prefer snowshoeing. It is sarcastically referred to as "slowshoeing," because you just can't travel as fast on snowshoes as you can on skis. I admit and accept this. But here's what you can do on snowshoes: You can go anywhere you please; you can clamber over fallen logs; you can travel on terrain that goes steeply up, then steeply down, then up again; you can easily switch between snowshoes, crampons and bare boots; you have the freedom to wander off-trail, cross icy snow, and tromp across patches of bare ground. To me, those were compelling reasons to stick with my snowshoes in the winter.

On my eternal quest for solitude, I learned that one sure way to veer away from people in the winter is to aim for summits.

Winter mountaineering has its challenges, so while most people will snowshoe and ski to cozy cabins in the woods, very few will venture out above the tree line. And that's for good reason — many winter summits are guarded by snow slopes that carry risks of avalanche and other hazards. It's important to learn about the special dangers that come with winter travel before attempting to climb mountains that time of year.

In March 2006, I set my sights on hiking to the summit of Mt. Jefferson, in the White Mountains of New Hampshire, with three friends. It was winter's last hoorah. The weather was cold with high winds forecast for the day. We took the Caps Ridge Trail towards the top of the mountain, which we lost almost immediately after missing a turn. At some point we encountered deep snowdrifts, which slowed our pace immensely. We were all too stubborn to put our snowshoes on, thinking that the drifts would be over shortly (they weren't). Despite our setbacks, we made it to the summit and back down. Winter threw us some curveballs, but we persevered and learned some lessons to apply the next time.

First, when encountering deep snow, it is almost always better to pause long enough to get your snowshoes on than think you're saving any time or energy by just continuing on without the right gear. Second, it's important to know your route and look for signs constantly when traveling in the winter. Snow makes even the most obvious trail difficult to follow. Our bodies like traveling in straight lines; it is remarkably easy to miss switchbacks and trail junctions in winter conditions. And third, know your partners' personalities and make decisions for them if you know they're too headstrong to suggest stopping to deal with a gear changeover.

Mt. Thielsen is known as the lightning rod of the Cascades. Its pointy summit pinnacle is scarred by lightning strikes. With no chance of a thunderstorm in winter, I set out with a partner to climb the mountain in February 2008. We snowshoed through deep snow to our camp located at the edge of the tree line. There we spent a night wrapped up in down, sipping hot beverages and waiting for the sun to come up.

The next morning we headed up steep snow slopes under a perfect blue sky. It felt magical to be up high on a mountain with no one else in sight. We climbed the steep shoulder of the mountain on beautiful snow. Just below "Chicken Point," we had to ascend an even steeper gully, which felt precarious to me.

Once we got on the ridge, I settled in for a long belay session.

It took about two hours of messing around with ropes, scouting out ascent routes, changing footwear, and trying to protect snow and rock to realize that we would not reach the summit that day. The mixed rock/snow/ice conditions were not favorable for the two of us to ascend any higher. As chunks of snow and ice rained down the mountain, we decided to turn tail and head back to camp. Winter summits are never guaranteed.

The following January I met up with a friend and his climbing crew to tackle Mt. Rose in the Olympic Mountains of Washington. With a trailhead elevation of only 840 feet, we were confident that it wouldn't be snowed in, but we were wrong. Fortunately, we had a very fit and determined crew that didn't mind adding a mile and a half of walking to each end of our hike. Once we reached the trailhead, we headed straight up the mountain. One advantage of snow cover is that nearly every surface becomes possible to walk on. There's no need to follow a specific trail when everything looks the same and you have a general idea of where you're headed. (Remember that navigating to a mountaintop is simple, but precisely making it back to your car is not as straightforward). We reached the top of the peak in gorgeous, summer-like weather and sunned ourselves as we ate lunch in our T-shirts. It was a far cry from that bitterly cold belay station on Mt. Thielsen.

While cold and snow present challenges in the winter, summer weather isn't always the best, either; it can get too hot to handle.

In 2015, Aaron and I took a trip to Zion National Park. We arose and started hiking early to avoid the midday heat. We also hiked as quickly as we could to avoid the rush of tourists that would most certainly arrive later in the day. Our efforts to begin hiking before most of the visitors were still snuggled in their sleeping bags were completely worth it. With hardly any shade along the route, we would have been extremely hot and tired attempting such a hike later in the day. Even after starting early, on our walk up Observation Point, we still felt the heat of the desert sun. The views overlooking Angel's Rest and the main canyon were tremendous, and worth every drop of sweat.

The next day, we grabbed the first shuttle out of camp,

wanting to get a head start on Angels Landing Trail. I'd seen dramatic pictures of this trail, and I was really excited to walk on the narrow section where iron chains had been bolted to the rock to be used as handrails. Despite the physical difficulty of ascending the section with the chains, I knew the biggest challenge we'd face on this trail would be jockeying for space in the crowds of tourists. Surely, that was more of a danger than the walking itself. We jumped off the shuttle and were among the first people on the trail. In the morning shade, temperatures were quite comfortable. But as the sunlight crested over the canyon rim, we got toasty pretty fast.

We flew up the chained section, as it was much less treacherous than I'd imagined. I met my goal of not using the chains for the entire hike up and back. Aaron, less comfortable with heights and exposure, grabbed onto them in certain spots. We enjoyed the view from the top and returned to the trailhead before 10 am. I couldn't believe how hot it was already getting. For the remainder of the trip, we'd have to be sure to drink plenty of water and be diligent about sun protection.

As we drove between parks in Southern Utah, I passed the time by leafing through my Zion and Bryce Canyon guidebook. I noticed a chapter in the back of the book dedicated to Capitol Reef National Park. Capitol Reef? What's that? As I read through the hike descriptions and glanced at our road-trip timeline, I started to think. Maybe we could make a quick detour and check the park out. As we turned northeast, towards the park, I read the hike descriptions a little more closely. Lower Muley Twist Canyon: fifteen miles long; a scenic walk through a remote desert canyon. I was sold. All I had to do was convince Aaron, and he did not take that much convincing.

The miles ticked away as we oohed and aahed over the epic scenery in Muley Twist Canyon. Massive rock walls towered over us. Pretty spring greens dotted the sandy desert wash. We raced from one cottonwood tree to the next in order to cool off beneath their broad canopies. Insects, birds and lizards also used this strategy; we saw wildlife at nearly every tree oasis. In some places, the huge canyon walls overhung ever so slightly, creating slivers of precious shade under their roofs. Entering those solemn spaces offered a more extended respite from the sun. The only water in the canyon sat in dank, still pools carved out of the rock by ancient geologic forces. Those water pockets provided drinking holes to the animals living in the hostile desert environment.

Pure silence filled the air. In nearly eight hours of hiking, we only saw two people. In a National Park. Pinch me, I thought. The toughest part of that long hike was the last five miles. By the afternoon, the sun was indescribably hot. We'd exited the shelter of the canyon and had to cross open desert with almost no shade until we reached the car. We sucked down all the water we had and made it back to the parking lot on fumes. The heat can really take a lot out of you.

By hiking in various places in all four seasons, I've learned a lot about how to prepare for various weather conditions. I have come to respect the different types of weather phenomena and am now able to manage my needs on the trail by wearing the right clothing, bringing the right supplies, and choosing the right hikes. In the process of my all-weather adventuring, I believe I've become more resilient and better able to adapt to changing and unexpected situations. As a bonus, I've had opportunities to cherish the unique beauty of rainy beaches, snow-frosted deserts, sun-baked meadows, and wind-swept mountainsides.

7

Finding My Way

We were twelve miles into a nineteen-mile day. The sun was getting lower in the sky. We lost the trail, got our feet wet crossing a stream, and started getting short with each other. We argued over which way the trail went. Someone whacked his head into a tree and started bleeding. We got mired in a beaver bog. And the sun finally went dark. We were lost.

Nine hours earlier, I met up with a hiking buddy and his longtime hiker friend. Both men were experienced in the outdoors, and while they had planned an ambitious agenda, I had complete faith that everything was under control. It was winter on a remote peak in the White Mountain National Forest.

We followed a mixture of marked and un-marked routes to the base of a rockslide that provided entry to one of the forty-eight highest peaks in the state, Owl's Head. We reached the summit after carefully picking a path up snowy rocks in our snowshoes. It took even more time to get back down, however, since the warm sun had turned the snow into a Slip 'N Slide. Somewhat behind schedule, we watched as the sun slid towards the horizon. We decided we should stick to official trails on the way back instead of following our tracks through the forest. Unfamiliar with all the trail sections, we got confused when the obvious trail disappeared into a tangle of fallen trees. That, combined with multiple stream crossings and the darkening sky, got us completely lost in the woods. From my January 13, 2006 journal entry:

I felt an uneasiness in the pit of my stomach. I had just come along for the ride; I had no idea where we were or where we had to go. I'd completely put my faith in my partners' skill and preparation. What was I thinking? And what do I do now?

We walked back and forth, retracing our steps. The arguments between my two partners became more panicky. They pulled out the map and argued some more. I imagined myself looking down upon the scene from a third-party perspective. What information could I gather to help us get out of this situation? I was no good at navigation. I felt like I had nothing to offer. I also felt helpless and stupid. How could I have let myself get into this mess? And then I noticed something.

It seemed that the one thing they could both agree on is that if we headed south, we'd run across the trail. South, south . . . Which way was south? I did not want to backtrack anymore, so I liked the idea of choosing a direction. But one of the men insisted that we'd have to cross the bog to go south and that would be dangerous, if not impossible. We'd get soaking wet and cold at best, and get completely stuck at worst. I pulled out my compass while they were quarreling about it. I knew how to read a compass!

According to the compass, south went through the trees, away from the bog. I felt compelled to speak up. I'd had enough drama for one day. I spoke with confidence that we'd have to walk into the forest to go south. And I showed them my compass to prove it. Not five minutes after we started walking south we came across an old road, which led to the relocated trail.

Getting lost at night with two experienced hikers was not fun. I was surprised at how I was able to remain calm and take control of a rapidly deteriorating situation. I didn't know I had that in me. Comically, my two companions totally downplayed our predicament for the remainder of the hike! I learned a few things from this experience.

First, it was my responsibility to plan ahead and prepare. Instead of leaving all the trip planning to my partners, I could have looked at the map before our trip, becoming familiar with the layout of the trails. I also could have paid closer attention during the hike in so that I would recognize landmarks and trail junctions on the way out. Sure, that would have been difficult information to use in the dark, but I think I would have been more place oriented if I had. Second, it was my responsibility to pack emergency gear for spending an unplanned night in the woods. Fortunately, it did not come to that, but it is not difficult to imagine how one small thing could have led to a much different outcome. What if my partner had sustained a more serious injury when he hit his head? What if one of us had become hypothermic after getting wet in the creek? What if we couldn't resolve our position in the woods until the sun came up in the morning? I did not have supplies to make shelter for the night.

Luck certainly played a role in the outcome of that scenario. We are not in as much control as we think we are. And because of that, it is important to be prepared for unexpected situations. Winter hiking presents more uncertainty and challenge than summer, which I would learn more than once.

Outdoor recreation in winter presents additional navigation obstacles. The weather can turn quickly. Places that are familiar in dry, summer conditions can appear completely foreign when covered in snow. This quickly became apparent during my first winter of hiking. In March 2006, a friend and I hiked out to Arethusa Falls in New Hampshire. We had to abandon our original plan because of the icy conditions and our lack of appropriate footwear. Without a map or compass we had difficulty finding a new route on the fly, so our day ended up shorter than we'd planned. We walked around in a disoriented state for a while before locating the trail back to our car. Fortunately, we hadn't made it too far before realizing we were ill prepared. Lesson learned.

From the beginning, navigation was a challenge for me. I remember hiking with my dad, who seemed to have a sixth sense about where things were. Even when we were driving around, he always knew how to get from A to B. As the roads twisted and turned, I lost all sense of direction, but he remained on track. I felt like the navigation center in my brain had failed to develop, since it just did not come intuitively to me.

When I hiked alone, I had many opportunities to practice and improve my route-finding skills. In November 2005, I took a casual walk up Mt. Chocorua in my beloved White Mountains. There are several trails on this mountain that converge into a confusing web of paths near the mountain's slabby summit. The rocks in November were covered in wet leaves near the trailhead and ice as the trail emerged from the trees. The ice provided less friction, so I was glad to have my Yaktrax with me.

Because I'd gotten a late start, I found myself chasing daylight coming down the mountain. The last mile or so, I hiked by headlamp. On the Piper Trail, I noticed tiny reflective pegs nailed into the trees that marked the way out. They shone brightly in the beam of my headlamp. The painted blazes were hard to see, so the reflectors were very helpful. I'm not sure how I would have been able to stay on track otherwise.

That hike was a big challenge for me. I found my mind wandering to curious places as I walked alone in the dark, guided only by the occasional gleam from the marked trees. I swore I heard voices in the woods. At one point I looked up at the trail ahead of me and thought I saw a man pushing a stroller. I blinked and the image was gone. Solitude mixed with fear is a powerful combination.

And while I was glad I allowed myself the opportunity to find my way alone, I knew I had a long way to go from being *proficient* to being *confident* in my navigation skills.

On a dreary February day in 2007, I joined the legendary Don Nelsen and some others on an off-trail mission to Cable Falls. Much of our hike involved hiking up and down steep, muddy social trails through a thick forest in search of hidden waterfalls. There were a few creek crossings, some snow and lots of rain. It was classic type 2 fun. I followed Don and the others closely, watching their step choices and listening in on their navigation discussions. I figured that learning how to find my way through the woods would involve a combination of book learning, mentorship and field practice. On this trip I had the opportunity to accompany a seasoned hiking veteran in his backyard playground and learn from him.

Later that fall I hiked up Cooper Spur on Mt. Hood with a

trusted friend and navigator. I bungled the directions right from the get-go, so we hiked thirty minutes steeply uphill in the wrong direction. Rather than retracing our steps to the last junction and fixing our mistake, we decided to hike cross-country towards our destination. On the way back, my partner wanted to chart a course navigating by compass instead of using the trail. That made me really nervous, but I went with it anyway and we arrived at the trailhead unscathed. I knew I still had a lot to learn about navigating in these mountains because being off-trail felt scary to me — I felt my heart race and my anxiety swell. My mind focused on all the things that I didn't know or recognize. My partner, on the other hand, was at ease. He had the skills and the confidence, aware that we were on the right path. I saw that and wondered if I would ever reach that point — to be able to walk calmly in the unknown with full faith in my ability to chart my own course.

Many of my off-trail adventures would be solo endeavors, however. In May 2007, I planned a hike to an old fire lookout site in Central Oregon on top of Horsepasture Mountain. I didn't intend it to be an off-trail hike, but lingering snow left me searching for trail signs for most of the day. While the hike was technically on a trail, I found myself using backcountry navigation skills to stay on route.

If you've never tried to walk on a snowed-over trail before, it might not seem that hard. But picture this: You're walking alone on a trail. How do you know it's a trail? Looking down at your feet, there is a clear brown path leading forward into the forest and backward to the trailhead. Take a step. The ground is hard, packed down by thousands of feet before you. Now step off the trail. Something is wrong. Your foot sinks into the soft moss and vegetation covering an untrodden forest floor. You quickly step back on the trail. Raising your head you can see the brown path weaving between the trees. Your body moves freely, with branches and shrubs trimmed back to provide a tunnel through the wilderness.

As you continue hiking you begin to notice patches of snow on the ground. Boot prints in the snow help guide you along the rapidly disappearing trail. The boot prints stop; you keep on going. Before long, you look up and the trail is no longer visible. Each gap between the trees looks like a path. You turn your head behind you; you can see your prints in the snow. Turning forward once more, you've really lost your sense of where the trail leads. Does it follow a straight line? Does it curve slightly to the right, between that tall tree and the stump? Or does it angle down and to the left, following the little creek? A sense of unease begins to rise in the pit of your stomach.

Pausing for a long moment, you focus on taking deep breaths. It's time to look for clues. Over there, you see a branch that appears to have been cut with a tool, not snapped in a storm. That's promising. Taking a few steps in that direction you notice a few more cut branches. So far, so good. Now your vision begins to soften. Subconsciously your eyes scan right to left, trying to extract relevant information from the noise. On the surface of the snow you notice a slight depression about the width of a trail. Surely that indicates you're on the right track. You become a little more confident but not overly so; it's too early to claim victory.

Wanting more confirmation, you pull the map out of your backpack. (Oh hey, you, good job for carrying a paper map!) You rotate the map, aligning it with your current direction, and find your last-known location. Based on how far you've come since then, you guess your approximate location and try to match what you're seeing in the real world with the topographic lines and features on paper. You can see that you'll hit a trail junction in about a quarter of a mile. Feeling a boost of confidence, you keep scanning the area for clues, following small hints of a trail as you walk at a fraction of your normal pace. Then, as you come around a large cluster of trees, you see it: a trail sign!

Using those strategies, I made my way to the top of the mountain, finding debris that was left after the fire lookout was destroyed in 1965. After poking around a bit I also found the little USGS summit marker. Seeing the marker was a sure sign that I'd reached the actual highpoint. The clouds parted for a quick summit celebration, and I was glad that I'd persevered through the deep snow and navigation challenges on my own. It would have been so easy to turn back. I would continue to stubbornly plot summit adventures in snowy conditions year after year. I actually grew to enjoy the hunt for summer trails under winter's blanket.

In May 2012, I set out to find another Central Oregon highpoint. Most of the high elevation trails were still buried under feet of snow, but I decided to take my chances at the Tumble Ridge trailhead near Detroit Lake. From there, I surmised, I could make it to the top of Dome Rock. I'd never been up there before, but I was in the area and figured I'd give it a try.

The trail started off very spring-like: snow-free and lined with early season flowers. I ascended rapidly uphill. Eventually, though, I ended up mired in snow. The trail signs in front of me did not match the information I had in my hiking book. Footsteps went off in unexpected directions. I went this way, then that. I thought back to previous feelings of being lost, except this time I was alone.

At least I had plenty of daylight and clear skies. I picked an upward direction and started walking. As I climbed I felt less and less certain that I was on the right track, but I pressed on anyways. After some struggle I made it up to a snow-covered clearing and dropped my pack. I sent a SPOT "OK" signal so I could check my location on the map when I got home. I had no GPS to see where I was.

SATELLITE MESSENGERS

The SPOT device is a one-way satellite messenger that allows users to transmit their location to family and friends at home. It also allows users to request help from Search and Rescue, all at the touch of a button.

This device gives hikers and their families peace of mind when traveling outside of cell reception.

Other satellite messenger devices include the Garmin InReach (which I began using in 2020) and Zoleo from Blue Cosmo.

At that point I'd all but given up on the hike. Despite *not* reaching the top, I sat and ate my summit brownie, a treat I carried to celebrate victory. I enjoyed a bit of shade and the occasional brush of wind as I pondered my situation. I noticed at the edge of my peripheral vision a rocky peak that was possibly Dome Rock. As I fixated on the peak, I tried to convince myself that it was too far away and I could not get there navigating through the trees. I packed up and retraced my steps until I stumbled across a sign of the trail. Walking along the now seemingly obvious trail, I popped out at the same place I'd veered off-trail on my way up in no time at all. Utterly confused, I dropped my pack again and started building a 3D topographical model of the surrounding area in my head. I could not resolve the incongruence between the book, the sign, and the land I was physically standing on. Some piece of information was wrong, and I knew the ground beneath my feet was the only thing guaranteed to be right. I took some deep breaths and gave it one more shot.

I know that I usually overestimate how far and how long I walk when I get "lost," so I adopted a strategy of taking pictures of certain geological features so I would have an objective measure of time. I followed my snowshoe prints back to the last spot that I knew for a fact was the actual trail. Then, I stopped to take my time-stamped picture and think rationally.

Originally, I had been thrashing around in snowshoes because I thought they would provide some flotation and support on the snow. However, the slushiness of the snow combined with constant side-hilling made the snowshoes a hazard, so I took them off and strapped them on my pack. By not wearing snowshoes, I could also be assured that I would not mix up my old tracks with my new ones. Besides, the deep footprints were much easier to see in the snow, so I could leave a breadcrumb trail to follow on the way back. I made one last attempt to progress from the confusing trail sign to the summit.

I occasionally noticed small rectangles of pink paint on trees along the trail. That, combined with some occasional pink or yellow flagging and the usual signature tree cuts made by trail crews, provided enough evidence to piece together the trail bit by bit. It was slow going and methodical, but I finally felt like I was making progress, and I no longer felt the anxiety of being lost. When I reached tricky spots where I thought I'd have difficulty seeing the trail upon my return, I dug my heel into the snow, carving big arrows pointing back the way I came.

At last I reached a tree with a sign that read "Dome Rock." The carved letters were so weathered that the sign was barely legible. The tree had grown over the entire upper lip of the sign. At that point, I had only half a mile to go, in some direction beyond the sign. Again, I carefully observed my surroundings. Soft, relaxed eyes did the trick. I spied the spur trail and a bit of pink tape just to the right of the main trail. Walking uphill I saw what appeared to be a well-defined ridge with nothing but blue sky beyond. I was lured up to the ridge, where I caught a view of the summit pinnacle. From there it looked like a straightforward walk up to the summit rock formation. I bobbed between the trees along the ridge after deciding the unpredictable cliff-top cornices were too dangerous for me. Once I saw a vertical rock wall ahead of me and an obvious ramp to my right, I knew I was back on the trail. Switchbacking up the rock, the anticipation built up inside of me like a popcorn kernel ready to explode. I flew up one last steep snow-covered slope, cresting the rocky top to be surprised with a spectacular 360-degree view. I was so excited that I'd found the place I'd worked so hard to get to, and the views were incredible.

Navigating through the snow does present its own challenges, but I like a good puzzle. Following an unmarked trail in the winter is kind of like going on a scavenger hunt. Looking for clues, it is possible to stay on track and find the prize at the end.

In December 2008, the Columbia River Gorge got slammed with a huge snowstorm. That was quite unusual for the area, so I headed out with a friend to see it in its white winter coat. We began at Wahkeena Falls, hiking up a snow-covered trail towards Devil's Rest. It was all so unfamiliar. Where were the lush ferns, green tree branches and damp moss? Where was the flowing water? The greenery was heavily flocked with snow and the water had mostly frozen to ice. It was like walking into an alternate universe.

Someone had hiked the trail before us. We followed their tracks all the way up to a viewpoint overlooking the Gorge, where the tracks disappeared. We navigated by GPS to Devil's Rest, stopped for lunch and enjoyed a lunch break. The return hike was easier, following our footsteps back to the car. It would take me some years before I would become comfortable using a GPS. Out of a combination of stubbornness and an unwillingness to be tethered to technology, I preferred using a map, compass and environmental clues to travel across the landscape.

In May 2011, I took my friend Sue on a hike to Henline Mountain and Henline Falls in the Willamette National Forest. May is a tricky time of year when it comes to snow cover. The trails can be easily navigable or totally snowed in, depending on the snow accumulation and weather patterns in a particular year. We had hoped the elevation was low enough that we'd avoid snow, but as luck would have it, we were wrong.

It looked promising at first, but as we gained elevation we saw that trouble was coming. Snow started appearing in patches, but it soon gobbled up the trail and everything around it. We kicked side-steps into steep snowfields. The snow had the consistency of snow-cone ice. We followed what appeared to be the trail as it wound itself up and around the mountain. Since it was my first time there, I was a bit disoriented. Eventually, I grew tired of trying to follow the trail, so we decided to make a beeline towards what we thought was our destination.

We angled directly up the slope, using snow steps, tree belays, and careful walking over forty-five-degree vegetation and dirt. My eyes settled on a wickedly cool rock ridge; we followed the ridge on rocks and snow until the trail magically appeared again. Taking the path of least resistance, we continued along our trek. In places, the snow formed a perilously thin and slushy layer over huge holes, created by heat radiating from the rocks below. I poked test holes with my hiking poles as best I could so we could travel safely. I had far more practice doing stupid stuff like wallowing through snow-covered terrain than Sue, so I took charge of finding the best footing and making nice snow steps.

After much bumbling around, we ultimately arrived at our summit, which was entirely surrounded by fog. Was it worth the effort? To me, it was. Completing a planned itinerary in spite of unforeseen obstacles filled me with a sense of accomplishment and pride. The views are never expected, but always appreciated. To Sue, well, she kept coming on my adventures, so I assume she had a good time too.

The following April we hiked in the Gifford Pinchot National Forest in Southwest Washington. We planned to complete a ten-mile loop hike with over 2,500 feet of elevation gain. In other words, it was a typical weekend outing. The hike started on clear, dry ground on a foggy, cool day. As we climbed higher and higher on the ridge, we hit some snow patches that ultimately turned into broad snowfields that completely covered the forest floor.

Up until we reached the junction with the logging road, Sue and I were able to follow the occasional pink ribbon in the trees and old footprints in the snow. We never felt like we got that far off track. At a trail junction, however, the footprints disappeared. We searched the woods for any sign of a trail, looking for cut branches and depressions in the snow. I found myself saying things like "this looks trail-y," and so the two of us kept moving forward in hopes of completing the loop. At that part of the hike, a logging road essentially paralleled the trail. Using the road as a handrail, we had some sense of where we were.

But once we left the safety blanket of the logging road behind, it became a search for sawed tree limbs and a logical path through the snow. I walked ahead in fits and starts, keeping the ridge to my left, rushing forward when I found a clue and slowing way down when I felt off track. I kept checking back with Sue for confirmation that it felt like we were going the right way. Since I had forgotten to pack my compass, I only had the hand-drawn map in the hiking book to guide us. Our amicable conversation paused during that miserable section of the hike. I think we were both bemoaning the challenging nature of walking in unpredictable and unforgiving snow as well as not being entirely certain of where we were or how far we had traveled.

NAVIGATION TIP: USING A HANDRAIL

Navigation without a compass or GPS is an art. By using context clues, you can often find your way.

A handrail is a geographical feature that is aligned in such a way that it can help keep you on track. For example, if you're hiking to a lake, you might be able to use an outlet river as a handrail—keep the river to your left and follow it all the way to the lake. Mountain ridges, cliffs, lava flows, meadow edges and roads are all helpful navigational handrails.

Miraculously, and after what felt like many hours of carefully following faint trail clues along the wooded slopes, we made it back to solid, dry ground. We rejoiced as our soggy feet and tired muscles settled back into easy walking on an actual trail. By paying close attention to our surroundings and working together patiently, we'd managed to stay on track and end up right where we needed to be to complete the loop hike.

Over time, I really began to enjoy hiking off-trail, route finding and piecing together my own agenda instead of following the same old popular routes. In September 2011, I went into the

Goat Rocks Wilderness in Southern Washington with Sue. Our mission was to climb Old Snowy, a non-technical peak in the Cascades. I also noticed a peak on the ridge that I thought we could add to our route, creating a slightly longer hike. There was no trail linking the two, but figuring out how to get from one to the other didn't look that difficult. I didn't have any specific details from my research besides "follow the ridge from Old Snowy to the summit of Ives Peak."

The route turned out to be surprisingly straightforward. We had to negotiate our way around several large gendarmes, or rock pillars, which looked more challenging to manage than they actually were. Along the way, we came across bits and pieces of climbers' trails and the occasional series of boot prints. There was a considerable amount of loose rock on our route that reminded me of climbing back in Oregon. We essentially followed the ridge as it rose and fell, passing by an interesting rock arch and other notable geological features, until we hit a steep talus slope leading to the base of the summit ramp. From the base of the ramp, we picked up a climbing path to the top. Hiking off-trail is adventurous and fun. It is more challenging than following a trail, but in a good way, a way that makes me use my brain a little bit more.

Most of the time, I'd research the area before an off-trail excursion or mountaineering trip. But I made an exception for Glacier Peak. I tagged along with a couple of people I really wanted to hike with and left the planning up to them.

The climb was supposed to take four days, round trip. My companions had planned to tag the peak and then keep going on a backpacking trek around the mountain. That was too much of a commitment for me, so I decided I'd part ways with the others once we safely descended the mountain, re-tracing the route to the car by myself.

On the first day, we hiked nearly ten miles up to a pass with stunning views of Glacier Peak. We got off to a late start the next morning and began hiking in the heat of the day. From the pass, the PCT dropped over 2,500 vertical feet in five miles. It was depressing to lose that much elevation after working so hard to get up there. We continued through bright meadows and dark forests, along snowmelt trickles and rushing streams. We were on the hunt for the Sitkum Glacier route. We had a couple of maps and a little bit of beta to go on, but no recent trip reports with updated conditions or directions. Regardless, we hiked for several more miles and then began looking for a cairn, a brushy trail, or any other indication of a climbing route. By 5:00 pm, with no route in sight and 3,500 vertical feet of climbing left to get to high camp, we knew our attempt was finished.

> CLIMBING LINGO
>
> Beta: information about a route.

The next morning my friends left to circumnavigate the mountain and I reversed our route towards the road. I tagged a small peak near the pass we'd crossed the day before and camped for one more night before hiking out.

I learned my lesson, yet again: Don't leave all the planning to someone else! The reason we couldn't find the route (I found out later) was because it had washed out years ago. No one went there anymore, for a pretty good reason.

Over the years I've found it helpful to have lists of hikes to work on. I love exploring new places and finding new routes instead of doing the same five hikes over and over again. Barbara Bond's *75 Scrambles in Oregon: Best Non-technical Ascents* has provided a wealth of fun ideas for hikes. In October 2017, I ticked off one of the scrambles in the book: Diablo Peak in the Oregon Outback. The adventure started along a dirt road on BLM land. There was no trailhead and there were no trails in the area. I took a group of hikers out there to experience what real cross-country desert hiking was all about. It was unseasonably warm for late October and we baked in the sun all day long. But it was fun to share the route-finding experience with a mixed group of people. We took turns looking at the route description, finding field navigation markers—like trees, canyons and Jeep tracks— and choosing a path to walk. Some had never done anything like it and gained a new respect for the art of navigation.

The Internet is another source of off-trail route ideas, especially when there are highpoints involved. There's a whole culture of "peakbagging," where the purpose of hiking is to reach the summits of mountains on a particular list. Probably the most well-known of these lists contains each of the fifty states' highest peaks. Other lists, like county highpoints or regional highpoints, are popular goals for truly dedicated peakbaggers.

Websites like *SummitPost.org* provide information on how to get to countless peaks. Since all the content is user-contributed, the quality of information varies from place to place. While researching summits to tag on a road trip through Utah with Aaron, I scanned a map for highpoints near our driving route. During this search, I stumbled across a page for the Silver Island Mountains near Bonneville Salt Flats. I'd never heard of those mountains before, but I quickly fell in love with the photos and descriptions of the area. We ended up spending two days exploring the rugged desert landscape.

One contributor on *SummitPost.org* had added some rough route descriptions to the website, and I chose a few for Aaron and I to explore. We negotiated unmarked dirt roads, rock outcrops, sun-blasted scrublands, and cliffy ridgelines to reach our destinations. Along the way, we discovered relics of explorers past, lots of speedy lizards, unique geology and views that went on forever. I loved walking across open spaces with hardly a road, building or human in sight. By a flickering campfire beneath a sky of endless stars, I wrote:

Today we were explorers. We climbed to two peaks without the aid of a trail. The mountains dictated our route. As we scrambled among colorful boulders striped with veins of agate, we became one with the desert. At the top of our first peak, we stood awestruck at the sight of the massive salt flat below our feet. It was as if we were on the top of a palm tree on a tropical island.

As I turned my gaze to take in the rest of the views around us, I caught a flicker of movement on a ledge below me. There, not thirty feet away, stood a pair of bighorn sheep. The big one, a mother, her dark eyes locking with mine in an intimidating gaze. The small one, an infant, barely able to wobble around on its toothpick legs. I yelled over instinctively to Aaron, "SHEEP!" We watched them for over thirty minutes as they lounged and explored the craggy ledges below the summit of the mountain. They climbed out of necessity, not fun, but I felt a sort of kinship with the pair. And my imagination ran wild with what we might see next.

I cannot overstate the sense of discovery and freedom I feel when hiking off-trail. In April 2018, we wandered off the beaten path in the Valley of Fire State Park in Nevada to escape its mobs of visitors. Our reward included quiet overlooks, beautiful land formations, and perspectives that differed from the photos in the visitor center. We created our own experience instead of mindlessly following in the footsteps of other visitors who came before us.

The previous summer we'd done the same at Steens Mountain in Southeastern Oregon. Hidden in plain sight, far from any developed urban area, the mountainous expanse is a dreamscape that has captivated me since the moment I set eyes on it. But with few developed trails, I wanted to see what I could discover on my own. With some savvy Internet research I stumbled across cross-country route descriptions that only a dedicated planner would ever find. Using those descriptions as a guide, Aaron and I got our own private tour of the Steens' alpine meadows and vistas. We were the only humans we'd see on our exploration.

I have learned that the best strategy for finding solitude is hiking off-trail. As public become more and more popular among tourists, it is a skill I will continue to develop in order to get what I'm seeking when hiking. But lest you get lured into the fantasy that cross-country hiking is nothing but pure delight, I'd like to share a few stories of misadventure.

In the summer of 2017, Aaron and I visited the Oregon Coast to escape the wildfire smoke choking Central Oregon. We were experiencing some cabin fever and were stoked to spend lots of time outside in the clean, coastal air. Turning to my trusty hiking guidebook, I envisioned a loop possibility based on the hand-drawn maps and meticulous hiking descriptions inside. I dreamed up an adventure that would have us ambling across pristine sand dunes with a sweet, ocean breeze caressing our faces as we listened to waves crashing on the shore.

While most of the day unfolded according to plan, I was snapped out of my fantasy when I realized why no loop had been placed on the map where I wanted one: a marsh. No problem, I said, let's just roll up our pants and quickly get across the wet, boggy mess. In no time we'll be on the other side.

Nothing tests a relationship quite like slogging through an

endless quagmire. The shrubs and trees were dense, making it difficult to see ahead or travel in a straight line. The terrain underfoot was a swampy mess, alternating in depth between a couple of inches and sometimes a couple of feet. Branches hid beneath the mucky sand, so we had to step carefully and delicately. By the numbers, the "other side" was not far away. But on the ground, it felt like a universe stood between ourselves and our destination. We slipped into silence, speaking only when necessary to discuss strategy. It took well over an hour to pop out of the wetland, in sight of a trail. Oh, what a relief that was.

I should have known better than to bushwhack at the coast. My first introduction to the joys of coastal off-trail travel was back in 2013. In June, I set out for a solo afternoon day hike while Aaron and his family relaxed at their beach house rental. In my trusty hiking guidebook, I found a ten-mile out and back hike that started at Cape Lookout State Park and traveled five miles down a sandy spit, just to turn around and return the same way. I packed a bag for the hike, took off my shoes and started walking at 1:30 pm.

In no time at all, I reached the end of the spit, read a chapter in a novel and dozed off for about an hour in the summer sun. As I wiped the sand out of my eyes, I thought about making things more interesting by turning my out-and-back adventure into a loop. From the map, it looked like I could walk along the bay on the other end of the spit, then walk across on its narrowest point, returning to the ocean-side beach. Simple. I was surprised that the author hadn't bothered to mention it as an option.

I walked south, through the grassy sand dunes, then cut left towards the shore of Netarts Bay. That side was much different. The low tide exposed expansive mudflats, pockmarked with holes from burrowing sand creatures. Broken scallop shells lay strewn across the ground. It was extremely pretty. I walked along the mud until it got really deep and squishy. Then I veered towards a welcoming grassy field.

The field turned out to be an exquisitely disguised wetland. As I proceeded across, a nearly invisible network of twisted water channels appeared beneath my feet. Some were shallow, water-filled gutters almost wholly covered in thick vegetation. Soon, they became waist-deep, mud-bottomed dugouts that turned far more precarious than they appeared at first sight. Since the grass was tall and bent over easily, the ankle-breaking channels were not easy to see until I was right on top of them. I walked slowly and cautiously, feeling very alone out there.

I looked ahead towards the ocean, which was barricaded by a wall of coastal forest. I looked behind me towards the bay and across the grass, which led to endless mudflats of unknown density and shoe-sucking muck. Not liking either scenario, I walked straight for a little while longer.

Meanwhile, I scoped out any opportunities for crossing back over to the beach through the thick forest. I knew the spit wasn't all that wide, so I could tolerate a little thrashing in order to make it back to the simple ease of walking on the beach. I angled towards the forest.

> ## PLANT LIFE
>
> Salal is an evil, I mean beautiful, evergreen shrub that produces little white flowers in the spring and dark-blue berries in the summer. On the coast, salal forms dense, woody thickets. These thickets are not suitable for safe passage without a bulldozer or machete. Bears and Native Americans ate salal berries for sustenance. Modern gardeners use salal as a decorative shrub. Coastal hikers fear salal for making bushwhacking very, very difficult. (See illustration at chapter start.)

The chest-deep grass led to a giant wall of salal, and I really mean giant. I started bulldozing my way through the impenetrable understory, regretting my choice of wearing a sleeveless shirt and shorts for my "mellow" beach walk. There was no path of least resistance. I could climb over, crouch under, or squeeze through the vegetation. Usually, over and under were not viable options. So I thrashed my way through, and the forest thrashed back. I was fortunate to have encountered very little blackberry or other thorny plants. However, the sticks and needles that dug into my skin didn't feel much better. Every time I paused to reassess my progress, mosquitoes reminded me to keep moving.

After forty-five minutes of that, I found a break in the trees. I happily exclaimed, "I'm back at the beach!" I stepped out of the woods and began traipsing through a tall, wild grassland. As I scampered towards the water, I wondered where the beach was, and if I was looking at the Pacific Ocean. I shouldn't be able to see across to the other side.

Against my better judgment, I neglected to get my compass out during the whole ordeal. Somehow, I'd managed to trace an arc through the trees, ending up back on the *bay* side of the spit. I looked at the time; it was 6:15 pm. I had people waiting for me in town, the clouds were rolling in, and I had no idea how I was going to get out of there.

NAVIGATION TIP: TAKING A BEARING

Here's one simple way to practice using your compass:

Hold the compass flat in your palm. Point the direction-of-travel arrow towards a point of interest (a tree, a house, a mountaintop, etc.).

Rotate the compass housing until the red half of the magnetic needle sits inside the outlined red arrow on the base of your compass.

Read the bearing at the direction-of-travel arrow. That is the direction you'll need to travel to get to your target, no matter how much salal you encounter in the meantime.

To learn this skill, take a map and compass navigation class, read a navigation book or watch lots of YouTube videos. I recommend doing a combination of all three, and practice every single time you go on a hike.

I thrust myself back into the trees. The pain of branches cutting into fresh wounds hurt even more the second time around. But I learned my lesson. I looked at my compass, took a bearing and walked straight, regardless of what lay ahead. I listened for the sound of the ocean, trying to correct the mistakes I'd made previously. I learned to make peace with the salal. I grabbed branches by the armful, pushing them down far enough to get a foot up, then walked on top of the salal until I could find a fallen log or other stable-enough surface to tread on. It was in this part of the forest that I encountered the spikiest evergreen trees I'd ever seen. The leaves felt like needles on my skin. I had to take a long-sleeve shirt out of my backpack and wrap it around my hand in order to grab branches without tearing my flesh.

It was slow going. But I just kept listening to the crashing waves, thinking that soon enough I'd be on the soft, cool sand once again. About half an hour after my forest re-entry, I reached that blessed sand. After making a quick phone call to Aaron letting him know I was on my way, I walked, jogged and ran up the beach to get back before sunset.

Can you see a pattern? I often found myself in those situations because I tried to craft a loop in terrain that did not facilitate a loop. I knowingly strayed from the maps and maintained trails to craft an adventure route of my own. In each of these calculations, I'd neglected one important thing: why no trail existed where I wanted one. Surely, if it made sense to build a trail there, then someone would have already built a trail. Instead, trails are built in places where it makes sense to do so. In trying to be clever, I put myself into difficult places that took much more time and effort to navigate than I accounted for. However, it is still possible to get disoriented and off-track when following (what you believe to be) an accurate map.

In September 2013, I noticed an interesting loop to Donaca Lake in a hiking guidebook. The hand-drawn map linked the current trail with some washed-out forest roads, returning to a logging road near the trailhead. Aaron had fond memories of doing trail work near the lake as a teenager, so he was happy to join me on this adventure.

Our journey began by first negotiating a maze of gravel forest roads to reach the trailhead. Once there, we walked on rarely used trails in the Middle Santiam Wilderness. The softness of the trails and the amount of brush encroaching on them signified that not many people had explored the area recently. The forest was lush and green and bursting with life. We reached the lake and explored its edges, including a rotting nurse log that had fallen into the lake. An entire ecosystem had developed on the log; I wondered how long it had been lying there. After lunch we headed back down the trail, looking for the alternate return route described in the book.

We turned onto an old forest road from the trail. The road had been reclaimed by the forest over the last few decades, giving it an eerie, post-apocalyptic vibe. Moss covered the old gravel surface. Blackberry runners streamed across the mossy coat, forming a loose mat of green vines. Trees grew over the road's edge, subtly in some places and boldly in others. As we continued along the old road, we enjoyed the soft carpet of greenery. It made walking especially easy and pleasant.

We came to a creek crossing where a concrete bridge had been removed, leaving what looked like a giant diving board on the other side. We dropped down to the water's edge, changed into water shoes, and waded across. From there, things got interesting.

We continued along the road for a little while longer, crossing a bridge over the Middle Santiam River. After that, the road narrowed and became more difficult to follow. At some point, we picked up a new trail that led us through the worst of the washed-out sections. Although this trail wasn't on our map, we figured it must lead the way out. We followed the trail until we popped out, surprisingly, at a well-manicured trailhead parking area. We found a Forest Service signboard with a wilderness permit box and a few miscellaneous signs. However, there was no name on the signboard or map to indicate where we were. It was not the same place we'd left the car; the parking lot was empty.

We followed the unmarked gravel road leading out of the parking area to another, nicer-looking gravel road, but again, there were no signs telling us where we were. Daylight was fading, we had no idea where the car was, and we were lost *on a road*. We had two choices, left or right. By our estimates and the compass direction, we guessed right.

We took off, quickly walking down the road, looking for any clue as to our location. We noticed a milepost marker, some large brush piles along the road, a few spur roads leading off the main drag, and nothing else. We walked for over a mile, with no success in finding our vehicle. "Well, maybe just a little further, around the next bend," we said over and over again. Ultimately, we decided we chose the wrong direction, and turned around.

The temperature was dropping fast. We were getting tired of road walking, and all I wanted was to eat dinner. We passed by the spur road to the mystery trailhead where we first knew we were lost, and kept going. We had to be on the home stretch.

Finally, we reached a road junction and sign that we recognized. Half a mile later, we collapsed at the car. Luckily, we had made it before dark.

Despite the occasional misadventure, I am still drawn to unusual routes, off-trail navigation and off-season outings. Even when my crazy ideas don't go according to plan, I always learn a thing or two about planning, hiking, decision-making or navigation. And when things do go right, I remind myself that all of my misadventures have taught me a lot about exploring the land, which is why I can confidently go out and satisfy my curiosity today.

8

Unique Experiences

The snow kept coming down outside my bedroom window. It was February 2014, and we were having an unseasonably snowy winter in Corvallis. Sixteen inches of powder covered the ground and more was on the way. It was a once-in-a-lifetime opportunity to see the local area in true winter conditions. I was thrilled; I knew that the time was golden to create a snowshoe route that linked up several trails, roads and parks into one epic adventure.

I asked Aaron to drop me off at a parking lot downtown, where I could begin my trek along a bike path. Having walked that path many, many times, it was fun to explore it in the snow.

I saw footprints and ski tracks, signs that other people were similarly inspired by the winter weather.

I snowshoed along the path, stopped into a coffee shop, and continued towards Bald Hill. It was there that I'd tag a highpoint, which always put a smile on my face. (It helps that my definition of highpoints is very broad, including hills, buttes, peaks, mountains and any point on the map that is higher than the land around it). There were plenty of people out and about, but most of them stuck to the paved trails below the hill. I struck out on a trail leading up to the summit, where steady snowfall obliterated my hope for a view from the top. Disappointed, I trekked back downhill to seek shelter and eat a snack. Next, I walked across the closed campus of Oregon State University, where even more people were out for a stroll. Everyone was grinning as they ventured through the fluffy snow. It made me happy to see so many people getting outside just for the fun of it.

I take walks in the city all the time, and I would not consider tracking them for the *Hike366* project. But that walk felt much more like a *hike* due to the snow conditions and the fact that I covered almost eighteen miles in one go.

When I think about all the hiking I've done, I'm intrigued by the breadth of experiences that I've had along the way. In this chapter, you'll be transported to a variety of these unique places and times. Whether I'm hiking in the city or among unusual geological formations, walking by moonlight in the evening or just catching the morning's sunrise, one thought always comes to mind: "This is a truly unique adventure!"

Hiking in urban spaces is one way to have a grand adventure without taking a big vacation. When you look past the shops, highways, crowds and noise, you will often find pockets of nature and interconnected trails. Those green spaces provide excellent opportunities to see a city in a novel way. Since many people don't consider city walks "hikes," I've put them into the category of "unique experiences." Included are several of my city walks that took place during unique times, such as the snowshoe walk just described. But you can conjure up an interesting urban hike in any conditions, any time of year.

How? Pull up a map of your local area and see what nooks

and crannies you haven't explored yet. Or choose a nearby city that is unfamiliar to you and plan a way to see it on foot. Pick a few points and play "connect the dots." You might be surprised what you discover along the way.

The city of Corvallis has several small parks worthy of exploration. It took this project to coax me into exploring more deeply a park that I thought I knew well. For years, I'd taught fitness classes at Martin Luther King Jr. Park three times a week, but we used the same area for every class. After poring over the city map, I realized there were trails all over the park that I hadn't explored.

In November 2015, I broke out of my rut. I started up a trail just to see where it went. That trail led to another trail. And that led to faint side paths. Fallen trees. Mushrooms. Deer bones. Colorful leaves. I wandered with no particular destination or route in mind. The park was small, so I wasn't worried about getting lost or going too far out. I was having a nature adventure.

That day, I realized that all it took to find a new place to hike was a mindset shift. I had to look no further than my own backyard to discover a new place to go. It also meant relinquishing a little control, something that I struggled with at first. I almost always showed up to a hike with a precise map and plan of what I intended to do. Walking without a fully developed plan broke all my hiking rules. I also realized through this experience that cities offered excellent hiking opportunities. Martin Luther King Jr. Park was right in the heart of Corvallis. I didn't have to commit to visiting a remote wilderness to have a meaningful outdoor experience.

A short drive out of town a month later brought me to the neighboring city of Albany. Albany is not well known for its outdoor recreation opportunities, but I'd heard good things about one park: Talking Water Gardens. On a dreary, gray December day I stepped foot into this park for the first time and it was delightful.

Talking Water Gardens is a manufactured wetland that's designed to "naturally" treat water before it flows back to the Willamette River. The park provides a space for native plants and animals to thrive. It helps decontaminate wastewater while converting a formerly industrial area into a natural space. Despite its function as a wastewater treatment facility, it's absolutely beautiful. It was teeming with bird life while I was there. While

I walked along the paths, I stopped frequently to look around, enjoying feeling like I was a part of nature. I completely forgot that I was in a city of over 50,000 people.

On the other hand, some cities are made for hiking. Bend is one of those cities; the twenty-mile long Deschutes River Trail runs right through the center of town. Other hiking and biking trails exist throughout the many parks of the city. In January 2017, I decided to take advantage of another heavy snowfall to concoct a hiking adventure across Bend.

I began from my house, traveling south on a mixture of shoveled and unshoveled sidewalks towards downtown until I could pick up a section of trail that would take me into a less urban part of the city. Following the Deschutes River, the trail entered a beautiful scene. Snow-covered ponderosa pines towered over the river. Ice clung to the river rocks. The air was quiet, save for the sound of water tumbling along beside me. The further I got from the center of the city, the fewer footprints I saw ahead of me. I walked and walked until I remembered that at some point, I needed to head back towards home.

As I re-entered the city, with streets and cars and nowhere to walk, I noticed I was not as relaxed as I was during my stretch in the woods. The walking paths on the city portion of my journey were not cleared for pedestrians, and cars were splashing through puddles of melted snow, sending ice-cold water hurtling towards me. It didn't feel like a safe place to be. I ducked into a coffee shop for a hot beverage to keep my spirits up for the remainder of my walk. All I could think about was a hot shower and a fresh set of dry clothes. Urban winter hiking is not always loads of fun, but on that day it sure beat staying home and shoveling the driveway.

In February 2018 I set off on a solo adventure through Dry Canyon in Redmond, Oregon. Like the Deschutes River Trail in Bend, the Dry Canyon Trail cuts through the middle of town, following the bottom of, wait for it . . . a dry canyon. The path bisected several parks with ball fields, a disc golf course, a climbing area, playgrounds, dog parks, and natural spaces. I enjoyed seeing the character of the trail change as I walked from one park to the next. There were all sorts of people enjoying the parks and using different sections of the trail. I was impressed that someone had the foresight to make the entire geological feature a public space that everyone could enjoy.

In 2016, Aaron and I spent some time exploring the parks and forests in Hawaii. But on the island of Kauai, we were rarely very far from a resort or developed land, like on our adventures near Shipwreck Beach. Our escapade began in Po'ipu, a town expanded on to accommodate tourists looking to relax at a beach-front resort, eat at expensive restaurants and go shopping. It was also a perfect place to go hiking.

Following driving directions from an old Hawaii guidebook that happened to be in our hometown library, we drove up a series of gravel roads to a pullout where we parked the car. With no particular trail to follow, we headed towards the ocean. The rest of the day we walked across quiet sandy beaches, scrambled over rocks and watched the waves crash into the shore. We saw monk seals, local fishermen and the occasional walker along the way. It was glorious. The blue sky, palm trees and sparkling seawater were so perfect it didn't feel real.

After walking past a golf course, we arrived at Shipwreck Beach, a sea of humanity located a few steps from the nearest hotel and parking lot. We took a quick break and then returned to the car, grateful to have found some peace and quiet among the busy beaches of Kauai.

There are secret pockets of quiet within every bustling city. Later that year I took a trip to New York City to attend a workshop. I found a place to stay in Brooklyn with one of the workshop participants. Since the conference was in Manhattan, I had a long commute on public transit to get there. But the Friday festivities didn't begin until the evening, so I decided to spend the entire day walking across the city. My host was a little flabbergasted by my plan, but despite his disbelief, I set out on foot in the morning.

PRO TIP

Use Google Maps to design your own urban hike.

Do a search for a city of interest to you. Zoom out and look for areas colored green. Pick a few locations on the map and search for directions. Click on the "person" symbol to get walking directions instead of driving directions. (This will sometimes direct you onto paths instead of strictly using roads.) You can also click on the route and drag it to other pathways to customize your trek.

Google Maps will provide the mileage of your route, so you can estimate how much time it will take you. However, their calculated time does not factor in your pace, exploring places of interest, or taking rest breaks. Add more time to the Google estimate to get a better sense of how long it will take you to complete your urban hike.

I geeked out on the map ahead of time, searching for as many green spaces as I could. The route I plotted took me through several unique neighborhoods and parks and over the iconic Brooklyn Bridge. I wove a path across the city that gave me a street-level view of daily life in New York.

One of the highlights was Prospect Park, a huge green space that included a pond, several walking paths, playgrounds and historic buildings. I lingered the longest in Brooklyn Botanic Garden, which contained plants from all over the world growing in one park. Each section of the garden highlighted a particular theme and geographic region. There were also indoor exhibits for the plants that could not thrive in New York City's climate. I admired the incredible diversity of cacti, aquatic plants and unusual trees from all over the world.

While my original plan focused solely on natural spaces, I ended up being the most fascinated by the urban jungle. I noticed how one neighborhood transitioned to the next, with obvious ethnic and cultural differences separated by just a couple of city blocks. I observed how identical row houses each displayed their own unique flair in an effort to distinguish themselves from their neighbors. And I was taken aback by how many people were out and about on foot. Living in a small city with poor pedestrian infrastructure, I wasn't used to seeing many people outside in their neighborhoods. But there, people were walking. They were biking. Riding scooters. Driving. It was loud and vibrant and pulsating and just *so* New York.

I covered over fourteen miles on my journey. My favorite part was walking across the Brooklyn Bridge. I'd admired paintings of the bridge ever since I was a teenage art student, and had not yet seen it in person. I relished the opportunity to step foot on the bridge and gaze up at its beautiful lines and angles.

Who knew New York City could be such an excellent hiking destination?

With an open mind and an insatiable curiosity, you can find special destinations within city limits. But some out-of-the-way places require a bit more tenacity and motivation to discover. Such locations may be found plastered all over the Internet, in books and in magazines; others may be carefully guarded by locals who keep them secret. The following stories take place in a variety of unusual locations, whose special features may be biological or geological.

Unique geological features, like canyons, volcanoes, hoodoos, mountains and waterfalls, have captured my imagination since I was a child. Now they're also a source of inspiration for trip planning. When I see photos or read about places that have their own special character, I enjoy figuring out how to get to them and how best to explore them on a hike or road trip.

On a brisk winter morning, our teeth rattled as we drove down miles of snowy gravel roads to access a remote location in Oregon. I'd convinced Aaron and another friend that this would be a good idea. I checked the directions as we rounded each corner. And then a small dirt parking area appeared. A nondescript brown sign indicated that we had arrived at our destination. Ours was the only vehicle in the lot. We put on our daypacks and started hiking.

I'd been there once before, but the ground was snow-free at the time. The conditions we were about to experience would be much different. We were headed for a narrow fissure in the earth created by the area's tumultuous volcanic past. In the vast, high desert landscape dotted with sagebrush and juniper, the fissure isn't noticeable until you're right on top of it. We walked along the edge of the two-mile long crack, peering down into its depths. In places it was just a few feet deep, filled with brown grass. In other places the crack plunged seventy feet down, its narrow walls creating dead-end caves and creepy, dark crevasses.

We put our explorer hats on and began walking within the walls of the crack. It was so interesting to see it blanketed with snow. We carefully stepped on the angular boulders that lined the desert floor; the snow made things extra slippery.

For hours we checked out side passageways, clambered up and down boulders and followed our curiosity to see where it led. Our hike wasn't about how far we could go or how high we could climb, but about how many hours of adventure we could enjoy. In an age where the data you post on social media proves how much of a badass you are, I was grateful to find a few partners who didn't care about such metrics. Instead, we enjoyed experiencing the wonder of being outdoors with no real agenda.

Inspiration sometimes comes from unexpected sources. A single photo in a AAA magazine piqued my interest in a place I hadn't heard of before: Cathedral Gorge State Park. Located in the middle-of-nowhere, Nevada, I worked a visit to this park onto our spring vacation driving route so that Aaron and I were able to check it out.

Prior to leaving, I did a little bit of research on the park, but I chose to leave some facts unknown. It's sometimes nice *not* to preview all the ins and outs of a place before visiting it. After all, you can only appreciate the elements of surprise and wonder when you're not sure what to expect. We hiked a half-mile interpretive loop on our first afternoon there to get ourselves oriented with the park. Halfway through the loop we saw a sign that read "Cathedral Caves." Curious, we strolled past the sign and into a labyrinthine network of narrow, cave-like structures formed by layers of volcanic ash deposited many millions of years ago.

As I stood in a long mud hallway just as wide as my shoulders, staring up towards a sliver of sky, my mouth gaped open in awe. *That* wasn't in the AAA magazine. No matter how much I travel and how much I see, there's always something completely new to discover on this incredible planet.

The desert offers some of the most remote and fascinating country I've ever seen. Geology comes to life on those desolate landscapes. In 2012, I took a trip to Colorado and spent a day hiking around the Garden of the Gods with a friend. Trails snaked around red rock formations, and the balanced boulders, rock arches and tall cliffs were stunning. I wasn't the only one enthralled by the rocks. Tons of tourists milled around near the major features of the park. Exploring the trails that dove into more remote areas provided us an escape from the noise and busyness near the parking lots.

While touring Utah with Aaron several years later, I drew some parallels between Garden of the Gods and my experience in Bryce Canyon National Park. Bryce Canyon's iconic rock towers drew scores of tourists with cell phones in hand. Every parking area was crammed full of people in flip-flops, stepping outside their cars just long enough to take a photo and then moving on to the next parking area. But something on the map grabbed my attention. It wasn't near the road, but I noticed a trail that passed nearby. "Hat Shop Trail"—it had a funny name, so I wanted to go. We left our car among the crowds and hiked down the trail.

As we walked, my anticipation built. About two miles down, we began to see our destination. The Hat Shop earned its name from a series of orange hoodoos topped with dark gray rocks. Each rock pillar looked like it was wearing a little hat. As we continued down, more capped hoodoos came into view. Beyond the hoodoos, we looked out at the magnificently colorful cliffs of the Grand Staircase. The whole scene was reminiscent of a children's fantasy novel. I imagined magical creatures hiding behind each of the delicate rock towers, just waiting for us to leave so they could scamper around. Along the way, we passed one trail crew and just a handful of hikers. Even in a bustling National Park, it is possible to find peace and quiet among unique natural features.

That was only one of several unusual places we explored in Utah. After many miles of driving down gravel roads in the middle of nowhere, we later arrived at Buckskin Gulch, one of the longest slot canyons in the Southwest. It was an otherworldly landscape. After a short walk in, the canyon appeared to be blockaded by impassable mud. The groups ahead of us had all decided to turn around, warning us about the conditions.

But with curiosity and determination we forged ahead; we

took off our shoes, rolled up our pant legs and waded through the icy water for a chance to see what lay beyond. Although temperatures outside the canyon rose into the 90's that day, we were bundled up in hats and fleece jackets. The canyon was so narrow and steep that sunlight couldn't penetrate its depths. We waded through thigh-deep water that lay stagnant in the cool, canyon bottom. We walked barefoot over pebbles, boulders and sand. We basked in the occasional sun patch when the canyon broadened. We craned our necks upward to admire the sheer, tall cliffs on either side of us. We walked alone in that quiet place for hours without a human in sight.

I've been obsessed with desert landscapes since I first set eyes on them. When I traveled across country from the East Coast to my new home in Oregon, I drove through long stretches of desert. In the South Dakota Badlands, I remember pulling out on the side of the road and walking aimlessly through the rock formations, wanting to see them up close. I didn't have much time to explore, but a few short jaunts from the roadside got me hooked.

I kept finding my way back into the desert. On the last day of 2012, Aaron and I strolled around Fort Rock State Natural Area in Central Oregon, not knowing that a few years later we'd get married there. As we walked through the newly fallen snow, following rabbit tracks through the sage, we were both struck by the beauty of the place. A semicircle of rock formed by volcanic activity, Fort Rock stood tall like a fortress in the high desert. Each nook and cranny in its rock walls looked as if it had been dusted with powdered sugar. The only sounds came from the dried-up shrubs rustling in a gentle breeze.

Across Oregon, there are many treasures to be discovered. As a newcomer, I was determined to step foot in every corner of the state. And still, after living here for over a decade, I know there's much more I need to explore.

In December 2013, Aaron and I took a road trip to Eastern Oregon, where there's more wildlife than people. We stopped at Borax Lake Hot Springs, which was unlike any hot springs I'd seen in the state; the boiling pools were far too hot for soaking. In fact, signs nearby stated: "SCALDING WATER," "GROUND MAY COLLAPSE," "CONTROL CHILDREN AND PETS." We cautiously walked among the pools without getting too close. I was amazed that such a place was open to the public without any walkways or fencing. I felt grateful for the opportunity to see something so wild. As national parks become more and more crowded with visitors, these precious natural wonders have to be fenced off and guarded as if they were displays in a museum. But out there, in wild and rugged Eastern Oregon, you can still venture out at your own risk. I only hope that thoughtless crowds don't start forcing local land managers to restrict access, making the area feel like a zoo.

Much of Oregon's landscape was created by volcanism. Nowhere is that more apparent than at Big Obsidian Flow in the Newberry National Volcanic Monument. In 2007, after climbing a nearby mountain, my friend Kevin and I wandered along a trail cut into the lava flow, reading all the interpretive signs and learning about the area's volcanic past. I got to see huge chunks of obsidian, a black, glassy rock used by Native Americans to make knives and arrowheads. It was something I'd only seen in museums and photos. Observing the rocks in context brought me a greater understanding of the land's geologic past and sparked my curiosity about the native people who once lived there. It was a great introduction to the state I would call home.

But the crown jewel of Oregon's unique places, in my mind, is Steens Mountain in the Eastern Oregon desert. Steens rises over 5,000 vertical feet from the flat desert playa at its base. It is the largest fault-block mountain in North America. At its 9,733-foot summit, you can see flowers that don't grow anywhere else. Unlike many other high mountain habitats, it has no coniferous trees. Surrounded by miles of desert in all directions, it is an unusual landmark in an otherwise desolate locale.

I'd been to the area around Steens Mountain many times, mostly in winter. But it wasn't until 2017 that I decided to make the drive for a summer hiking trip with Aaron. The timing was impeccable; wildflowers were in peak bloom and the weather was warm and sunny. Over three days we drove the loop road that skirted the mountain's summit, swam in an alpine lake, hiked the trails, rambled cross-country and breathed in sweet desert air. The landscape was like none other I'd ever seen in Oregon. I felt like I was driving onto a movie set; it was an oasis of lush mountain life surrounded by dry desert sage in all directions.

I loved every second of my trip to Steens Mountain. Places like that are rare and special. I can only hope that Steens' isolation will protect it from a visitation explosion and increased development.

Oregon isn't the only state with hidden treasures. Earlier

in 2017, I drove down to Southern California for a festival. I decided to pad a few extra days onto each end of the trip so I could break up the long drive by checking out some parks and trails. The timing was just right to see the poppies blooming, so I made a short detour to the Antelope Valley California Poppy Reserve. As I approached the entrance, I couldn't believe what I saw: cars upon cars upon cars. It was like pulling into a crowded ski resort or amusement park! Apparently, word had gotten out about how incredible the poppies were that year.

Since it was a unique event in a unique place, I chose to sit in traffic and wait for my turn to get in. As soon as my feet hit the dirt, I knew I'd made the right decision. There were poppies as far as the eye could see. The hills looked as if they had been painted orange. It was an impossible display of colors, like nothing I'd seen before. Among the Technicolor orange poppies, other flowers put on a show: owl's clover, goldfields, lacy phacelia and many more.

Many lush landscapes are hidden across the California deserts. In 2013, Aaron and I took a trip to Death Valley National Park. While it is well known as one of the driest and hottest places in the United States, it is less known for its grasses, pools and waterfalls!

One of my favorite hikes in Death Valley was to Darwin Falls. That surprising oasis in the desert provided cool shade, running water and a plethora of wildlife. Birds sang. Frogs floated in the water. Raptors built immense nests among the rocky cliffs. It was a haven for people, animals and plants. Compared to the rest of the park, there was so much green. Although the hike was only a couple of miles long, we spent several hours there. Around every corner was a new treasure to explore and celebrate. We found a quiet viewpoint near the upper falls that was free of people, and we just sat there taking it all in. What a magical place.

❦

Below ground, there's even more to discover. Northern California's Lava Beds National Monument contains over 400 lava tubes. About two dozen caves have marked entrances inviting visitors to enter and explore. Once you go inside the caves, however, you're completely on your own. I discovered that in March 2011 while on a road trip with a friend.

Literally all of our plans were ruined by unusually high levels of snow that winter. As we drove, I pored over the maps in the car to see what we could salvage of our trip. I noticed Lava Beds National Monument marked in the road atlas and, having no idea what to expect there, set a course for the park's entrance.

When we arrived, the ground was covered with snow, but the parking lot was plowed and the visitor center was open! We learned that the hallmark destinations were the caves, and the park rangers pointed out a few that we could visit during our stop. The "introductory cave" was developed, with signs and lights, and was really not that interesting to me.

But once we wandered into some of the other caves, I was hooked. The ice formations around the cave openings were quite impressive. Once inside the caves, there were no lights. There were no navigation arrows. There were no signs of human intervention. It was just us, our headlamps and the great unknown. We poked around the caves, learning about the unusual rocks and ice not by reading signs but by investigating with our senses. I left that year with a new appreciation for caves and their potential for adventure.

Several years later, Aaron and I returned to Lava Beds with a little more knowledge and preparation. That time, we bought a book from the visitor center that contained a basic map of the most complex cave system: the Catacombs. The rangers warned us that to explore Catacombs Cave we'd need to bring multiple light sources, be prepared to crawl on our bellies, and budget up to four hours to see the whole thing. Four hours in a cave sounded like a really long time! I was curious and a little nervous, but my experience with park rangers led me to believe that they'd never recommend anything remotely dangerous—the cave couldn't be that bad.

Aaron and I spent some time in a few of the park's other caves before attempting the Catacombs. As we approached the entrance to the cave, we turned on our headlamps, took in one last glimpse of the outside world and then walked down the metal stairs into the darkness below. The features inside the Catacombs were similar to those in the other caves: tooth-like projections dripping down from the cave ceilings, reflective gold spatter covering the walls, broken rock strewn across the floors. But what made that cave different was its network of interweaving tunnels: left, right, up and down. Without a map or a keen eye for features, it would be easy to get disoriented and not know which way was out. That thought alone was terrifying, so we moved slowly in order to stay aware of our location in the cave.

During our adventure we learned how to read a cave map, tested our claustrophobia boundaries and discovered some interesting cave geology. We crawled and dragged and wiggled our bodies through some tight spaces, but I was too freaked out to shimmy through the narrowest corridors. We left half the cave unexplored because of my unwillingness to go further, but the sense of adventure I felt, alone in the darkness of the cave, was something I hadn't experienced in a long time. After two hours in the darkness, we emerged from the cave's opening, delighted and grateful that we took the opportunity to do something really different.

In 2015 we visited another type of cave in Great Basin National Park. That cave experience was entirely different. The Park Service only granted access to tour groups, so we entered Lehman Caves with a ranger guide and a small crew of visitors. Electric lights illuminated the rooms in the cave, so we could see across its vastness. Unlike the basalt caves at Lava Beds, Lehman Caves is made of limestone. Rock formations protruding from the ceiling mimicked the shapes of jellyfish, columns and shields; it was a spectacular sight to behold. Hiking through the caves, I felt transported to another world.

By actually making an effort to explore a few caves for myself, my previous assumption that caves are dark, damp and uninteresting places was shattered. I learned to appreciate the subtle and dramatic beauty hidden inside these underground spaces.

While the subterranean world held many secrets for me to discover, most of the unique places that have drawn my attention are above ground. On a drive across Southern Idaho in 2015, Aaron and I camped and hiked at Bruneau Dunes State Park. The park contains the largest single-structured dune in North America. At nearly five hundred feet high, it is a unique formation to find in the center of a desert basin. Since the local winds blow equally in all directions, the dunes hold their shape over time instead of shifting or eroding away. We arrived at the park just in time to participate in their night sky program. Aaron enjoyed looking at the stars through the telescope, but my mind was busy contemplating a night hike of the dunes. It had become somewhat of a tradition, exploring sand dunes at night. So as soon as he had his fill of the stars, we put on our backpacks and headed for the hills.

It was challenging finding the trail in the darkness. We kept getting mired in thick vegetation at the edge of the pond abutting the sand dunes. But once we made our way through the tangle of shrubs, it was easy-going along the soft sand. That is, the navigation was simple, but it did not feel easy on the legs. For every step we took, we slid half a step back. As the sand slope got steeper, it got more and more difficult to walk forward. Eventually, we were forced to crawl to the top of the biggest hill. After a quiet ridge walk, we ran down the hill, fumbled our way around the lake and crashed back into camp.

Oregon has its fair share of dunes, too. The Oregon Dunes is one of the largest stretches of coastal sand dunes in the world, extending for forty miles along the Oregon Coast. The area is a haven for off-highway vehicle (OHV) riders, hikers and wildlife. I've visited this area several times and each time I've had a different experience.

In September 2014 I took Aaron to some of my favorite spots at the dunes. We hiked on boardwalks and soft sand. I spent most of the day with my shoes tied to my backpack, feet free to explore the sand. Walking barefoot, I felt a real connection to the earth. I noticed the changing textures beneath my feet: dry, wet, coarse, fine. My feet took me across long, smooth pieces of driftwood washed ashore. Under a thick gray sky, Aaron and I walked the beach side by side, not a soul in sight. We watched the waves roll into the shore. As we turned our backs to the ocean, we found bear tracks behind the foredunes. Neither of us had any idea that bears roamed the coast! What an interesting discovery. When you approach a hike with an exploratory mindset, it is easier to see something new. We capped off our journey to the coast with plates full of delicious fresh-caught seafood. I can't not get seafood when I'm at the Oregon Coast.

It is often the prospect of seeing a new and unique natural feature that motivates me to plan a trip. For our 2016 trip to Hawaii, I immediately started planning out some adventures on our chosen islands: Maui and Kauai. Each island has an array of special places that we explored on our visit.

We hit the standard highlights but set aside time to seek

out some less-favored attractions as well. On Maui, we drove the Hana Highway and took a hike on the rightfully popular Pipiwai Trail. The trail terminated at a tall, thin waterfall that was nothing spectacular. (Clearly I've seen my fair share of waterfalls.) But one portion of the walk passed through a dense bamboo forest. The whole place felt manufactured, like we were walking through a cartoon. The tall, thin bamboo creaked and groaned as a gentle breeze blew overhead. It sounded like the whole forest could collapse at any moment. It was strange yet magical, and it was worth braving the crowds to experience that surreal walk.

In Kauai, we hiked along the Na Pali Coast on the famed Kalalau Trail. I think every single person who visits Kauai visits that trail. Much of it was only open to backpackers, so we took the same route that all the other day hikers take: a heavily touristed section from the parking area to Hanakapi'ai Falls. We arrived early so as to see the landscape in a wilder, less crowded state. Along the way we enjoyed spectacular ocean views. The turquoise water to our right seemed too colorful to be real, but the mud beneath my feet and the salty air reminded me that it was not all a dream. The thick tropical trees and flowers growing in all directions made me feel very small and insignificant. The sheer beauty of the place combined with the challenging hiking conditions completely justified the predawn wakeup time.

However, I was shocked by how crowded the trail was on the way back. I did enjoy hiking barefoot through the jungle, seeing the wild and rugged coastline and admiring the crazy trees and plants growing along the trail, but my soul craves solitude. I knew I'd get a better shot at being alone if I found a less well-known hiking area. That desire brought us to Koke'e State Park—a place I'd researched in a guidebook before leaving on our trip—where we drove to the end of the road and ventured out towards Alaka'i Swamp on foot. The hike began on a muddy trail that was deeply rutted with footprints. I laughed a little at how back home in Oregon, land managers warned visitors to stay off muddy trails because it ruined them! Here in Hawaii that seemed to be impossible to do. We slid around in the tacky muck until we reached something that looked like the swamp. Technically a boggy forest, the Alaka'i Swamp was unlike anything I'd seen before. Fog bathed the thick vegetation, giving the area a spooky ambiance. Dilapidated boardwalks crossed the most flooded areas, where building a trail would be all but impossible. Some of the boards were so rotten they sunk into the water as we stepped on them. Uncertain we'd be able to complete the walk without drowning in the swamp, we proceeded cautiously and with a heightened awareness of our retreat options. There were few visitors in that wonderfully dynamic landscape. At last, I'd managed to find an area on the island that wasn't packed with people, which was great because there were no passing zones on those creaky, narrow boardwalks! That unique trail through the bog gave me a great appreciation for the wild areas of Hawaii.

Occasionally, I find joy in visiting places where the main attraction is not natural but man-made. One of those places is the Pont du Gard, a UNESCO World Heritage Site in southern France. The Pont du Gard is a three-tiered aqueduct bridge built in the first century AD to carry water across the Gardon River to the city of Nîmes, and is one of the most complete ancient Roman aqueducts still standing in modern times.

> **LIFELONG EXPLORING**
>
> Want a sightseeing list that will take you a lifetime to finish? Try the list of UNESCO World Heritage Sites. As of 2019, there are 1,092 properties in 167 countries on the list.
>
> I don't think I can even name 167 countries.
>
> Good luck!

When Aaron and I visited, we spent a good portion of the morning chasing trails, "finding" bits of stonework and ruins, and searching for secret viewpoints. A small trail network in a nearby park provided a pleasant way to see the surprisingly stout structure. Eventually, we made our way to a cute little wildflower meadow with excellent views of the Pont du Gard.

One of the best parts of our impromptu exploration was that few other visitors had decided to go exploring. We had our own private hiking trails for hours. The park was full of people, but they mostly remained within a half mile of the gift shop.

After some creative scrambling, we made it down to the river and hopped along the rocks to get a view of the aqueduct's underside. We could hear lots of people on the deck above, but no one was down on the river. Again, it felt like our own special place. The river ran slowly and smoothly. Swallows flitted above our heads, diving in and out of the nests they'd built on the aqueduct. The giant structure provided welcome shade in the heat of the day.

While the Pont du Gard had not been on my to-do list when we planned our travels in France, I now can't imagine doing that vacation without making an effort to visit that site. Sometimes last-minute plans turn out to be the best part of a trip.

What is it about sunrise and sunset that captivates us? Is it the dramatic shift from day to night? Is it the color display? The feeling in the air? The general sense that something is *different* as the sun crosses the horizon? That special something has inspired me to time certain hikes in such a way that I can experience those ephemeral times of day.

In April 2017, I was driving across Southern California and made a stop at the Mojave National Preserve. I knew the hike to the huge dunes would be mobbed with people, so I put off my visit until sunset. Pulling into the parking lot at 5:30 pm, I noticed a few cars in the lot and small groups of people out on the dunes. Most of the groups were heading back towards the parking lot. I started up the biggest dune, making barefoot tracks in the steep sand. Walking slowly and methodically, I stopped to admire the wildflowers, some of which were just peeling open in the evening's cool temperature. An interesting assortment of animal tracks captured my curiosity, and I tried to envision which critters were making which tracks.

As I crested the top of the dune, there was a group of twenty-somethings with cameras and tripods, talking loudly and taking up lots of space. I feared they had the same idea as I did—to watch the sunset before hiking back. I said hello, found my own little perch at the edge of the dune, and within minutes the noise stopped. I looked back and saw that they had gone.

Alone on the dune's top, I nestled into my seat for the big light show. The sun dropping through the clouds created streaks of color across the sky that changed every second. The sand dunes glowed under the light of the setting sun. I held my breath as I looked around me, mesmerized by the one-person concert of light. Just before the sky went totally dark, I ran down the dunes and back to the car, reaching the trailhead at dusk.

Mountaintops make for good sunset viewing too. In August 2017, Aaron and I hiked up Tumalo Mountain, just outside of Bend, to catch the sunset from the summit. 2017 was a horrible year for wildfires in Oregon, and we were really feeling the oppression of the smoke in town. We hoped that at least on the mountain we could enjoy a stunning view as sunlight filtered through the layers of smoke in the air. As we ascended the steep trail, we stopped often to catch our breath. I pulled a bandana over my face to try and filter out some of the smoke particles. By the time we reached our viewpoint, it felt like we were standing in the coals of a fire pit. The smell was strong and the air was thick. We watched the fluorescent orange sun dip down in the sky, waiting for the grand finale. But the sun hit one thick gray layer of smoke and simply vanished, not to be seen again. We'd been robbed of a sunset!

Highpoints aren't the only way to do sunsets. In August 2016 I left town in the evening to take a hike at the beach. I walked on the sand alongside the waves crashing on the shore. I watched in awe as the moon and stars replaced the sun. Darkness crept across the sand, creating mysterious shadows. The beach looked so much different at night. The inky blackness shrunk my world; I could sense the deep abyss beyond my strained vision and felt my isolation more acutely. To break that somewhat uncomfortable feeling, I pulled out my headlamp and used it to help me navigate back to my car. The beach is even more quiet and magical at night than it is in the daytime. The sunset was an extra perk.

Hiking at night has its own special allure. In 2013, while on a Death Valley road trip with Aaron, we drove out to a remote section of the park in order to see some big sand dunes. During the day, hiking the Eureka Dunes would have been unbearably hot. So I was curious to explore the rolling hills of sand at night, when the air was cool and a full moon would be overhead. Well after sunset, we made our foray, barefoot, into the sand.

Words to describe this adventure escape me now, as they did then. Here are some notes from my journal:

Atop the grandest sand dune, we stopped to look all around us. There was a ridge leading out towards the opposite side of the dunes that looked like it might be a little taller, so we ventured out there. Several bumps later, we arrived at the end of the ridge, which dropped down to the dry lake basin several hundred feet below. Here we determined our turnaround point, where we sat for a long time. The adjectives needed to describe how I felt in those long moments have yet to be invented. It was at once surreal, mysterious, serene and blissful. We snacked on gummy dinosaurs as we tried to express to each other just how awesome it was to be there, in the moonlight, together. I'd say this was one of the most unusual and memorable hikes I'd ever had.

Timing a hike for sunrise is a little more challenging because it means getting up extra-early and starting a hike in the dark. But while we were in Hawaii, Aaron and I decided to overcome these obstacles for a chance to watch the sun rise from Sleeping Giant.

Sleeping Giant, also called Nounou Mountain, is a prominent bump on the island of Kauai. Several trails wind their way up to viewpoints near the summit, where a web of user-created trails sprawl out over its insecure, muddy cliffs. On our ascent we encountered several novel things that I would not have expected. For one, the trail was laden with bullfrogs that we had to maneuver around because they sat in complete stillness. They looked out with creepy, staring gazes, as if they were all fixated on some distant point. It was startling at first and then unnerving as we stepped over an endless string of frogs.

Secondly, we struggled to stay on-trail because the tread had washed out in some areas. And finally, since there was no marked route to the true summit, we had to do a little scouting. While there were several other people out there who also wanted to see the sunrise, they were perched on precarious overlooks near the edge of the mud walls. We took the wiser route, situating ourselves on the vegetated, stable and quiet *true* summit. A quick rainstorm blasted across the sky right before sunset, but the colors were even more beautiful than I could have imagined. It was worth the early start!

The simple act of hiking has led me to see a diversity of landscapes in an intimate way. From walking through pockets of forest in New York City to ambling across ancient aqueducts in France to crawling across dark cave floors in California, I have found myself in many places that have challenged my definition of hiking and changed my perspective of the world. I have come to love hiking at unique times, such as sunrise, sunset and after dark, as each of them brings their own charm and surprises. Think about how you define hiking for yourself; chances are you don't even realize what constraints you've constructed. Try dismantling one of your constraints, and let your curiosity open you up to new possibilities.

9

Leave No Trace

The rain poured relentlessly as my partner and I hiked toward our objective. I was dismayed at the state of the trail; it was flooded. In places, the puddles were so deep that I was afraid of getting my feet wet. Sure, I had waterproof footwear, but I didn't want the water to come up over the tops of my boots. I carefully hopped from side to side, avoiding the slightly depressed trail surface. My buddy cut in front of me. "No, like this; walk right down the middle. Don't widen the trail surface!"

"Huh?" I thought. "But my feet!" I watched her happily slosh through the water, stepping on rocks when she could but keeping her feet centered on the trail. I reluctantly did the same.

To my amazement, my waterproof boots did just fine, and I kept my feet warm despite traipsing through the puddles. It never occurred to me that my choice of foot placement could leave an impact on the vegetation outside the trail. I was just trying to keep my feet dry. In that moment, I started to realize that there was more to learn about hiking than I had originally thought.

When I started hiking, I only worried about two things: getting lost and getting caught in the dark. I focused my attention on what I believed were the most important factors that would ensure my safety and enjoyment of the trails. As I accumulated more and more trail miles, talked to hikers of various ages and experience levels, and started to read books about hiking, I became increasingly aware that my choices could affect future visitors. Each partner I had taught me new things about hiking responsibly, and soon enough, I started reading books and articles on how to minimize my impact as well.

As the population grows and more and more people fall in love with outdoor recreation, we each have a responsibility to learn about how to use public land so that our limited resources will be preserved for future generations. I am disheartened when I see photos and videos of people exploiting and abusing the land with complete disregard for our natural resources and other people. At the same time, I am thrilled that so many people are excited about getting outside, being more active and trying new things. I am hopeful that people are willing to learn from their mistakes and will strive to be more mindful each time they visit public outdoor spaces.

Through hiking in various landscapes, taking outdoor skills classes, and reading books and blogs, I have learned what methods of camping and hiking leave minimal impact. Every year, I continue to learn and practice new strategies. On each trip I do my best to apply the seven principles of Leave No Trace (LNT). These principles were established to help arm hikers, climbers, hunters, skiers, kayakers and all other outdoor explorers with the information they need to take care of shared resources. In recent years, I have made it my mission to not only apply the principles myself but also to educate others about LNT.

Principle 1: Plan Ahead and Prepare

The first LNT principle establishes a code of conduct that not only protects the land but also the people recreating on it. When you fail to plan ahead and prepare, there are many things that can go wrong.

In May 2012, I set my sights on the Devil's Peak lookout tower, which would require hiking nine miles from the trailhead and navigating through lingering spring snowpack. I had a plan and a backup plan just in case the snow made route finding difficult. Since I would be hiking alone, I didn't want to risk getting lost.

I got an early start, arriving at the trailhead with a full daypack and a pair of snowshoes. Within a couple of miles I began seeing patches of snow on the trail, and before long, the ground was completely covered. The snow never got very deep, but it was wet and saturated my GORE-TEX shoes with water.

PLAN AHEAD AND PREPARE

- Know the rules and regulations of the area you're visiting.
- Prepare for weather, trail conditions and emergencies.
- Avoid high-use times of year.
- Visit in small groups.
- Minimize waste.
- Know how to navigate with a map and compass.

I walked along in quiet solitude, following the occasional bit of pink tape dangling from tree branches, dreaming up a story to explain the snowshoe tracks I began seeing in front of me. Someone had been up there recently, probably the day before. The tracks all pointed uphill, so I guessed that a solo backpacker had come up to camp for the night. I figured I'd run into the tracks' owner once I got higher. I did some creative profiling. A male, most likely, since I didn't often come across solo female hikers. And someone between the ages of 35 and 55 who was in pretty good shape for hoofing it up the mountain alone. I couldn't explain why the person had worn snowshoes in what couldn't have been more than an inch or two of snow—mine were still strapped to my backpack. I passed the time by detailing the story in my head as I continued up the trail.

As I entered a small open meadow, the tracks suddenly veered off-trail, heading to my left. Weird. I kept walking, thinking that I must be near the person's campsite, but I soon came across snowshoe tracks facing in the opposite direction. That was a curious development. Cruising along, I worked on revising the story unfolding in my head, when my eyes glanced up from the ground and fixed upon a figure. It was a man in his late twenties standing right in front of me on the trail, eyes open wide. I said hi and smiled. He shouted, "Oh my God! I'm lost! Can you help me?"

Bewildered by this exclamation, I thought for a minute that he must have been joking. For all the people who have warned me about the dangers of hiking alone, there I was, face-to-face with the one-in-a-billion chance of running into a psychopath in the woods. Surely, I thought, I wouldn't go down like that.

After a few minutes of talking with the man, I got a sense of his situation; he was truly disoriented and in need of assistance. He said he'd hiked up the previous day and planned to spend the night at the Devil's Peak lookout tower. He was unprepared to navigate through the snow and walked in circles in search of his destination. Giving up, he pitched a tent and camped in the woods. In the morning, he awoke, completely lost and afraid.

I walked him a few minutes down the trail—past the confusing snowshoe tracks he'd left behind—back to where the trail was blindingly obvious to follow. He said he had already called his girlfriend, who had contacted Search and Rescue. He was uninjured, had food and water, and was confident he could make it out safely, so we said goodbye to each other at that point.

I continued uphill in my search for Devil's Peak. As I walked, the snow got deeper. I climbed over fallen trees, crossed a stream, climbed another hill and realized that I too could become disoriented. I also began to feel really guilty for leaving that guy by himself. If something happened to him on his way out, I'd never be able to get over it.

As soon as I reached an open viewpoint with cell service, I sat down to call Search and Rescue, letting them know what I learned in my conversation with the lost hiker. I ate my lunch, followed my tracks back to the trail, and decided to head back down the peak. Once I reached bare ground, I ran down the trail, eager to catch up with the lost hiker. Not long after I reached him, the Search and Rescue team appeared.

It was easy to see how he got himself lost on a snow-covered trail in fading sunlight. Alone, with only his thoughts to guide him and fear clouding his judgment, he walked in circles and lost his bearings. If I hadn't been prepared, that could have been me. But I gave myself plenty of sunlight to accomplish my goal, and I knew that reaching Devil's Peak was not mandatory. I felt comfortable turning around, even though I was probably within a half mile of the highpoint I was seeking. I knew it was always okay to turn back.

To the hiker's credit, he did several things right. He had sufficient food and water. He had shelter and the ability to stay warm. And he had a cell phone and used it to call for help. We can't prevent *every* emergency situation from happening, but we can arm ourselves with the supplies and information we need in case our plans fall through.

I learned that lesson myself on a solo overnight trip to Little Crater Lake. In over a decade of hiking and climbing, I've been fortunate to have only sustained minor injuries in my time outdoors. There were the usual cuts, scrapes and bruises. There were lots of tired legs, strained muscles and achy backs. There were plenty of bruised egos, too. But on one particular trip, I was faced with some challenges I'd never encountered before, and it ended with a trip to the emergency room.

In 2007, I was still pretty new to Oregon. I made plans to backpack around Timothy Lake in the Mt. Hood National Forest. It was the end of March and I was on spring break, itching for an adventure. I drove out towards the trailhead and noticed something I hadn't anticipated: snow. The road leading from the highway to my intended starting point was completely snowed in. Whoops, I guess I missed that in my research.

Coming from the East Coast, I wasn't too familiar with the concept of snowpack, and specifically snowpack that lingered through the spring. Already I was racking my brain for plan B. Instead of my original plan to circle the lake, I decided to follow the Pacific Crest Trail (PCT) from the highway to the lake, coming back the same way. It was a popular trail, so I assumed it would be well-marked, even in the snow. I was wrong. Later, I thought long and hard about the effects of my poor planning, writing about it in my journal:

Without snowshoes or a decent trail to follow, I struggled to even make it to the lake. I relied solely on my map and compass skills, and collapsed in a fit of exhaustion when I reached my destination.

The purpose of the trip was to spend a night in the woods by myself, where I could practice using all of the emergency supplies I dutifully carried in my pack. I tried starting a fire with a magnesium block. I tried building snowshoes with some cord, green branches and my brand-new knife. I failed at both of these things and crawled into my bag, admitting defeat. Before leaving the next morning, however, I had to dismantle the "snowshoes" I'd crafted the night before. It was too much work to try and undo the knots, so I whipped out my knife and started hacking away at the cord. And that's when it happened.

The knife slipped and I nicked my middle finger. I felt no pain, but when I looked at my hand I saw blood pouring out of the cut. I dropped the knife and pulled out my first aid kit. I wrapped up my finger in gauze and tape. Not five minutes later, the gauze was completely soaked through. I rustled through my pack. What else could I use? I reinforced the gauze with a tightly folded bandana and stuck my toe warmers inside. The toe warmers helped to dry out the wet bandana, warm up my frozen hand and act as a splint for my finger. I then wrapped the whole contraption in duct tape and made my next decision.

> ### PRO TIP
>
> It is easier to prevent problems than to solve them in the field. Do your homework before going out on a hike.

According to my map, I had two options to get out. I could retrace my steps, following the deep post-holes I'd made on the way in, or I could follow some Forest Service roads back to the highway and hitchhike to my car. I knew that I'd be able to move faster and I'd be less stressed out about route finding on the roads, so even though that route was a couple miles longer, I decided to break trail on the roads. I had to get out of there quickly and efficiently, alone, without losing my mind.

I started walking. The miles ticked away. I was hungry, thirsty and hot. I was so intent on reaching the road that I hardly stopped to take care of myself. It took me only three hours to reach the highway, at which point I took a deep exhale. Walking along the highway, I stuck out my (bleeding, wrapped up) hand in order to hitchhike the last few miles to my car.

No one stopped. Several people honked their horns at me, which I found infuriating, as if they were mocking me in my time of need. I rarely ask for help, and this experience did not make me anymore inclined to ask for help in the future. Although, I thought, I wouldn't pull over and let a hitchhiker in my car, even if they didn't have a bloody wound!

At the ER, I calmly explained my situation and eventually learned that the cut was so deep I had nearly severed my extensor tendon. They stitched me up for the time being and told me I'd need to follow up with a hand surgeon to repair the tendon. Surgery! I'm glad I decided to seek medical attention instead of chalking it up as just a stupid cut and driving home. I had no idea that I'd injured myself so badly.

While the end result of my poor planning was a serious hand injury, I was grateful that I had the resources I needed to stop the bleeding, and the skills to navigate back to my car. Whenever someone asks if it's worth the weight to carry extra supplies, like a first aid kit and spare clothing, my answer is always an emphatic "Yes!" Had I done my research better and practiced my survival skills in my backyard first, I might have avoided the whole debacle. While I can't change the past, I can use my experience to make more thoughtful decisions in the future.

Principle 2: Travel and Camp on Durable Surfaces

In October of my first year in Oregon, I hiked with a friend up Mt. Hood's Barrett Spur. Some of the meadows were trampled from humans walking every which way. That got me thinking about whether or not it's a good idea to divulge route information for off-trail travel on the Internet. The hike was mentioned in many places online and in print. In some places on Barrett Spur there were clear social trails, in some places the route was flagged, and in others there was no trace of a path. An official trail would concentrate people's impact to one area.

Because there is currently no official trail, and more traffic will only continue to destroy the area, is it a good idea to keep publishing route details and promoting the hike? According to the Leave No Trace website: "Travel damage occurs when surface vegetation or communities of organisms are trampled beyond recovery. The resulting barren area leads to soil erosion and the development of undesirable trails. Backcountry travel may involve travel over both trails and off-trail areas."

Since the path we took was an unofficial route, the LNT ethic would seem to suggest dispersing use. But it was a somewhat popular unofficial route, so it would also seem prudent to concentrate use to one path. In that particular area, I couldn't determine what the preferred method of travel should have been. However, it was obvious that hikers should not be walking over sensitive meadow vegetation and instead stick to bare rock and gravel when possible.

I learned more about durable surfaces on a trip to Utah's Kodachrome Basin State Park in 2015. Signs located near the nature trail cheerfully stated, "Don't bust the crust!"

The "crust" the sign referred to was cryptobiotic soil. This special soil is formed by millions of microorganisms working together to build a symbiotic community. It is able to absorb and retain water more rapidly than sand and other soils, and it is more resistant to erosion. Because cryptobiotic soils have the ability to retain water in extremely arid places, they help to support desert plants and other wildlife.

There's one thing that cryptobiotic soils are not good for: enduring the impact of human footprints. Walking across cryptobiotic soils destroys the surface structure, exposing the loose sand below to wind and erosive forces. It can take decades for the cryptobiotic soil crust to re-form, stabilize the earth and support a plant community. Therefore, the most prudent way to travel in these landscapes is on trails. I was glad to learn about that so I did not inadvertently disrupt the landscape on an off-trail ramble.

Interpretive signs often provide such useful information, especially for visitors who are unfamiliar with the local terrain. The next time you visit a park or wilderness area, take a few minutes to read the signage at the trailhead or along the trail.

You might learn something that you didn't know, which could affect your adventure decision-making.

As tempting as it may be to plop your tent in the middle of a field of wildflowers, imagine what the colorful meadow would look like if hundreds of people did that each summer. Know that you set an example each time you recreate on public lands (and even more so when you share your actions on social media!). You are one person who can influence the behavior of many. Choose to create a positive influence. We can all take part in minimizing our impact on the landscape when we go hiking, climbing and camping so that our public lands remain intact for future generations.

Principle 3: Dispose of Waste Properly

When I mention Leave No Trace, the third principle is the one most people think about first. While on a hike in Corvallis' McDonald Forest, I observed an interesting attempt to raise awareness about the waste issue. At the trailhead, I saw a sign explaining an ongoing campaign designed to combat a chronic issue: people not picking up their dogs' poop on the trail. Apparently, volunteers had sprayed all the dog waste (including waste left in plastic bags) they found near the trail with orange paint in order to make people painfully aware of how big the problem was. As I hiked I wondered if the type of people who leave their dog waste on a trail would also be the type of people who would respond positively to such a campaign.

> ### DISPOSE OF WASTE PROPERLY
>
> - Pack out all trash and leftover food.
> - Manage human waste by digging a 6 to 8 inch deep cat hole, using a backcountry toilet, or using a WAG bag.
> - Pack out toilet paper and hygiene products.
> - Wash camp dishes 200 feet from water sources, and scatter strained dishwater or bury in a cat hole.

Following the dog-waste awareness experiment, I read newspaper editorials and online discussions regarding the topic. There were fierce debates about the issue. People were either strongly for the approach taken or really defensive, saying how dog poop on the trail isn't a big deal.

Here's why dog poop *is* a big deal: It carries pathogenic bacteria, which then gets passed along to wildlife, the soil and the water. Birds and other critters may pick at those plastic poop bags left on the trail, which means the animal is ingesting plastic as well as bacteria-laden dog poo. And it makes the trail less sanitary for the next hikers who come through.

But dog poop is not the only waste being left behind on the trails. Human waste and human-generated garbage is an all-too-common sight on public lands. It is a rare hike when I return to my car without ever seeing garbage on the trail. I have gotten into the habit of picking most garbage up; although, I will not touch other people's toilet paper or any kind of feces on the trail.

While social media is often touted for encouraging irresponsible behavior in the wild, it's not all bad. One positive outcome of social media has been the development of global campaigns designed to tackle the trail waste issue. The 11th Essential is a project dedicated to encouraging people to pack a trash bag in addition to the ten essentials when they go hiking. One quote I love from their website is: "Through every adventure, with every bag, with every person we start a conversation with—we can make a difference and spark change." I wholeheartedly agree. Incorporating an act of stewardship into every outdoor adventure can only serve to deepen our connection with the land and the people we share it with.

On that note, when you see trash along the trails or in campsites, pick it up! I often carry a spare plastic bag that I can put trash in. I commonly see things like food wrappers, single-use water bottles, beer cans, cigarette butts and food-related items on the trail. These are easy to stow away in a mesh pocket on the side of your backpack if you don't have a plastic bag.

People also often leave organic materials, like banana peels, orange peels, apple cores and pistachio shells, on the ground. You may think that since these items are natural and biodegradable, it may be beneficial to leave them to decompose along the trail. However, it can take orange peels and banana peels years to decompose. Pistachio shells remain for years even within the hot, moist environment of compost bins! So the orange you peeled near that viewpoint bench, added to the many other oranges, bananas, pistachios and other organic trash people leave behind while admiring the view, adds up fast. If you don't see your orange peel when you visit that site six months later, it's probably because someone else picked it up for you. In the meantime, discarded organic matter will attract wildlife, creating future problems for both animals and humans in the area.

Pack it in; pack it out.

Principle 4: Leave What You Find

In April 2018, I visited Wupatki National Monument in Northern Arizona. The monument preserves ancient structures left by Native Americans hundreds of years ago. The stone shelters, pottery shards and other signs of human life found there are protected so that modern visitors can learn more about how this land was used. Seeing the structures as they were left hundreds of years ago provides a deeper sense of place and purpose than reading about them in a book. Before that trip, I had not spent much time exploring ruins such as those. It held many lessons for me.

Aaron and I walked the trail, interpretive guide in hand,

admiring the work it must have taken to build and maintain massive stone rooms without the luxury of modern power tools and machines. The guidebook explained how people captured and stored water in the blistering heat of the desert. How they broke and moved rocks to construct these buildings. How they gathered and farmed. How they played games and forged relationships between tribes. Sure, I *could* have read about all of this stuff on the Internet in my house, but by physically being there I was thrust into the story and eager to learn. I was inspired by being in that place, walking from structure to structure and connecting the story in the text with the physical remnants that I could see and touch.

LEAVE WHAT YOU FIND

- Do not touch or remove cultural artifacts.
- Leave nature as you find it; don't carve into trees, pick flowers or disturb rocks.
- Avoid transporting non-native species.
- Do not build things or dig into the ground (cat holes excluded).

Parks like Wupatki exist all over the world. The only reason they provide a meaningful place to learn about our past is because ancient artifacts are left in place. Before LNT was established in the 1960s, it was more common for people to take interesting things found on public lands, but there are heartbreaking stories even today of stolen art, tools, bones, jewelry and pottery from historical sites.

Along with leaving artifacts in place, Principle 4 suggests that you avoid altering nature with signs that will last. Hundreds of years ago, well before digital cameras and Instagram, the only way to let someone know you'd been somewhere was to leave a physical mark of your presence. I've seen initials carved into rocks, caves and canyon walls by travelers in the 1800s and early 1900s. Those carvings are historical artifacts. In 2019, we have the technology to record our travels in ways that leave no trace. Times have changed—take only photographs; leave only footprints.

✿

Principle 5: Minimize Campfire Impacts

I'm not much of a backpacker. I much prefer taking day hikes and then retreating home or to a roadside camp where I have access to all of my heavy stuff at the end of the day, so I have a lot of experience making fires in a fire pit at a developed site. Building a campfire in that situation is easy. Building fires in the backcountry, however, takes more thought and preparation.

In my research for this book, I read about the best practices for building fires in the forest and why those practices are recommended. The potential impact of backcountry fires that do not follow LNT principles can be devastating. Across the American West, wildfires destroy millions of acres of land each year. Smoke from the fires fills the air in cities nearby and many miles away. People lose their homes, businesses, and lives as a result of these fires. According to estimates, up to 90 percent of wildfires are caused by humans (campfires being just one of the causes).

MINIMIZE CAMPFIRE IMPACTS

- Use a camp stove instead of building a fire.
- If you must have a fire, be sure it is permitted for the place and time in which you're camping.
- Keep fires small.
- Use only dead sticks (no wider than your wrist) harvested from the ground.
- Burn all fuel into ash. Completely extinguish your fire with water. Scatter the ashes.

Those aren't the only impacts of wildfires. Heat kills microorganisms beneath a campfire, which sterilizes the soil. In some habitats, like in the high mountains, vegetation is scarce.

Using live or dead wood for campfires in those places reduces the overall biomass in that environment, meaning fewer homes for animals, less nutrients to build up the soil, less stabilizing vegetation to keep soil in place. In addition, popular backpacking areas may become littered with rock fire rings and burn scars, providing a far-from-pristine experience.

In 2017, despite a horrible fire season in Oregon, I took a small group of hikers up Mt. Bailey in Southern Oregon. The smoke from a nearby wildfire was thick, making it hard to breathe. We walked uphill at a pace we could manage, and once we got out of the trees things got worse.

It looked like Armageddon was upon us. At midday the skies were gray and heavy. We could see plumes of smoke coming up from the distant forest. There were no pretty mountain views, as we were essentially walking through a massive campfire. It made me wonder why anyone would even dream of having a campfire in the middle of a dry summer. Despite having fire bans in place, it only takes one careless camper to set the whole forest ablaze.

I almost always build a campfire when I go car camping, so I understand the innate draw humans have to fire. I've heard the argument: "Well, why even have a fire at all?" While I appreciate that sentiment, and I agree that not building a fire would have the least amount of impact, there's nothing inherently wrong with campfires. Fire creates heat, light and ambiance. Fire can make the difference between a pleasantly chilly night and a miserably cold one. When managed properly and situated in the right place, you can have a fire that is comfortable, safe and enjoyable.

I do much more camping in the fall and winter than I do in the summer, when fire danger is at its highest. During those low-risk times of year, it is much safer to have a fire. The next time you take off for a camping trip, learn about where you're camping; some places require fire permits during part of the year, or ban fires during some or all of the year. Check the regulations beforehand so you can plan ahead and prepare.

If you use Principle 5 to guide your fire-making decisions, you can build fires without harming the environment. The U.S. Forest Service and other outdoor agencies have published guides that demonstrate best practices for building a campfire that complies with Leave No Trace principles. Do a quick search online to find out more information on how to build and extinguish campfires safely. And always remember to put your fire out completely before leaving it.

Principle 6: Respect Wildlife

> **RESPECT WILDLIFE**
>
> - Observe wildlife from a distance.
> - Never feed the animals (on purpose or by accident).
> - Store food and food waste securely.
> - Control pets or do not bring them with you.
> - Respect closure areas due to nesting, rearing young, and mating.
> - Do not touch wildlife or move animals for any reason.

In September 2009, I excitedly packed for a trip to Olympic National Park in Western Washington. In preparation for my trip I researched backcountry camping options. I was joining a team for a multi-day trip that included a mountain climb. Since there was a large population of bears in the park and those bears had come to enjoy human food, we would have to hang up our food using bear wires provided by the park. I'd hung my food before to keep it away from squirrels and other little critters, but I never had to think about bears. We took care to hang our food and trash properly, spending several days in the forest without encountering any bears.

The more humans expand into the backcountry, the more accustomed wildlife gets to our habits. Human food is very calorie dense and easy to acquire, so it's no wonder animals are attracted to it. Parks with large bear populations have infrastructure in place to keep them away from human food. Many national parks and forests have bear-proof trash cans and storage lockers for visitors to store their food in, safe from curious bears. In Yosemite National Park, for example, the bears have become so accustomed to human visitors that they'll break into your car if they see a food wrapper lying on the floor! Be sure to read the signage at the entrance to any new park you visit to become familiar with the particular guidelines that park has regarding animal safety.

Even good intentions can turn bad, for humans and animals alike. It is difficult to watch animals suffering. If you see an animal that appears to be in distress and you want to help, the best thing to do is report your observation to the local land manager. Don't put a bison in your car. Don't try to rescue a wild animal. Don't take home baby animals to keep as pets. This may sound silly, but people do these things every year!

It is also tempting to wander close to wildlife to get a better look at them. In December 2009, my mom flew to Oregon to spend time with me during the holidays. We took a trip to the coast on a gorgeous winter day and hiked along Nehalem Bay. We walked down a long sandy beach for miles until it dead-ended at a rock jetty. From there we hiked across a log-strewn spit on a trail until we could drop back down onto the sand. Suddenly, my mom yelled, "Look ahead!" In the distance we saw a large group of seals, maybe fifty individuals, sitting together by the edge of the water. Neither of us had ever seen a pod of seals like this before, so we walked closer out of excitement and curiosity.

I stopped, paying close attention to the seals' behavior as my mom inched even closer for some photos. As soon as they became agitated I asked her to back off, which she did with some dismay. We were in their home, their place to relax out of the water. We were only visitors on that beach. Although we could not get as close as we wanted to, it was really something special to be able to see those animals in their natural habitat, even if they were far away.

Remember that the land you're walking on is home to thousands of animals, from the tiny insects beneath your feet to the large, charismatic mammals lumbering through the trees. Wild animals are disturbed by our behaviors and the behaviors of our pets. It is important to consider how we can coexist in the same spaces with animals while minimizing our disruption to their lives. Animals are not in the wilderness for our entertainment. Watching them through binoculars or zoom lenses are exciting ways to observe wildlife without affecting their well-being.

Keep in mind, too, that domestic animals and wild animals are two different things. Surely your dog loves to run wild and free in nature, but that has an impact on native species. Off-leash dogs terrorize other animals by barking, threatening them and running at them. Uncontrolled dogs can also harass and bite other people who are out enjoying a hike. Keeping pets under control (or leaving them at home when appropriate/required) is a simple way to practice Principle 6.

Principle 7: Be Considerate of Other Visitors

It's rare to be truly alone on the trails. In August 2017, I hiked up Mt. Bachelor, a popular local ski destination. When I learned there was a summer hiking trail to the top, I knew I had to go check it out. Only a handful of people were hiking the trail on that lovely summer day. One pair in particular stood out in my mind. I could hear them before I could see them; they were hiking with music blaring from a cell phone. Since much of the trail crossed a wide-open slope, I could hear them for half the hike. I rushed to try and get in front of the pair so I could leave that awful music behind. I simply don't understand why people choose to do that. It is a blatant violation of Principle #7. With advances in technology comes more ways to make noise and detract from the wilderness experience.

> ### BE CONSIDERATE OF OTHER VISITORS
>
> - Respect other people and avoid infringing upon their experience.
> - Yield to other trail users: bikers yield to hikers, bikers and hikers yield to horses. Downhill hikers yield to uphill hikers.
> - Take breaks and camp away from trails and other people.
> - Avoid making loud noises and use a soft voice.
> - Keep pets under control.

On a lovely forest hike in Maui's upcountry, Aaron and I got a little more than we bargained for. Not far up the trail we started hearing music. It got louder the further we walked. Was someone having a party up there? As we turned a corner we bumped right into the source of the noise. A young man was pulling what looked like a piece of rolling luggage behind him. *It was a full-sized* speaker. Yes, the music was booming out of a speaker that was half as tall as me. I couldn't believe it. Here's a suggestion: If you want to listen to music while hiking, that's totally okay. Plug headphones into your device and listen away. Understand that everyone else is not going to enjoy your music the way that you do. Let nature's sounds prevail.

Drones are another new source of noise in the backcountry. I've encountered people with drones on several occasions, including in places where it's illegal to fly them. Drones are incredibly loud and invasive. Drone operators are not always great at maneuvering their new toys, either. A man crashed a drone into me on top of Larch Mountain as I was enjoying a summit rest with my friends. Luckily, I was wearing a thick down jacket, where most of the damage was relegated. Still, I was pretty upset, and the drone flyer didn't even bother to apologize before packing up and slinking away. While the Leave No Trace organization has chosen not to take a particular stance on drones, they do remind users to abide by the rules and regulations of the areas in which they fly them. Drones are not allowed above National Park Service lands, federally designated wilderness areas and many state parks. Check the rules before you choose to fly.

There are many other ways your choices can impact other visitors in a negative way. Off-leash dogs that do not readily obey voice commands bother not only wildlife but other people as well. And on multi-use trails or popular trails, it is important to understand that you are sharing a resource that many other people have come to enjoy too. Try to leave space between groups, take breaks away from the trail, and be aware that your idea of a good time might not mesh with other people's ideas of a good time.

By being a little more aware of each other and our surroundings, we can all enjoy public lands for generations to come. I am optimistic that the wave of newcomers to the outdoors is eager to learn and play a positive role in how they interact with others and the natural world. I am encouraged that so many hiking groups dedicated to educating marginalized communities, like Unlikely Hikers, Outdoor Afro and The Venture Out Project are springing up and inviting more people into outdoor spaces. I am excited that people are recognizing the value of spending time in nature and providing avenues for folks who have felt excluded from these spaces to get outdoors. Everyone belongs outside.

With that excitement and eagerness must come responsibility. We each need to be accountable for our own actions and our influence on other people. We need to understand the consequences of our decisions and the impact they have both near and far. Through this project, I learned so much about myself, my biases, my needs and my ability to share my story with others. I strongly believe that hiking is an activity that anyone of any ability can enjoy throughout the year. Hiking can be easy or challenging. It can create a sense of peace or a sense of pushing the limits. It can introduce us to worlds beyond imagination. It can foster a passion for the outdoors and drive a deep need to protect it.

I hope that parts of my story resonate with you in a meaningful way. I encourage you to hike more, share your love of the outdoors with people you care about, take time to learn more about Leave No Trace, and dedicate time to preserving your favorite places. Whether your talents lie in education, conservation, legislation or putting in some hard labor on the trail, you can make a difference that will last many lifetimes.

Epilogue

Continued Growth

After writing this book, 2020 happened. It was a reckoning for me and much of the rest of the world. The global COVID-19 pandemic shook the foundation of what we've taken as "normal" and revealed to my comfortable, white, middle class self how the systems in the United States have been built to exclude, oppress and marginalize many communities across the country. I knew anecdotally from all the hiking I've done that the majority of people using trails, campgrounds and parks are white, able-bodied people, but I never thought about why that is.

From seemingly small things like access to outdoor spaces to critical support systems like healthcare, housing, education, employment and the criminal justice system, it finally became apparent to me that these systems were designed for, and continue to benefit white people. After the horrific murder of George Floyd by a white police officer in broad daylight, I forced myself to convene with other nice white people to learn more about our roles in our community and what we needed to learn as well as how to take action for change.

I had never been interested in social justice, because I didn't have to be. So, I quickly found I was poorly informed about how things worked, and I had a lot of catching up to do. I committed to listening to people who did not share my experience in America, including Black people, indigenous people, LGBTQ+ people, immigrants, disabled people and homeless people. I picked up actual books for the first time since I was assigned reading in college. The stories I heard helped me develop empathy for those who didn't walk through the world as I did, and helped me understand that being a nice person and not an outright racist was simply not good enough. Over time, I learned to acknowledge my privileges: as a white, cis-gender, thin, able-bodied human, I am granted safety and access to spaces that others are not. This does not mean that everything in my life has come easily, but it does mean that my life was not made more challenging because of the characteristics I was born with.

Sitting at home as the pandemic raged on, I found myself with an abundance of time to read, think, connect with new people online and develop a better sense of the big picture. Just as I was able to learn so much about myself on the trail, I was able to learn about others from my living room. This new understanding motivated me to donate to nonprofits dedicated to equity and access, join an allyship group to help me see my blind spots and contact my elected officials to support systemic changes. Inherently, we want to believe that all people are created equal and that we're all navigating the same waters, but once it becomes clear that some people are given yachts and others are given leaky rafts, it's difficult to buy into the myth that we all have the same opportunities for success.

Life is like a chapter book; you need to complete one before proceeding to the next. If I hadn't finished the *Hike366* project, if I hadn't felt comfortable in my own humanity, if I hadn't developed my confidence through hiking, I'm not sure I would have been ready to turn the page to the chapter on fighting for social justice. Learning is a lifelong pursuit if you choose to look at life through that lens. I learn something new on every hike, on every day at work, with every book I read. Be less afraid of being wrong than of receiving feedback and criticism; this is true for hiking and life. As author Maya Angelou once said, "Do the best you can until you know better. Then when you know better, do better."

Now that you've read this book, what's next? I pose this challenge to you: Start your own *Hike366* project. Open up a notebook or set up a clean spreadsheet and start documenting your hikes. If you already have an extensive record of your hiking history, then you can begin penciling in the hikes you've already completed. You might notice something. Do you have loads of hikes in the summer but nearly nothing in the winter? Do you see a ton of repeat destinations? Do you strictly hike on weekends or do you have a collection of after-work, weekend and vacation hikes? Do you only hike in nice weather? How do you define hiking?

Maybe you finish the list and maybe you don't. Either way, I guarantee you'll learn something. I hope that you'll come to value hiking and being outdoors in various seasons, weather conditions, locations and times of day as I have. And I hope you'll share those experiences with others, both in person and online. Tag your photos on Instagram with #hike366 to share the message and help build a diverse community of thoughtful, resilient and inspired hikers.

Appendix

List of 366 Hikes

Month	Date	Year	Location
January	1	2014	La Pine State Park, Oregon
January	2	2013	Oregon Dunes, Oregon
January	3	2015	Finley National Wildlife Refuge, Oregon
January	4	2013	Heceta Head, Oregon
January	5	2016	Minto-Brown Island Park, Oregon
January	6	2016	McDowell Creek Falls, Oregon
January	7	2016	Bald Hill, Oregon
January	8	2016	Willamette Mission State Park, Oregon
January	9	2018	Otter Bench, Oregon
January	10	2017	Pilot Butte, Oregon
January	11	2017	Dry River Canyon, Oregon
January	12	2017	Smith Rock, Oregon
January	13	2006	Owl's Head, New Hampshire
January	14	2017	Vista Butte, Oregon
January	15	2006	Cannon Mountain, New Hampshire
January	16	2012	Cape Horn, Oregon
January	17	2009	Mt. Rose, Washington
January	18	2017	Deschutes River Trail, Oregon
January	19	2014	Cape Perpetua, Oregon
January	20	2013	Black Butte, Oregon

January	21	2007	Hamilton Mountain, Oregon
January	22	2006	Mt. Moosilauke, New Hampshire
January	23	2011	Wyeth Trail, Oregon
January	24	2014	Marys Peak, Oregon
January	25	2016	Fitton Green, Oregon
January	26	2017	Gray Butte, Oregon
January	27	2017	Chimney Rock, Oregon
January	28	2012	Smith Rock, Oregon
January	29	2012	Scout Camp, Oregon
January	30	2011	Saddle Mountain, Oregon
January	31	2017	Steelhead Falls, Oregon
February	1	2017	Sahalie Falls, Oregon
February	2	2018	Deschutes River Trail, Oregon
February	3	2007	Mt. Hood, Oregon
February	4	2018	Shevlin Park, Oregon
February	5	2017	Nordeen Long Loop, Oregon
February	6	2018	Dry Canyon, Oregon
February	7	2014	Corvallis trails, Oregon
February	8	2015	Nestucca Spit, Oregon
February	9	2016	Peavy Arboretum, Oregon
February	10	2006	Sandwich Dome, New Hampshire
February	11	2006	Arrow Slide, New Hampshire
February	12	2011	Coyote Wall, Washington
February	13	2010	Lookout Mountain, Mt. Hood National Forest, Oregon
February	14	2014	Eula Ridge, Oregon
February	15	2016	Callaghan Country, British Columbia
February	16	2008	Mt. Thielsen, Oregon
February	17	2013	Marys Peak, Oregon
February	18	2018	Tumalo Canal, Oregon
February	19	2018	Tumalo Creek, Oregon
February	20	2018	Bessie Butte, Oregon
February	21	2009	Huckleberry Mountain, Oregon
February	22	2006	Mt. Monadnock, New Hampshire

February	23	2016	Newport Beach, Oregon
February	24	2007	Cable Falls, Washington
February	25	2017	Maiden Peak Shelter, Oregon
February	26	2011	Angel's Rest, Oregon
February	27	2016	Brandenburg Shelter, Oregon
February	28	2015	Coffin Mountain, Oregon
February	29	2016	Butte Creek, Oregon
March	1	2015	Wizard Falls, Oregon
March	2	2014	Cape Kiwanda, Oregon
March	3	2013	Marys Peak, Oregon
March	4	2018	Crack-in-the-Ground, Oregon
March	5	2016	Cone Peak, Oregon
March	6	2010	Mt. Hood, Oregon
March	7	2016	Spencer Butte, Oregon
March	8	2009	Larch Mountain, Oregon
March	9	2018	Feather Falls, California
March	10	2007	Cape Horn, Oregon
March	11	2006	Mt. Jefferson, New Hampshire
March	12	2017	Cone Peak, Oregon
March	13	2016	North Bank Ranch, Oregon
March	14	2016	Peavy Arboretum, Oregon
March	15	2017	Reynolds Pond, Oregon
March	16	2014	Cone Peak, Oregon
March	17	2013	Eagle's Rest, Oregon
March	18	2018	Smith Rock, Oregon
March	19	2006	Arethusa Falls, New Hampshire
March	20	2010	Yosemite National Park, California
March	21	2014	Silver Falls, Oregon
March	22	2011	Lava Beds National Monument, California
March	23	2014	Mt. St. Helens, Washington
March	24	2010	Joshua Tree, California
March	25	2013	Telescope Peak, California
March	26	2012	Garden of the Gods, Colorado

March	27	2013	Darwin Falls, California
March	28	2013	Eureka Dunes, California
March	29	2007	Little Crater Lake, Oregon
March	30	2014	Henline Mountain, Oregon
March	31	2017	Santiago Oaks Regional Park, California
April	1	2018	Valley of Fire State Park, Nevada
April	2	2016	Horse Rock Ridge, Oregon
April	3	2011	Klickitat Rail Trail, Washington
April	4	2017	Antelope Valley California Poppy Preserve, California
April	5	2015	Opal Creek, Oregon
April	6	2017	Kelso Dunes, California
April	7	2018	Sunset Crater Volcano and Wupatki National Monuments, Arizona
April	8	2007	Illumination Saddle, Oregon
April	9	2016	Little North Santiam, Oregon
April	10	2018	Buckskin Gulch, Utah
April	11	2018	Snow Canyon State Park, Utah
April	12	2018	Cathedral Caves, Nevada
April	13	2018	Juniper Draw, Nevada
April	14	2012	Siouxon Creek, Washington
April	15	2012	Madrone Wall, Oregon
April	16	2018	Suttle Lake, Oregon
April	17	2014	Pont du Gard, France
April	18	2010	Cape Lookout, Oregon
April	19	2015	Wheeler Peak, Nevada
April	20	2015	Lehman Caves, Nevada
April	21	2015	Observation Point, Zion National Park, Utah
April	22	2015	Angel's Landing, Zion National Park, Utah
April	23	2015	North Guardian Angel, Zion National Park, Utah
April	24	2015	Hat Shop, Bryce Canyon, Utah
April	25	2015	Figure Eight Loop, Bryce Canyon, Utah
April	26	2015	Fairyland Loop, Bryce Canyon, Utah

April	27	2015	Kodachrome Basin State Park, Utah
April	28	2015	Lower Muley Twist Canyon, Utah
April	29	2015	Hickman Bridge, Utah
April	30	2006	Rumney, New Hampshire
May	1	2015	Rishel Peak, Utah
May	2	2015	Shoshone Falls, Idaho
May	3	2015	Bruneau Dunes State Park, Idaho
May	4	2014	Crescent Mountain, Oregon
May	5	2007	Horsepasture Mountain, Oregon
May	6	2012	Hunchback Ridge, Oregon
May	7	2011	Vantage, Washington
May	8	2011	Vantage, Washington
May	9	2016	Baskett Slough, Oregon
May	10	2018	Belknap Traverse, New Hampshire
May	11	2013	Browder Ridge, Oregon
May	12	2006	Ethan Pond, New Hampshire
May	13	2012	Dome Rock, Oregon
May	14	2011	Henline Mountain, Oregon
May	15	2010	Smith Rock, Oregon
May	16	2010	Smith Rock, Oregon
May	17	2016	Beverly Beach, Oregon
May	18	2013	Lookout Mountain, Ochoco National Forest, Oregon
May	19	2013	Smith Rock, Oregon
May	20	2016	Mt. Pisgah, Oregon
May	21	2016	Waihou Spring, Hawaii
May	22	2011	Indian Point, Oregon
May	23	2016	Pu'u Ola'i and Big Beach, Hawaii
May	24	2016	Pipiwai Trail, Hawaii
May	25	2013	Hager Mountain, Oregon
May	26	2013	Campbell Rim, Oregon
May	27	2006	Presidential Traverse, New Hampshire
May	28	2005	Welch-Dickey Loop, New Hampshire
May	29	2016	Alaka'i Swamp, Hawaii

May	30	2016	Shipwreck Beach, Hawaii
May	31	2010	Tieton, Washington
June	1	2016	Sleeping Giant, Hawaii
June	2	2016	Napali Coast, Hawaii
June	3	2016	Awa'awapuhi Ridge, Hawaii
June	4	2016	Secret Falls, Hawaii
June	5	2011	Unicorn Peak, Washington
June	6	2015	Tidbits Mountain, Oregon
June	7	2016	Luckiamute Landing, Oregon
June	8	2014	Scar Mountain, Oregon
June	9	2007	Mt. Hood, South Side, Oregon
June	10	2012	Duffy Butte, Oregon
June	11	2017	Echo Basin, Oregon
June	12	2016	Pilot Butte, Oregon
June	13	2017	Lava Cast Forest, Oregon
June	14	2013	Mt. St. Helens, Washington
June	15	2016	Crescent Mountain, Oregon
June	16	2014	Bigelow Hollow State Park, New Hampshire
June	17	2012	City of Rocks, Idaho
June	18	2011	Leavenworth, Washington
June	19	2011	Leavenworth, Washington
June	20	2012	City of Rocks, Idaho
June	21	2013	Proposal Rock, Oregon
June	22	2013	Netarts Spit, Oregon
June	23	2012	City of Rocks, Idaho
June	24	2006	Baldface, New Hampshire
June	25	2011	Lower Gorge, Smith Rock, Oregon
June	26	2005	Jackson, New Hampshire
June	27	2012	Dog Mountain, Washington
June	28	2009	100-Mile Wilderness, Maine
June	29	2014	Iron Mountain, Oregon
June	30	2013	Diamond Creek Falls, Oregon
July	1	2005	Caribou-Speckled Mountain Wilderness, Maine

July	2	2005	South Baldface, New Hampshire
July	3	2013	Bald Hill, Oregon
July	4	2014	Middle Pyramid, Oregon
July	5	2009	Mt. Monadnock, New Hampshire
July	6	2007	Mt. Shasta, California
July	7	2013	Red Butte, Oregon
July	8	2012	Loowit Trail, Washington
July	9	2009	McNeil Point, Oregon
July	10	2015	Independence Rock, Oregon
July	11	2015	Marion Lake, Oregon
July	12	2015	Middle Pyramid, Oregon
July	13	2014	Black Crater, Oregon
July	14	2013	Diamond Peak, Oregon
July	15	2005	Tripyramids, New Hampshire
July	16	2007	Mt. Shuksan, Washington
July	17	2009	Paradise Park, Oregon
July	18	2017	Three Sisters Wilderness, Oregon
July	19	2014	Bald Hill, Oregon
July	20	2014	Dome Rock, Oregon
July	21	2011	Middle Sister, Oregon
July	22	2017	Steens Mountain, Oregon
July	23	2017	Two Gorges, Oregon
July	24	2009	Boston Basin, Washington
July	25	2009	Boston Basin, Washington
July	26	2012	Grizzly Peak, Oregon
July	27	2010	Brown Mountain, Oregon
July	28	2012	Marion Mountain, Oregon
July	29	2014	Glacier Peak, Washington
July	30	2010	Harris Beach State Park, Oregon
July	31	2007	Mt. Olympus, Washington
August	1	2015	Chip Ross Park, Oregon
August	2	2013	South Sister, Oregon
August	3	2006	Badlands, South Dakota
August	4	2006	Devil's Tower, Wyoming

August	5	2006	Amphitheater Lake, Wyoming
August	6	2015	Black Crater, Oregon
August	7	2015	Belknap Crater, Oregon
August	8	2015	Hand Lake, Oregon
August	9	2017	Tumalo Mountain, Oregon
August	10	2015	Millican Crater, Oregon
August	11	2007	Boundary Trail, Washington
August	12	2007	Multnomah Falls, Oregon
August	13	2017	Mt. Bailey, Oregon
August	14	2011	Midgard Peak, British Columbia
August	15	2015	Panhandle Gap, Washington
August	16	2017	Mt. Bachelor, Oregon
August	17	2017	Pine Mountain Ridge, Oregon
August	18	2014	Mt. Thomson, Washington
August	19	2005	Mt. Garfield, New Hampshire
August	20	2012	Four-in-One-Cone, Oregon
August	21	2012	Belknap Crater, Oregon
August	22	2014	Bear Point, Oregon
August	23	2013	Luna Peak, Washington
August	24	2014	Tenas Lakes, Oregon
August	25	2016	Waldport Beach, Oregon
August	26	2017	Baker Beach and Dunes, Oregon
August	27	2012	Sahale Peak, Washington
August	28	2009	Austera Peak, Washington
August	29	2009	Austera Peak, Washington
August	30	2009	Eldorado Peak, Washington
August	31	2008	Weldon Wagon Trail, Oregon
September	1	2007	Mt. Thielsen, Oregon
September	2	2007	Big Obsidian Flow, Oregon
September	3	2005	Arrow Slide, New Hampshire
September	4	2006	Mt. Defiance, Oregon
September	5	2010	Rooster Rock, Willamette National Forest, Oregon
September	6	2010	McDowell Creek Falls, Oregon

September	7	2014	Marys Peak, Oregon
September	8	2012	West McMillan Spire, Washington
September	9	2013	Donaca Lake, Oregon
September	10	2015	Fitton Green, Oregon
September	11	2005	Kinsman Mountains, New Hampshire
September	12	2009	Mt. Cruiser, Washington
September	13	2009	Mt. Cruiser, Washington
September	14	2014	South Sister, Oregon
September	15	2015	Finley National Wildlife Refuge, Oregon
September	16	2006	Devil's Peak, Oregon
September	17	2011	Smith Rock, Oregon
September	18	2015	Beazell Memorial Forest, Oregon
September	19	2010	L.L. Stub Stewart State Park, Oregon
September	20	2013	Peavy Arboretum, Oregon
September	21	2014	Oregon Dunes, Oregon
September	22	2012	Mt. Washington, Oregon
September	23	2016	Brooklyn to Manhattan, New York
September	24	2011	Old Snowy Mountain, Washington
September	25	2006	Elk-Kings Mountain, Oregon
September	26	2010	Table Mountain, Washington
September	27	2008	Clatsop Spit, Oregon
September	28	2015	McDonald Forest, Oregon
September	29	2013	Salal Hill, Oregon
September	30	2015	Siuslaw National Forest, Oregon
October	1	2005	Franconia Traverse, New Hampshire
October	2	2005	Wildcat-Carter Traverse, New Hampshire
October	3	2014	McNeil Point, Oregon
October	4	2005	Lincoln-Lafayette Mountain, New Hampshire
October	5	2014	Mt. Hood trails, Oregon
October	6	2012	Lower Gorge, Smith Rock, Oregon
October	7	2017	Strawberry Mountain, Oregon
October	8	2015	Snag Boat Bend, Oregon
October	9	2016	Mt. Scott, Oregon

October	10	2006	Barrett Spur, Oregon
October	11	2015	Little Cowhorn Mountain, Oregon
October	12	2016	Three Sisters Wilderness, Oregon
October	13	2013	Multnomah Falls, Oregon
October	14	2015	Tahkenitch Dunes, Oregon
October	15	2005	Mt. Moosilauke, New Hampshire
October	16	2011	Yocum Ridge, Oregon
October	17	2006	Tanner Butte, Oregon
October	18	2013	Tidbits Mountain, Oregon
October	19	2016	Four-in-One-Cone, Oregon
October	20	2013	Cowhorn Mountain, Oregon
October	21	2015	Bald Hill to Fitton Green, Oregon
October	22	2005	Mt. Carrigain, New Hampshire
October	23	2011	Steins Pillar, Oregon
October	24	2009	Salmon Butte, Oregon
October	25	2013	Echo Basin, Oregon
October	26	2013	Linton Lake, Oregon
October	27	2012	Smith Rock, Oregon
October	28	2017	Diablo Peak, Oregon
October	29	2011	Smith Rock, Oregon
October	30	2005	Davis Path, New Hampshire
October	31	2009	Salmon-Huckleberry Wilderness, Oregon
November	1	2015	Alsea Falls, Oregon
November	2	2014	Fuji Mountain, Oregon
November	3	2015	Iron Mountain, Oregon
November	4	2007	Cooper Spur, Oregon
November	5	2005	Franconia Traverse, New Hampshire
November	6	2005	The Twins, New Hampshire
November	7	2015	Leadbetter Point, Washington
November	8	2013	Marys Peak, Oregon
November	9	2014	Maxwell Butte, Oregon
November	10	2011	Table Mountain, Washington
November	11	2005	Mt. Chocorua, New Hampshire

November	12	2005	Mt. Washington, New Hampshire
November	13	2015	Martin Luther King Jr. Park, Corvallis, Oregon
November	14	2009	Mt. Mitchell, Washington
November	15	2013	Newport, Oregon
November	16	2014	Marys Peak, Oregon
November	17	2013	Niagara and Pheasant Falls, Oregon
November	18	2017	Paulina Peak, Oregon
November	19	2006	Silver Falls, Oregon
November	20	2015	Nisqually National Wildlife Refuge, Washington
November	21	2015	Oyster Dome, Washington
November	22	2012	Gold Lake, Oregon
November	23	2006	McGraw Creek, Hells Canyon, Oregon
November	24	2006	Hells Canyon, Oregon
November	25	2017	Catacombs Cave, California
November	26	2006	Herman Creek, Oregon
November	27	2015	Warner Peak, Oregon
November	28	2013	Maiden Peak, Oregon
November	29	2013	Maiden Peak, Oregon
November	30	2008	Coffin Mountain, Oregon
December	1	2012	Yaquina Head Outstanding Natural Area, Oregon
December	2	2006	Mt. St. Helens, Washington
December	3	2005	Mounts Tom, Field, and Willey, New Hampshre
December	4	2005	Middle Carter Mountain, New Hampshire
December	5	2010	Elk-Kings Mountain, Oregon
December	6	2015	Mt. Pisgah, Oregon
December	7	2014	Peavy Arboretum, Oregon
December	8	2012	Wahclella Falls, Oregon
December	9	2006	Trillium Lake, Oregon
December	10	2016	Lookout Mountain, Ochoco Mountains, Oregon
December	11	2011	Mt. Hood, Oregon

December	12	2015	Crater Lake National Park, Oregon
December	13	2014	The Watchman, Oregon
December	14	2013	The Watchman, Oregon
December	15	2013	Garfield Peak, Oregon
December	16	2008	Teacup Lake, Oregon
December	17	2005	Jackson, New Hampshire
December	18	2012	Fields Peak, Oregon
December	19	2008	Devil's Rest, Oregon
December	20	2012	Potato Hill, Oregon
December	21	2014	Marys Peak, Oregon
December	22	2015	Talking Waters Garden, Oregon
December	23	2016	Blitzen River, Oregon
December	24	2009	Nehalem Bay, Oregon
December	25	2011	Jordan Craters, Oregon
December	26	2010	Bald Butte, Oregon
December	27	2013	Pueblo Mountains, Oregon
December	28	2013	Borax Hot Springs, Oregon
December	29	2014	Warner Mountain Lookout, Oregon
December	30	2014	Warner Mountain, Oregon
December	31	2012	Fort Rock, Oregon